An Expert's Guide to Top

101 ENTRY-LEVEL JOBS

FOR MBAs and GRADUATES

A graduate of IIT Chennai and IIM Ahmedabad, **T. Muralidharan** is a first-generation entrepreneur and Founder-chairman of the TMI Group, one of the top five recruiting firms of India. Since 1991, Muralidharan and the group have helped over 100,000 professionals get jobs in the private sector. A regular speaker on various national forums, his articles on issues relating to education and employment can be read in a number of leading newspapers and magazines, including *The Hindu, The Week,* and *Sakshi.*

He is a member of the National Board for Micro, Small and Medium Enterprises (MSME), Government of India; a national board member of the Federation of Indian Chambers of Commerce and Industry (FICCI); former Co-chair of FICCI Skill Development Forum; and the Founder of JobsDialog, India's first mobile-based recruitment platform exclusively for small and medium enterprises.

To know more, visit www.careerdialog.com.

Praise for the author's previous book
An Expert's Guide to Your Right First Job
(Career Dialog Series #1)

Media:

'These tips are very valuable because the author shares his experiences as an assessor for the various employers.'
—*The Hindu*

'The book is marked by crisp and to the point writing which makes it unputdownable. […] it should be referred to by every final year graduation student before they decide to enter the industry of their choice.'
—*Businessworld*

Academia:
'Read the book with interest. Certainly written in a very friendly style.'
—Dr Bhaskar Ramamurthy, Director, IIT Madras

'Our hearty congratulations to Sri T. Muralidharan for bringing out this excellent book which will be of great help to fresh engineering graduates and our thanks for encouraging us to provide this book to our students.'
—Dr P. Narasimha Reddy, Executive Director, Sreenidhi Institute of Science and Technology

An
Expert's
Guide to Top

101 ENTRY-LEVEL JOBS

FOR MBAs and GRADUATES

T. Muralidharan

RUPA

Published by
Rupa Publications India Pvt. Ltd 2016
7/16, Ansari Road, Daryaganj
New Delhi 110002

Sales Centres:

Allahabad Bengaluru Chennai
Hyderabad Jaipur Kathmandu
Kolkata Mumbai

Copyright © T. Muralidharan 2016

The views and opinions expressed in this book are the author's own and
the facts are as reported by him which have been verified to
the extent possible, and the publishers are not in
any way liable for the same.

All rights reserved.
No part of this publication may be reproduced, transmitted,
or stored in a retrieval system, in any form or by any means,
electronic, mechanical, photocopying, recording or otherwise,
without the prior permission of the publisher.

ISBN: 978-81-291-3716-6

First impression 2016

10 9 8 7 6 5 4 3 2 1

The moral right of the author has been asserted.

Printed at Nutech Print Services, New Delhi

This book is sold subject to the condition that it shall not,
by way of trade or otherwise, be lent, resold, hired out,
or otherwise circulated, without the publisher's prior consent,
in any form of binding or cover other than that in which it is published.

*This book is dedicated to two people:
my mother, Mrs Jayalakshmi Rajan
and
my father-in-law, Mr S. Radhakrishnan*

CONTENTS

Introduction ix

Section 1: Organizational Basics
1. Understanding Organizations and Stakeholders 3
2. Common Elements Across All Job Roles 9

Section 2: Entry-level Job Roles in Regular Organizations
3. Marketing Department 21
4. Sales Department 37
5. Operations Department 56
6. Finance and Accounts Departments 69
7. Information Technology Department 91
8. Human Resources Department 100
9. Legal Department 126
10. Supply Chain Department 133

Section 3: Entry-level Job Roles in Industries
11. Automotive Sector 141
12. Civil Aviation 149
13. Banking 159
14. Education 176
15. Insurance 189
16. Construction, Building, and Infrastructure Sector 205
17. Information Technology (IT) Sector 217
18. IT-enabled Services (ITeS) 240
19. Logistics 256
20. Media and Entertainment Sector 268
21. Retail Sector 285
22. Telecom Sector 294
23. Travel, Tourism, and Hospitality 308

24. Pharma and Healthcare Sector 321
25. Other Popular Job Roles from the Financial Services Sector 347

A Quick Index 357
Notes 361
Sources 365
Acknowledgements 369

INTRODUCTION

Young Indians are the future of our nation and around 5 million-plus youngsters graduate from various educational institutions annually. Most of them start looking for jobs shortly before and immediately after graduation. Under extreme placement pressure, most choose the first available job and realize within three months that it is not the job they want to do.

So the first question every youngster must answer is, 'How do I identify a job, the right first job that I will enjoy and eventually excel in?' Making that one correct choice is the secret to a long and fulfilling career. How to choose that 'Right First Job' (RFJ) was the subject of my first book, *An Expert's Guide to your Right First Job*, published by Rupa Publications in February 2015. The book has received an excellent reception.*

This next book, the first of its kind, examines the job market and identifies the top 101 entry-level job roles available in India for graduates and freshers. Its main purpose is to make readers familiar with these 101 job roles and also explain each and every aspect of each job.

This book will help the youth narrow their search, identify which job role suits them the best, and help them in making an informed and eventually a very fulfilling career.

WHO WILL BENEFIT FROM THIS BOOK?

Graduates from any stream—BE, BTech, BA, BCom, BSc, BBA, BCA, BPharm, MBBS, any other graduation, diploma-holders in engineering and other disciplines—can definitely benefit. MBAs, especially from the smaller cities, and postgraduates—Chartered Accountants, Cost

---

*An Expert's Guide to Your Right First Job also provides numerous tips and tests. The book is currently available in leading bookstores and online book portals.

Accountants, Company Secretaries, and MCAs—will also benefit immensely.

This book will help candidates who are in their final year of graduation/post-graduation and preparing for placement or anyone who is actively looking for her/his 'right' job.

WHY SHOULD PARENTS AND CLOSE RELATIVES OF GRADUATES ALSO READ THIS BOOK?

Parents or close relatives—uncles, aunts, elder brothers, and sisters—are natural counsellors for young graduates. They have an obligation to ensure that the advice they give is based on facts and market reality, and should, therefore, read this book.

Recruitment experts or job practitioners have first-hand information on jobs and this book is based on this practical knowledge.

WHY SHOULD PLACEMENT OFFICERS AND JOB COUNSELLORS READ THIS BOOK?

This book is designed to be a guide for placement officers and job counsellors.

There are five reasons to read this book:

- this book is a complete list of 101 popular jobs in the market for graduates and MBAs. A first of its kind in India.
- job descriptions of each of these 101 jobs is available in one place.
- the organizational context for each job is explained, which makes the job description meaningful.
- industry write-ups and job forecasts from a job-seeker point of view is captured from multiple sources. This is again not easily available under one umbrella.
- this is the only book which provides details like salary, targets, challenges, and so on for each job authentically. This is again a first of its kind.

HOW WILL THIS BOOK HELP STUDENTS/FRESHERS?

Job roles cannot be understood in isolation. They have to be understood in the context of the organization. This book attempts to throw some light on how organizations work, in simple language, using analogies and examples that readers can easily relate to. We have also attempted to explain the working of various departments in an organization and the entry-level job roles available in each department. We have interviewed practitioners to capture their experiences.

Coming to job roles, students have some simple questions such as 'What will I be doing if I get this job?', 'What are the challenges in the job?', 'What are the career prospects, salary?', and so on. These have been answered with the help of practical knowledge and contemporary data.

WHY THESE 101 ENTRY-LEVEL JOBS?

This book covers 101 job roles of which 69 are specific to the 15 industries/sectors covered and 32 job roles in 8 functions common to all organizations. The selection of the top 101 jobs listed in this book is based on the perceived demand for these roles in the private corporate sector, from two sources. The first was the National Skill Development Corporation's (NSDC's) recently published 'Human Resource and Skill Requirements reports' across multiple sectors, based on a survey conducted by KPMG, a leading consulting company. Some of the jobs were selected based on this survey. Additionally, the expertise and experience of the TMI Group, one of India's largest talent acquisition companies with a large hiring experience of fresh graduates, was used to finalize the 'Top 101' list.

In our estimate, the 101 job roles covered across 15 sectors will see creation of 2 million vacancies for graduates at the entry-level in the next six years.

The TMI Group has been involved in sourcing, assessing and counselling, and placing over 100,000 experienced Indian professionals across various sectors—like Information Technology (IT), Information Technology-enabled Services (ITeS) Banking, Financial Services, and Insurance (BFSI), Fast Moving Consumer Goods (FMCG), Manufacturing, Telecom, Petroleum, Construction, among others— filling job vacancies in over 400 multinational corporations (MNCs), and in large- and medium-sized corporates in the private, public, and government sectors.

The TMI Group has set up Youth Employability Services (YES)

Centres in cities like Hyderabad, Mumbai, Noida (NCR), Bengaluru, Kolkata, and Chennai where students can walk in and speak to counsellors.

In the six months preceding the writing of this book, thousands of young graduates have walked into TMI Group YES Centres. We have trained and hired 8,000 and assessed close to 50,000 candidates in this short period. The above domain knowledge proved useful not only in making the Top 101 list, but also in providing an insight on job roles.

Disclaimer: We are covering only a few entry-level job roles specific to the sector/industry in Chapters 11 to 25 in this book. This does not mean that these are the only roles available for freshers. We have selected these job roles based on the demand. Most of the roles common to all sectors are separately covered in Chapters 3 to 10.

WHAT PRACTICAL INFORMATION IS COVERED IN THIS BOOK?

While writing this book, we realized that the knowledge of organizations—how are they structured, what the various departments do, and so on—is minimal among fresh graduates, and so Chapter 1 is devoted to understanding organizations.

There are many common elements across all the job roles discussed in the book and these are listed in Chapter 2, to avoid repetition in every chapter.

The book from Chapter 3 to Chapter 10 covers eight departments and job roles in every large manufacturing/service organization, irrespective of the industry/sector.

Chapters 11 to 25 cover fifteen industry/sector highlights and the job roles exclusive to that industry. Why industry highlights? Because one should know the industry from an employee point of view—industry structure, current economic situation, employment potential, future business, and employment growth—before deciding to work in the industry. A brief write-up on an industry doyen is also provided in some chapters to inspire the reader interested in joining that sector.

HOW BEST CAN THE READER NAVIGATE THIS BOOK?

The best way to read this book is to read Section 1: Chapter 1 and Chapter 2. Thereafter you can move on to Section 2, Chapter 3 to Chapter 10. You can read Section 3 and the chapters on various industries in sequence, or read them selectively, depending upon your interest.

I hope you will enjoy reading this book as much as Ms Asha Donkar and I enjoyed writing it.

Section 1

Organizational Basics

1

UNDERSTANDING ORGANIZATIONS AND STAKEHOLDERS

When I was a child, I always used to wonder why my father maintained meticulous records of income and expenditure, and why my mother gave accounts to my father regarding paper bills, milk bills, groceries, vegetables, and so on. I always wondered why there was a division of roles and responsibilities between my mother and father. Why couldn't one person manage everything? But as I grew up and started understanding the world, I learnt how difficult it is to run a household and why it is so important to plan, divide, organize, and prioritize work. Each one of us is born into an organization. Yes! It is a household that I am talking about.

During my childhood, my father was the 'income generator', who worked day in and day out to ensure that we received all the luxuries, and my mother the 'money distributor' who decided how much and where to spend the money so that at the end of every month, there was a 'profit', which in a household context means 'savings'. An organization is said to be successful if it is able to make profits regularly, just as a household is said to be successful when it is able to save some money, every month.

The reason I am giving you this scenario is because I feel that running a household successfully and running a business organization successfully, are very similar. At home, the head of the family strives hard to see that all the needs and wants of his/her family members, are fulfilled. In the same way, a Managing Director of a company strives hard to see that his shareholders and his employees are taken care of. The values, priorities, and goals might differ but the purpose is the same.

UNDERSTANDING ORGANIZATIONAL STRUCTURE AND ROLES: A CASE STUDY

I am sure most of you must have travelled by an inter-state bus at some point or the other. Have you ever wondered how the bus is so neat and clean when you board it and how it manages to reach its destination on time? Obviously, a lot of people work behind the scenes in the bus company to make sure you reach on time and in a clean and safe environment. I plan to use a hypothetical bus company as an example to explain how business organizations are run, and the role and importance of the various departments in these organizations.

Operations Department

Let's start. A bus cannot run without a driver and a conductor. Since they are required to operate the bus, they are part of the Operations Department. The bus must run and reach its destination without breaking down on the way. Who is responsible for the performance of the bus? It is the Maintenance Team. Maintenance Team members, including engineers and mechanics, are part of the Operations Department.

Marketing Department

From here we move on to a bus company's need for passengers to fill bus seats on every journey, so that the company can run without losses. What is it that makes passengers choose our hypothetical company's bus over another? It could be an advertisement on TV or radio, or in a newspaper, or even word-of-mouth recommendations. So who is in charge of deciding what types of advertisements have to be placed in various media, and when? It is the people from the Marketing Department. All the people in this department have only one goal—ensuring adequate demand for seats in the company's buses.

Sales Department

After choosing to travel by our hypothetical company's bus, your next requirement is a ticket and you need to know where you can book your seat. The company may have a ticketing stall at the bus-stand, or a website, or a booking office in the city, where a Salesperson or Ticketing Executive books your seat. He/she belongs to the Sales Department.

Customer Service Department

If you lose your baggage in transit, this is the department you will contact. Imagine if there were no Marketing Executives, Salespersons, Customer Service Executives, or Ticketing Executives in this bus company. What would happen?

Very few, if any, people would know about the company; even those who did, would not know where to get the tickets from—thus nobody would use these buses; the company would become bankrupt and shut down.

Other Departments

While Marketing, Sales, Customer Service, and Operations are the **core departments** in any business organization, there are many more. For instance, the Maintenance Team at the Operations Department in our mythical bus company depends upon the **Purchase Department** to meet its ongoing needs for spares such as tyres and batteries. In fact all other departments rely on it to ensure they have the supplies that they need. The Purchase Department takes care of all the buying of equipment—from paper clips to buses—for our bus company.

The Purchase Department requires someone to stock and transport equipment to the maintenance workshop and this is done by the logistics team which is part of the **Supply Chain Department**. When a Purchase Executive needs money to buy spares the person who arranges the money, works in the **Finance Department**. S/he works with the person who keeps the accounts in the **Accounts Department**. But which department decides employee salaries and perks? It is the **Human Resources (HR) Department**. This department also decides the number of leaves and holidays per year, negotiates with unions or disgruntled employees to resolve issues, and is overall in charge of ensuring that employees have a safe, amiable working environment and thus remain motivated and productive with regard to their roles in the organization.

Our hypothetical bus company also has another department, the **Legal Department**—which ensures that the company meets all its legal obligations to the Regional Transport Organization (RTO). And finally in today's digital age, its computers are managed by the **Information Technology (IT) Department**.

To summarize, our hypothetical bus company needs operations staff to ply its buses, and marketing, sales, and customer service staff to ensure that there are enough happy customers like you and me in the bus. These core people are supported by the Purchase, Finance, Accounts, HR, IT, and the Legal Departments—who are called the Support Staff.

In any business organization, like our hypothetical bus company, the maximum number of staff members belong to the Operations Department. This is how organizations work. You would have also noticed that every person is important and plays a critical role because without these people and their services, organizations cannot run efficiently.

Every organization is set up with a purpose and tries to attain sustainability through customer and employee satisfaction by following legal, transparent, and ethical practices. It is set up with the objective of overcoming all hardships and continuing to grow. Figure 1.1 shows us how departments are organized within an organization.

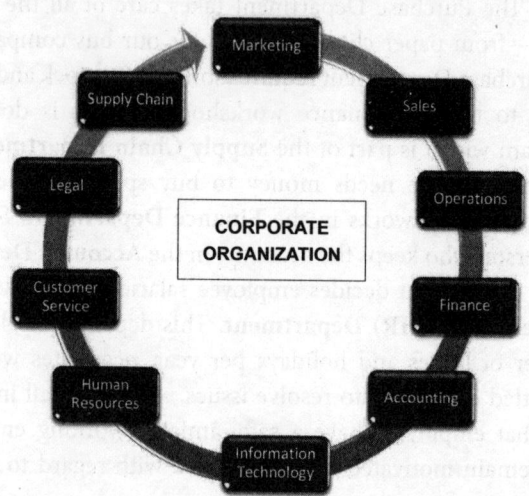

Figure 1.1: Departments Within a Corporate Organization

To understand what makes the organization run better, why team effort is so important and how it affects the overall performance of the team, let us take the simple analogy of how a cricket team works.

Each cricket team has players with different talents who make up the team led by the Skipper/Captain. There are batsmen, bowlers, wicket-keepers, and all-rounders. During a match, what will happen if only the batsmen perform well but the bowlers and fielders don't deliver their best? The team will end up losing the match. Therefore, for a team to win, it is very important that all the players play well and give their 100 per cent. It is team effort that will help any team attain victory. The playing 11 members need the Support Staff to win, consistently. Therefore, each team also has a Team Manager, a coach, a physical trainer, and a physiotherapist to take care of the needs of the team. In the same way, for organizations to remain sustainable, it is very important that all the departments function effectively. That's why we have shown the organization in circular form to reflect the interdependence among departments

Now let us move on to another important term often associated with an organization—its stakeholders. You need to understand these stakeholders because every job in an organization is created to meet the expectations of one or more stakeholders.

Who are an Organization's Stakeholders?

Stakeholders are people who have a stake or interest in the company. A stake could imply a financial stake (such as **Shareholders** have), or an emotional stake a **Customer** has in a product or service. For instance, by preferring one soft drink brand over another, or preferring to choose the services of one hospital or airline over another, customers show their commitment.

The person who has started/provided the funds to start the company is the promoter and his/her role in an organization is to primarily meet customer needs and in the process make money for himself/herself. The **Promoter** needs employees who work for the benefit of the company and equity investors who invest in the company. Apart from them, organizations must satisfy the needs of a few more sets of people such as **Financial Institutions, Trade Unions, Suppliers,**

Government Agencies, the **Press,** and the **Public** at large. These people are also stakeholders of an organization.

In other words, stakeholders are those individuals or groups or institutions that are affected directly or indirectly by organizational achievements or failures. They can affect or be affected by the organization positively or negatively. Every stakeholder has self-interests and expectations. A company becomes successful only when it is able to align all the interests and expectations of all its stakeholders and then tries to meet them.

2

COMMON ELEMENTS ACROSS ALL JOB ROLES

Before we take a look at different job roles, there are a few aspects that are common for all the roles. Let's take a look at them in detail.

SALARY

Before joining an organization, everyone wants to know how much salary they can expect. But the way an employee looks at salary is different from the way an employer looks at it. A salary to an employee is the money that is transferred into her/his bank account every month. This is often called the 'take-home salary'. But the employer looks at the total expenses incurred by the company, which is often called 'cost to company salary'. So you need to understand the various ways salary can be defined and the various components of the salary. The appointment letter and the company's Human Resources (HR) manual has to be read carefully to fully understand the compensation. The components that make up a salary are classified as follows.

Basic Salary

This is the fixed pay that the employer pays the employee for the work done. Retirement benefits like Provident Fund (PF) and annual payments like bonus are often given as a percentage of the basic salary.

Allowances

These include house rent allowance, dearness allowance, conveyance allowance, special allowance, and so on, which are often paid so that the employee has a good quality of life.

Annual Performance Pay

These include variable payments linked to employee performance, and an annual bonus specified under the law. Often, variable performance pay is paid as a percentage of salary which depends on how you are rated against your peers. The annual bonus may also include other bonuses like retention bonus, project completion bonus, and so on.

Retirement Benefits

These include PF payments, gratuity, and superannuation contributions. Typically, the company contributes 12 per cent of the basic salary for PF while the employee is also expected to contribute 12 per cent, which is deducted from the monthly salary. The Government of India is planning to exempt employees from contributing the 12 per cent shortly, for certain salary levels. Gratuity is payable only if the employee stays for five years or more and is payable at the rate of 4.15 per cent of the basic salary for every year of completed service. A few MNCs also contribute to superannuation funds, which may go up to 15 per cent of the basic salary; this money is invested and the employee gets the money back in instalments post-retirement.

Employee Expenses

These include the cost of the car/bus pick-up, free or subsidized food provided, cell-phone expenses, medical insurance, and accident insurance paid by the company.

Employee Deductions

The entire salary paid by the employer does not reach the employee. There are monthly deductions. The biggest deductions are the employee's contribution to the PF, and the income tax payable by the employee based on the salary.

Stipend

Some companies pay a fixed amount per month during training and this fixed amount is called a stipend. Normally, there are no other payments in addition to a stipend. Once the training is over and the person is confirmed as an employee, she/he gets an appointment letter which specifies all the compensation benefits.

HOW IS COMPENSATION (ANOTHER WORD FOR SALARY) DECIDED?

The next question is how is salary determined? Every job is different and hence requires a different compensation, so first we must understand how the employer fixes the compensation for each job role. Compensation depends on five important factors.

Size of Role

Salaries paid by big corporates are higher as compared to the salaries paid by mid-size and small organizations for the same role because the larger the size of the company, larger the size of the job. For example, the Company Secretary of a large company has to do a lot more work compared to the Company Secretary of a small organization.

Complexity of the Job

The role of an Accountant in a listed company is much more complex when compared to the role of an Accountant in an unlisted company. This is because, in a listed company, the Accountants have to provide reports and updates to the stock exchange on a regular basis. But in an unlisted company, the Accountant largely performs book-keeping duties.

Location

Let us take the case of a company that has various branches across India in cities like Hyderabad, Mumbai, Delhi, and Kolkata. There are Managers in all the locations, but a Manager working in Mumbai and Delhi will get at least a 30 per cent higher salary than a Manager working in a state such as Odisha, because the cost of living in Mumbai or Delhi is much higher.

Qualification

Compensation may also vary depending on the qualification of a person. For example, an Accounting Executive with only a BCom degree will be paid at least 15 per cent lesser compensation as compared to an Accounting Executive with an MCom degree. This is very unique to India.

Experience and Expertise

Experience and expertise determine a person's productivity on the job. Therefore, the greater the experience/expertise, the larger the pay packet.

Based on the above factors, the compensation paid will be different for different people performing different roles within the same company.

WHY DOES COMPENSATION VARY ACROSS PEOPLE DOING THE SAME JOB ROLE?

People doing the same job but in different companies may get paid differently. It is also possible that people doing the same job in the same company may also get paid differently. This range of compensation across different people doing the same job is called the compensation band/range. Let's understand the reasons behind this.

Compensation across Companies

The compensation band varies from company to company, based on the size of the company and ownership of the company. For example, MNCs pay better salaries than Indian companies and large corporates generally pay better salaries than small enterprises.

Variation in Compensation for the Same Job Role within the Same Company

People doing the same job have different levels of experience and different qualifications. For example, for Accounts Assistant roles, one person may be a BCom with two years' experience, another may be an MCom with no experience, while a third may be an MCom with one year of experience. All three will get different compensation packages even though all of them are doing the same job.

Compensation Band indicated in this Book

Therefore, while indicating compensation in this book, we have indicated the compensation in a band. The lowest part of the band corresponds to a small employer and a candidate with minimum qualifications and minimum experience, and the maximum will correspond to an MNC employer, higher qualifications and maximum experience. The minimum wages are being revised upwards by the State Governments regularly. The minimum compensations indicated in this book are based on the minimum wages applicable for the year 2014-15 and hence will need to go up to be on par with the revised minimum wages.

Source of Compensation Data

The compensation band mentioned in this book is based on data collected from various job boards and is based on the thousands of job requirements received by the TMI Group during the year 2014-15. As compensation varies from year to year, it is a good idea to visit websites like www.payscale.com, to get the latest compensation brackets.

TRAINING AND ON-THE-JOB TRAINING

Training is another aspect that most freshers worry about. Being fresh out of college, they worry if they will be able to perform a particular job role or not. Nowadays, most corporates induct freshers to the job, and training gives them an idea about the company and what the company expects from them. Some corporates also prefer giving on-the-job training so that instead of understanding the job role theoretically, they can gain practical knowledge by working on the role.

However, lately there is a trend to minimize the induction training for a variety of reasons. Therefore, new employees have a handicap and are still expected to perform.

DEALING WITH PHYSICAL AND MENTAL STRESS

No job is a bed of roses. We all live in a very competitive world. To survive the tough competition, an individual is expected to be one above the crowd and not one among the crowd. So with expectation, comes stress. All jobs—desk jobs and field jobs—can be stressful. Stress can be physical and mental. Desk jobs do not involve travel, but people can experience mental stress since deadlines have to be met. In field jobs, employees experience physical stress when they have to travel to meet clients, go for meetings, get orders, meet suppliers/customers, and others. For example, take the role of an Accountant. It is a desk job. But there are times when the company has to close the books of accounts. During this period, Accountants experience maximum stress as they spend long hours at office. This causes both physical as well as mental stress. Similarly, take Human Resources (HR). During performance appraisals they also experience heavy stress. So targets are embedded in almost all roles.

Stress due to Targets

There is a misconception that only sales jobs have targets and hence are stressful. This is not true. Stress is inherent in every job. We at the TMI Group conducted a survey of 6000 graduates from Tamil Nadu and Andhra Pradesh. Most did not want to take up Sales or Customer Service jobs because of targets. There is a high level of phobia among students regarding targets. So we want to take some time explaining the relationship between targets, job stability, and stress.

What is a target?

It is nothing but an outcome that you are asked to achieve within a particular time-frame. It can be as simple as preparing a PowerPoint presentation or meeting sales targets, meeting deadlines in the IT industry, and so on. Stress comes with uncertainty. When does uncertainty arise? It arises because of poor planning and execution.

Handling stress

Ask yourself, 'Can I manage stress?' Yes! You can. Please understand that companies assign targets because they are achievable. No one will give you an unrealistic target. So:

- plan your work;
- prioritize your activities;
- start working from day one; and
- focus on your target and work hard, because there is no substitute for hard work.

Over a period of time, you get used to the stress.

SHOULD WOMEN AVOID SOME JOB ROLES?

Most of the jobs in the corporate world can be deemed safe for women.

There are two parts to a woman employee's career—what happens at the beginning of her career before marriage and what happens after she gets married. It is true (especially in the Indian context) that once a woman gets married, her responsibilities increase and therefore, she may not be able to dedicate too much time to her career. So this should not stop her from selecting a job that she wishes to do at the beginning of her career. Various entry-level jobs give an opportunity to women to explore the corporate world and the number of opportunities is immense. So women can venture into any job they want to after understanding the challenges involved.

HIRING AND FIRING

A fear that exists in the minds of most youngsters is about getting fired. What if the company asks me to leave the job? What will I do in such a situation? Where will I go? How will I face my family?

Relax!! Hiring and firing depends upon three aspects—individual performance, the state of the economy, and the company's overall performance. If your individual performance is not good, you will lose the job anyway. The current state of the economy impacts the performance of most employers. If the economy is booming, job opportunities will increase and if the economy is on a downturn, companies will be forced to reduce jobs and so they fire employees. A financially secure company will keep all its jobs during an economic slowdown/recession. But if a company is unable to bear the brunt, then good performers will be retained while non-performers may be fired. If you are a good performer, there is no risk.

So being fired is not a risk for a hard-working and performing employee. Even if that happens, there are many competitors who will pickup that person.

BASIC SKILLS A CANDIDATE MUST POSSESS

Every job role demands certain skills from candidates. Skills can be basic or job-specific skills. Basic skills that are commonly required across all job roles are covered in this section.

Communication Skills

The most important and the most crucial skill that any job role demands from candidates, is basic communication skills—to converse with people, write emails, and so on. Companies expect candidates to know basic communication etiquette, so that it is easy for them to survive in the corporate environment.

Very often communication skills are misunderstood as communication skills in English. This is not true. For many job roles, English is a big advantage. But even if you are not very good at English but can still communicate well in the vernacular language that is spoken in a specific region, you will succeed. Another misconception is that good communication skills means being a great public speaker. This again is not true at the entry-level but is required at higher-level jobs.

There are four aspects to communication.

Think clearly

You must always think before you say something to anyone. If you don't think before you speak, you might end up saying something else and hence create confusion.

Articulate/phrase clearly

You must always use the right words and phrases while communicating with people.

Take feedback

Always wait and assess if people have actually understood what you are trying to say. If you keep talking and there is no reaction from the other party, it means you have failed in communicating. But if they show some reaction like laughing or nodding their heads, then it means you have made your point.

Get a positive outcome

The purpose of communicating, especially in an organizational context, is to get the person to appreciate your viewpoint. Even when you criticize, you want the other party to listen to your views and accept your criticism, which will happen only if you speak in a persuasive and non-offensive manner. This aspect is often missed out.

Multi-tasking Skills

Multi-tasking is the ability to plan and start multiple activities so that all your tasks progress simultaneously. For example, chess is a mind game that is not easy to master, but there are people who are called Grandmasters. A Grandmaster can challenge multiple players at the same venue, moving from table to table responding to the moves of each opponent. They are great multi-taskers.

Time Management Skills

Many people think that only if one manages time well, one will be able to maintain a work–life balance. Why is time management so important? Because inefficiency in managing time can make you miss deadlines. Managing time effectively is an art. There are some simple rules of managing time. We would like to call them the 4 Rs of Time Management.

Realize that deadlines are important

You need to plan your activities by keeping in mind that every task requires a certain amount of time, has a deadline, and your time is also limited. So prioritizing your tasks is very important.

Review before you commit

Once you are given a task, you must always make a work plan to meet the deadline before accepting it.

Review after you commit

Once you start working on something, make it a point to take some time out and see if the activities are taking place in accordance with the work plan. If you don't do so then things might not go your way at the last moment and you may have to miss your deadlines.

Revise your deadlines

Once you realize that due to some reason, the project might take a little longer than expected, it is always better to negotiate with your boss and revise your deadlines by giving him/her the real reasons.

If you follow these four Rs, then you will definitely be able to manage your time well.

Team Skills

Most jobs in organizations are done in teams. So you need to be a team player to perform well. You may be a part of the team. To be a team player you have to share information, share the work load, and be positive. Every team loves a person who gives more than s/he takes and who is a problem-solver.

For instance, if you are working in the Production Department of a company you will need the help of many people to manage production—the Maintenance Engineer (to ensure that the equipment is in working condition), Procurement Executive (to ensure that all the raw materials are in place), Industrial Relations Manager (to ensure that the factory workers are reporting on time for their shifts and working properly). Many of these people may even be senior to you. You need to get their cooperation.

People Management Skills

When you are leading a team, you have to understand that each team member is different and cannot be managed merely by authority. You have to be empathetic, a good listener, a good motivator, good at delegating the task to the right person to be a good people Manager.

Decision-making Skills

Taking decisions is part of every job. To decide, you have to be analytical and also intuitive. Some decisions will go wrong, but you should know how to take corrective action.

Analytical Skills

Analysing is the science of drawing inferences from data and events that happen. The most important questions—why did something happen? What is the real cause? What is likely to happen if you do something? Analytical skills help you answer some of these questions.

Apart from these basic skills, every job role demands sound technical skills as well as specialized skills based on the nature of work. These are highlighted in the individual job profiles.

Section 2

ENTRY-LEVEL JOB ROLES IN REGULAR ORGANIZATIONS

3

MARKETING DEPARTMENT

Before going on to the entry-level job roles, let us understand why the role of a Marketing Department in an organization is so important, through a simple example. Most of us come across vegetable vendors either sitting by the wayside or pushing their carts through colonies in our day-to-day lives. Have you ever wondered how they market their vegetables? To understand the importance of effective marketing and before coming up with a marketing strategy, it is important to concentrate on the 4 Ps of Marketing.

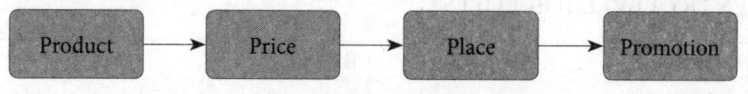

Figure 3.1: The Four Ps of Marketing

Product

The vegetable vendor must first identify customer needs and expectations. Accordingly, he must decide if he wants to sell non-perishable goods like potatoes and onions or, for example, sell only fresh green vegetables. Thus he has to choose the product to sell first.

Price

Next he has to decide the price at which he will sell—how much margin should he charge on his purchase cost? The product should be priced in such a way that it is easy on the pockets of customers as well as profitable to the vegetable vendor.

Place

He now has to decide if he wants to stand at one strategic place and attract customers, or if he wants to go around streets and sell vegetables door to door. He decides on 'where' to sell.

Promotion

It is imperative he makes people aware of his vegetable shop. He can choose to shout on the streets or he can blow a horn letting people know that he has come. This is how a product is promoted.

Similarly, once a company is set up, it is important for it to create a continuous demand for its goods and services. Effective marketing done by managing the 4 Ps has a very strong impact on achieving profitability and boosting sales. A Marketing Department plays a very vital role in helping the company cope with heavy competition and also in bridging the gap between ever-changing consumer needs and services through new product launches.

Thus there are many functions that a Marketing Department performs. Of them the most important are mentioned below, along with some entry-level job roles.

ENTRY-LEVEL JOB ROLES

CODE	ROLE
MKTG 1	Market Research Analyst
MKTG 2	Brand Executive
MKTG 3	Media Executive
MKTG 4	Creative Copywriter
MKTG 5	Design Artist Assistant
MKTG 6	Digital Marketing Specialist

MKTG 1 MARKET RESEARCH ANALYST

Job Description

The organization must know what the demands of customers are, who the competitors are, how their advertising campaign meets the customer needs, among other factors. Whose job is it to collect all this data? It is the job of a Market Research Analyst. This person is a very important part of the Marketing Department.

Market research (MR) is a specialized area and many companies also outsource this function to specialist market research agencies. So this role is also available in MR agencies.

This role is about analysing information to measure the demand for a potential product or service. Some companies develop marketing and sales strategies based upon the information procured by Market Research Analysts.

Typical Responsibilities

- Collecting data on customer demographics, preferences, needs, and buying habits to identify potential markets and factors affecting product demand.
- Analysing collected data.
- Preparing reports of findings, illustrating data graphically, and translating complex findings into simple action items.
- Measuring and assessing customer satisfaction.
- Forecasting and tracking marketing and sales trends.
- Conducting research and measuring the effectiveness of marketing, advertising, and communication programmes and strategies.
- Attending staff conferences to provide management with information and proposals concerning the promotion, distribution, packaging design, and pricing of company products or services.
- Gathering data on competitors and analysing their prices, sales, method of marketing and distribution, to help companies determine their position in the marketplace.

Market Research Analyst: A Profile

Likely salary with 1–3 years of experience	Rs 150,000–Rs 350,000 per annum.
Targets	All the research activities have to be conducted at the lowest cost in minimal time without compromising on the quality and produce crucial consumer insights, every time. This creates daily work pressures and deadlines.
Challenges	The biggest challenge is making sense of the data collected from field research. Most often the respondents that you survey may not tell the truth or may tell only part of the truth. So how to draw conclusions based on reliable data is the biggest challenge. To meet this

	challenge one needs experience in designing the research plan, watching out for research mistakes, and so on. Developing end-to-end knowledge about market research techniques and staying abreast with the latest developments is another challenge.
Skills	Apart from some basic skills that are mentioned in the beginning of the book, one must have: • excellent analytical and statistical skills; • good planning skills; • be detail-oriented; and • have good critical thinking and report writing skills.
Stress	Moderate.
Travel on the job	Very limited.
Impact on stakeholders	The Marketing Team is directly impacted by this role.
Career prospects	You can go on to become a Senior Research Analyst after three years of experience and then become a Lead/Manager, heading a team of Market Research Analysts.
Future salary with 5–7 years of experience	Rs 500,000–Rs 800,000 per annum.

A Practitioner's View
Market Research Analyst, Prachee Kukreja, Thane

Ms Kukreja has some experience in the field of market research. When we spoke to her and asked her why she would recommend this role to a fresher, she said:

'Market research to me has always been creativity applied to exploration. Exploring facts, figures, statements then comprehending reasons, working on causes and effects, all need creativity. I love the field because it makes me think "beyond" every aspect of the subject. I worked with the ice-cream brand TOP 'N TOWN as an Assistant Market Research Analyst and that was the time when I actually learnt how the ice-cream industry actually works. The competitors are around waiting to grab your market share and your efforts will help marketing wizards design strategy to beat them. The best part is, it allows you to make errors. It is a serious job but is coupled with fun! Trust me, I learnt a lot while working in this role and so will you!'

BRANDING AND ADVERTISING

It is the responsibility of the Marketing Department to attract new customers and retain existing customers by constantly striving to create a positive brand image of the product through advertising. The Branding and Advertising Department works along with departments like Sales and Customer Service to protect and increase the brand preference of the product.

So let's look at the 'branding' side first.

MKTG 2 BRAND EXECUTIVE

Job Description

A Brand Executive (also called a Product Executive) is the champion of the brand and is responsible for the communication material required to inform the customers about the brand attributes. In addition she/he is responsible for various events like music shows to promote existing brands or organizing big media events to launch new products.

Typical Responsibilities

A Brand Executive is also responsible for standardizing brand guidelines across all brand communication materials. Apart from this, overseeing and approving all promotional and branding materials, managing the creative advertising agency (that creates the branding communication), and coordinating activities with event management companies and press relations agencies are also the job of the Brand Executive.

- Planning and scheduling brand campaigns.
- Assisting the Brand Manager in product launches.
- Planning and taking part in exhibitions.
- Approving vendor bills in advertising, PR, and event management areas.
- Keeping track of brand budget utilization.
- Doing a brand sales analysis and submitting periodic reports to the top management.

- Preparing press releases and coordinating with PR agencies.
- Developing consumer and dealer promotion campaigns.
- Coordinating with outdoor media.
- Most importantly—ensuring that all the money spent results in continuous sales increase.

Brand Executive: A Profile

Likely salary with 1–3 years of experience	Rs 300,000–Rs 500,000 per annum.
Targets	To ensure brand promotion activities are scheduled and executed on time and within budget. To ensure extensive press coverage. To measure effectiveness of 'ad spend'—the amount being spent on various communications, including advertising. To ensure that the dealers of the product are incentivized to achieve their targets.
Challenges	Managing vendors against tight deadlines. Staying up-to-date on the new media and promotion options.
Skills	Up-to-date knowledge on branding and communication. Analytical and quantitative skills. Creative thinking. Good report-writing skills.
Stress	Moderate.
Travel on the job	Extensive travel to conferences and exhibitions and market visits.
Impact on stakeholders	The Sales Team is highly impacted by this role.
Career prospects	Become a Senior Branding Executive with two-plus years of experience and then go on to become a Brand Manager with five years of experience.
Future salary with 5–7 years of experience	Rs 600,000–Rs 1,000,000 per annum.

A Practitioner's View
Brand Manager, Piya Vas, Delhi

When I asked Piya what she liked most about her job, she said:
'The knowledge base I was able to garner from working in this marketing function over the last six years has been vast and rich. I have had the opportunity to manage projects and campaigns in customer relationship management (CRM), digital, print, events, media, public relations (PR), product launches, retail promotions, ground activation, outdoor media and exhibitions. In addition to this, I was also able to work on budget allocations, activity/calendar planning and vendor sourcing and management. My presentation skills have been honed to the extent that I am approached even by senior management to assist with PowerPoint presentations. Brand management is one aspect of marketing where you can successfully combine creative, analytic, and strategic skills to excel in the field.'

JOB ROLES IN ADVERTISING

Consumers are bombarded with as many as 100 advertisement communications in a single day and the advertiser's communication must stand out in this crowd at minimal cost. Three departments work together to achieve this. The Media Department places this communication in a public media like TV, or newspapers; the Copy Department creates the communication, and the Art Department designs the communication visually. Here we look at the entry-level job roles in these three departments—the Media Executive, the Copy Writer, and the Designer.

Most of those in advertising work in an independent advertising agency, because most companies prefer to outsource these activities, though some large companies—especially in the IT industry—have these three departments in-house.

MKTG 3 MEDIA EXECUTIVE

Job Description

Let's assume that you want to release an advertisement in a newspaper to sell your house. You now have to decide where to spend the money. Should you release a classified advertisement in an English daily, or a vernacular? Or should you place an advertisement on a property website? When should you release the advertisement—on a weekday or a weekend? Should you put the advertisement in one newspaper or in many?

These are the many questions a Media Executive/Manager has to answer on a daily basis. The various options for advertisement releases are called media options. A media plan is the way you spend the budget across various media options.

Typical Responsibilities

As a Media Executive/Manager, your day will buzz with activity. Your typical day starts with a client (also called an advertiser) meeting, to understand the target audience, the budget, and the timelines.

You then spend one or two hours understanding the reading habits of the target audiences and studying the readership/viewership of various media options. Then you make a tentative media plan which will list the media you would like to use. This will be followed by media negotiations with the Sales Team of the respective media.

You finally make the media plan, discuss it with your advertiser and get his/her approval. You release the advertisement through the selected media. In addition to the above, you also manage vendor payments; communicate updates regarding market trends to the management, make changes to media policies as and when required, and negotiate with the media. After the advertisement appears in the media, the Media Executive is responsible for raising the media invoice on the advertiser and for making timely payment to the media.

Media Executive: A Profile

Likely salary with 1–3 years of experience	Rs 200,000–Rs 400,000 per annum.
Targets	Meeting daily deadlines for media releases. Continuously negotiating concessional rates with the media for the advertiser. Bringing down the cost of media spend, through innovative and targeted media like digital media.

Challenges	Biggest challenge: Negotiating with the media because you want to get the lowest prices. Your boss will judge you by the cost-savings that you bring. Second challenge: Measuring and tracking the media reading/viewing habits of your target audience. You may need to keep a track of the latest readership surveys.
Skills	Have a strong outgoing personality with excellent communication skills. Be able to build and maintain healthy relationships across various media.
Stress	Moderate except when media releases are re-scheduled. Initially this can create stress, but over a period of time you adapt to these challenges.
Travel on the job	You may need to travel occasionally to conduct media events like press conferences.
Impact on stakeholders	The clients and business leaders of an organization are impacted by this role.
Career prospects	In two years you can be promoted as Senior Media Executive and in five to eight years you can become a Media Manager.
Future salary with 5–7 years of experience	Rs 500,000–Rs 700,000 per annum.

A Practitioner's View

Media Manager, Afroze Shabana, Hyderabad

Mrs Shabana from Hyderabad worked as a Media Manager for five years. She has hands-on experience in the field of media management, digital marketing, preparing media plans and costing for clients. She says:

'Working in this role has helped me understand media and its management in a better way. Interacting with clients, conducting research, media buying, creating display ads for social networking sites, interest me a lot. The scope in this role is extremely high and so is the learning.'

CREATIVE ROLES IN ADVERTISING

There are two entry-level roles that exist in a Creative Department—those of a Creative Copywriter and a Visualizer/Designer.

MKTG 4 CREATIVE COPYWRITER

Job Description

A Creative Copywriter's job is to take client briefs and develop creative and catchy communication, by using the right words/copy. Copy is the written content of the advertisement, which includes the headline and the other written material. Copywriters also write slogans, catchphrases, and messages for printed adverts, posters, banners, and leaflets. Copywriters are involved in writing text for web advertising, as well as scripts for radio jingles and TV commercials. They integrate the copy with various visual and audio components. It's a very interesting role.

Typical Responsibilities

The duties of a Copywriter include the following:

- Attending meetings to take client briefs.
- Conducting research about clients, competitors, and audiences.
- Coming up with creative ideas/concepts based on client demands.
- Presenting/discussing your work with seniors/Project Managers.
- Understanding the target audience and writing copy accordingly.
- Proofreading the written copy for any spelling errors.
- Working/re-working advertisements, posters, leaflets, and other materials until the final communication is accepted.
- Working on multiple clients and multiple briefs, amidst tight deadlines.
- Submitting reports to the Manager on work done.

Creative Copywriter: A Profile

Likely salary with 1–3 years of experience	Rs 200,000–Rs 500,000 per annum.
Targets	Your target will be ensuring that you produce the most appropriate copy that will help in promoting a product or a service. You will have to write copy on a wide variety of products and services.
Challenges	Understanding the target audience and then writing a copy. For example, if one has to write a slogan or a headline for a fashion show being organized by youngsters, then the copy should be eye-catching; one that will grab everyone's attention. In the same way, if it is for a corporate brochure then the slogan on headline should be more formal. Working on multiple accounts at the same time. Completing work according to the given deadlines.
Skills	Excellent communication skills and command over the used language. A creative and inquisitive mind. Keen observation. Able to work under pressure.
Stress	This job is moderately stressful for a genuinely creative person due to deadlines and rework but will be very stressful for others because creativity is difficult to acquire.
Travel on the job	No travel, this is a desk job.
Impact on stakeholders	Product Managers and customers are impacted by this role.
Career prospects	You will start off as a Junior/Trainee Copywriter and within three years can become a Senior Copywriter. Within the next five to six years you can become a Copy Director, heading a team of Copywriters.
Future salary with 5–7 years of experience	Rs 500,000–Rs 1,000,000 per annum.

A Practitioner's View
Senior Copywriter, Akkinepally
Bharani Kumar, Hyderabad

Mr Kumar is currently working for a leading FM Radio channel and has around six-plus years of work experience in the field of advertising. He says:

'My career in advertising began in January 2008 as a Junior Copywriter, in a small advertising agency. It's been five years now and currently I am working as a Senior Copywriter for a leading FM Radio channel in Hyderabad. I started writing for print ads and went on to write for radio, TV, and web content. Advertising has always been a domain that picks various situations of life and uses the dreams, fears, fun, and emotions of people to convey how a product makes life better. In this process of showcasing each product as a thing that makes life better, my life has become better. It enabled me to think differently, because as a Copywriter it's essential that we not just show one solution, but give multiple choices to the client. That makes you think differently and find solutions from different viewpoints. Last and most important thing this job has taught me is not to get disappointed over any kind of remarks or scathing criticism and always THINK BIG.

'It makes you a better person; it gives you great confidence to do anything you wish to do later in life. It sharpens your intellect and overall understanding of business, people, and the world. It helps emotionally as well; you develop equipoise, because in advertising one day is desolation and the next day, elation. I recommend this especially to those who love challenges.'

MKTG 5 DESIGN ARTIST ASSISTANT

Once the copy is written, it has to be visualized that is, converted to a visual form. This visualized form is called a 'layout'. The layout typically has a headline, written matter called 'body copy' that elaborates upon the headline, plus one or many graphic elements. All these items have to be laid out within the given size of the communication material.

The department which carries out this work is called the Art Department headed by an Art Director and a team of Design Artists who work under the Art Director. The entry-level role in the Art Department is the Design Artist's role.

Typical Responsibilities

- Assist in creating and designing various promotional materials like print advertisements, brochures, catalogues, posters, leaflets.
- Maintain an in-house image bank so that the company can use the required images as and when required.
- Help the core team in planning and executing various advertising campaigns.
- Create various design templates by doing a thorough quality check of the same.
- Assist in day-to-day printing of promotional materials to meet required deadlines.
- Get the ads reviewed by a Senior Design Artist before release.
- Following advertising and printing guidelines while designing material.

Design Artist Assistant: A Profile

Likely salary with 1–3 years of experience	Rs 180,000–Rs 300,000 per annum.
Targets	Ensuring that your designs are contemporary, visually appealing, and achieve the desired outcome.
Challenges	Working on multiple designs at the same time. Meeting demanding deadlines. Keeping up with current trends.
Skills	Develop a creative approach. Strong knowledge of design software applications like Corel Draw, PageMaker. Ability to work under pressure.
Stress	Moderate.
Travel on the job	It is a desk job.

Impact on stakeholders	The Art Director of the company and the target audience of your creative efforts will be impacted by this role.
Career prospects	You will start as an Assistant and, within three years become a Design Artist. You could become an Art Director in seven to ten years.
Future salary with 5–7 years of experience	Rs 350,000–Rs 600,000 per annum.

A Practitioner's View
Design Artist, Kamalakar Miryala, Hyderabad

Mr Miryala has been working as a Design Artist for three years now. He has hands-on experience in the field of designing promotional material. He says:

'Working in this role has helped me understand the importance of design in the field of advertising and branding, in a better way. There is freedom of thought and I get to show my skill and expertise in designing branding materials. I love working on various new design application softwares. The scope in this role is extremely high and so is the learning.'

MKTG 6 DIGITAL MARKETING SPECIALIST

Digital marketing (DM) involves marketing a product/company by using the internet, computers, tablets, even smart phones to communicate with prospective customers.

Job Description

As a Digital marketing Specialist, you will research on the internet first to identify the online habits of your target segment and identify where they are spending time—online discussion groups, websites, blogs, online stores, social media sites like Facebook and others. Identify sites and forums where your target segment posts maximum complaints and queries. You will then reach out through these discussion groups and sites by creating an online marketing strategy and a plan. You will be a part of the Marketing Department of a company and work closely with the Brand Manager, the Creative Team, and with social media specialist agencies. You will handle all digital projects and maintain all web content. You will track the competition's online strategy and research on the effectiveness of various online media options.

Typical Responsibilities

- Identify target audiences.
- Prepare an online marketing plan and digital marketing strategy.
- Visit job boards and social media sites and connect with prospective customers.
- Develop digital communication content.
- Finalize digital marketing budgets and track utilization of the budgets.
- Work with online media agencies.
- Track and counter any negative perceptions posted online.

Digital Marketing Specialist: A Profile

Likely salary with 1–3 years of experience	Rs 300,000–Rs 600,000 per annum.
Targets	Maximizing the number of sales leads received online. Attracting unique visitors and large numbers of page views to your website. Improving the ranking in Google on relevant key words. Attracting a large number of click-throughs in case of banner advertisements. In short, a Digital Marketing Specialist is responsible for getting value out of every rupee spent on the digital media, and ensures that it results in increased business.
Challenges	The biggest challenge is tracking the online behaviour pattern of your target audiences as this changes very fast. Every day new web properties are launched, new technologies are released. One has to be on top of these.
Skills	Deep understanding of web technology, web analytics, content management, and online marketing techniques. Strong project-management skills.
Travel on the job	This job does not involve travelling since most of the time is spent on the internet.

Impact on stakeholders	Digital Marketing Specialists directly impact customers.
Stress	Stress is moderate if you love the internet. The stress lies in convincing others of your ideas, especially when they are not familiar with digital media.
Career prospects	Within five years you can become a Digital Marketing Manager. Or you can become an entrepreneur and start your own digital marketing agency.
Salary with 5-7 years of experience	Rs 800,000–Rs 10,00,000 per annum.

A Practitioner's View
Digital Marketing Specialist, Sachin V. Shenoy, Bengaluru

Mr Shenoy has been working as a Digital Marketing Specialist for the past two and a half years. He has hands-on experience in web analytics, digital media, and social media. He says:

'As this is a booming area of work, most companies are aiming to up their spending quotient. It is very good to be working in this space. Once you develop enough expertise—both tactical and strategic—you can expect a lot of demand in the market and also expect good pay rises. Personally, you become more social in approach and stay up-to-date with the latest trends and also challenge yourself to try out new things and bring out quantifiable outcomes.'

4
SALES DEPARTMENT

This chapter is divided into two sections. Section 1 is a background on the many aspects that go into setting up successful sales organization, no matter what the product is, and Section 2 lists the entry-level job roles in the Sales Department

SECTION 1
SALES: A BACKGROUND

When I was in my management college, my marketing professor used to always give us an example of an individual who used to sell washing powder. This person manufactured and sold the product himself going door-to-door on a bicycle. He sold the washing powder at a very competitive price, and as many people liked the product, his sales started to grow gradually through word-of-mouth publicity.

Yes! I am talking about Dr Karsanbhai Patel who is the brains behind 'Nirma', one of the biggest names in the FMCG industry.

There are various sales techniques available today, but he adopted the most common and most effective form of selling, that is, door-to-door selling/direct selling. But as his market grew, his sales strategy changed to the distribution model typical of the FMCG industry.

IMPORTANCE OF DISTRIBUTION

Dr Karsanbhai had to set up a distribution system for his product to reach customers in different locations, and also ensure that the price of the product did not change.

Therefore, we can see that 'distribution' is the process of delivering the goods from a manufacturing location to a retail location that is nearest to the customer, in the right pack sizes, in a planned manner, at the right cost, and then ensure that the goods are continuously replenished.

Before moving on to the entry-level job roles in the Sales Department, let's look at different ways of selling, that is, 'How you sell', and different types of customers 'to whom you sell'.

CLASSIFYING SALES BASED ON 'HOW YOU SELL'

Consumable sales

The most common and easy type of sale is a consumable sale. Here, the buyer consumes the product, knows about its features, attributes, and benefits and buys it regularly. Good examples would be any consumer goods like soaps and toothpaste.

Concept sales

This is a very difficult form of sale as the seller has to first sell the idea/benefit of the product and then once the customer is convinced, the seller actually sells the product. For example, when selling time-shares in vacation/holiday homes (for instance, selling a time-share in Mahindra Holiday Resorts), one has to first sell the concept ('time-share') and then the product.

Capital equipment/Consumer durable sales

This type of sale usually refers to selling an asset to the consumer. The equipment is sold to the consumer, but the benefit of buying the asset can be felt over a period of time. For example, an inverter is purchased only once by the consumer but he experiences the benefit of this purchase over the coming years.

CLASSIFYING SALES BASED ON 'WHOM YOU SELL TO'

Various sales techniques are adopted by companies to fulfil their sales targets. The type of sales technique that a company adopts depends mostly on the buying behaviour of consumers.

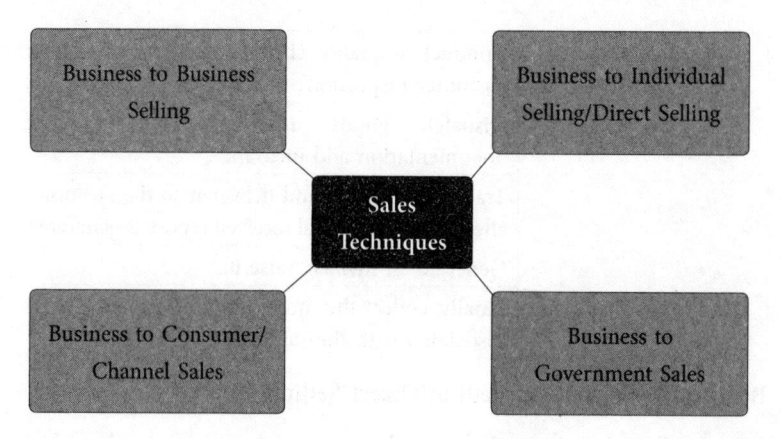

Figure 4.1: Types of Sales Techniques

- Business to Business Selling
- Business to Individual Selling/Direct Selling
- Business to Consumer/Channel Sales
- Business to Government Sales

(Sales Techniques)

Business to Business (B2B) Selling

B2B sale involves one company selling its products, goods, or services to other companies or enterprises. This could be a manufacturing company selling goods to a consumer goods company. For example, a company manufacturing glass bottles sells to a company that is planning to launch a new liquor brand. This is called business to business or B2B selling. Here the sales process is more business-like and the sales-cycle time is longer. The typical B2B sales process is given in Table 4.1.

Table 4.1: Industrial B2B Sales Cycle

Industrial business to business sales cycle	Marketing Department generates an enquiry
	Respond to the enquiry by sending proposals/estimates.
	Handle objections raised by the other party.
	Pick up the order and accept it.
	Take an advance and pass on the order to the Production Department.
	Follow up with the Production Department to complete the order on time.

	Conduct a quality check and also arrange for customer inspection.
	Dispatch goods after checking all the documentation and insurance.
	Track the dispatch and deliver it to the customer, after which a 'material received report' is generated.
	Generate an invoice, raise it.
	Finally, collect the money and all the documents associated with the sale.

Business to Individual Selling/Direct Selling

Direct selling involves selling products, goods, or services, directly to consumers. Here the manufacturing company directly reaches out to consumers and sells products. For example, Eureka Forbes is a water-purifier company that directly reaches out to customers, provides them free demonstrations on how to use its water-purifiers, and if the customer is convinced, a sale takes place.

Business to Consumers/Channel (B2C) Sales

This involves selling products, goods, or services through different sales channels—stockists/distributors, wholesalers, and retailers—to reach consumers. Consumer goods like toothpaste are typically sold using this model depicted in Figure 4.2.

The toothpaste manufacturer sells his product to various stockists/distributors at different locations who stock these items in their warehouses and in turn sell them to wholesalers. The wholesalers club various other goods along with the toothpaste, and deliver them to retailers to minimize transportation costs and finally, the retailer sells it to the end-user, that is, the consumer.

Business to Government (B2G) Sales

This type of sale is a slightly complicated one, because all government purchases have to be transparent and everyone must be given an opportunity to sell. If you want to sell something to a government, then you must first send an application with facts such as your tenure of business, type of business, your qualifications, and get yourself

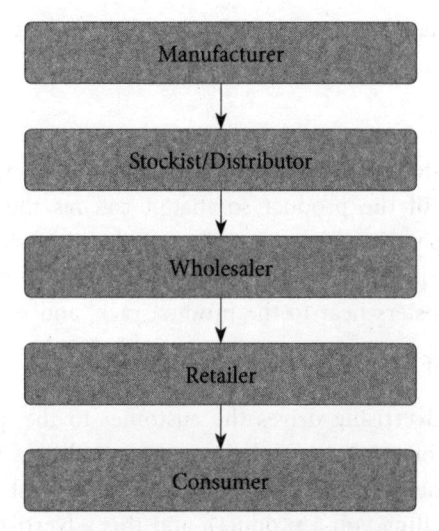

```
Manufacturer
    ↓
Stockist/Distributor
    ↓
Wholesaler
    ↓
Retailer
    ↓
Consumer
```

Figure 4.2: Parties Involved in B2C Sales

registered through an expression of interest (EoI). They will then call for tenders and various bidders will be invited to bid and win the contract. The bids are technically evaluated and those bids which are technically not suitable are rejected at this stage and the price bids of the remaining bidders are opened. Whoever bids a lowest price, wins the contract. Due to so many factors involved, this mode of buying is mostly adopted by public sector companies and government departments.

Now that we have gained an understanding of some of the major modes of selling we can move on to the role of the Sales Department in a consumer goods company.

PRODUCT AVAILABILITY AND DISTRIBUTION

Why was Dr Karsanbhai Patel so successful in his endeavour? It is because he had done considerable research to identify where his prospective customers are and how to reach the product to them.

In the same way a Sales Department of a company is responsible for proper distribution of goods to various locations by using channels like distributors, wholesalers, and retailers or reach the product directly to the consumer. Unless and until the product is easily accessible to customers, they will not be interested in buying it. So the key challenge is to ensure that the product is purchased and stocked by the retailer.

Merchandizing

Once a retailer stocks the product, it is important to work towards effective display of the product so that it catches the attention of customers. The space in which the product is placed can be highlighted using additional lighting, placing point-of-sale (PoS) materials like small danglers/posters near to the product rack, and so on.

Effective Point of Sale Communication

Effective mass advertising drives the customer to the 'point-of-sale', that is, the location where the sale is made (could be a retail shop, a wholesale warehouse, or even your own front door if it is a door-to-door salesman selling you a product), and this advertising has to be further reinforced by PoS communication material like danglers and posters to convert an inquisitive prospect into a customer.

The Sales Department must ensure that a strong bond is established between customer and product by constantly explaining the product's features, attributes, and benefits (FAB) to customers through effective PoS communications.

Close the Sale

Once the product's FAB quality is established in the prospect's mind, the next step is to close the sale. When you are selling a consumer product like toothpaste, the sale is made by the retailer. In case of industrial products (B2B sales), the Sales Department is responsible for closing the sale, that is, 'Converting an enquiry into cash'.

Let us understand this through a simple example. A company manufactures generators, its Marketing and Advertising Department puts in enormous efforts to advertise the generators. When a prospective buyer calls, influenced by the advertisement, an enquiry is said to be generated. Now it is the responsibility of the Sales Department to convert that enquiry into a sale. So the Sales Executive contacts the prospective buyer, makes various presentations to him, overcomes any objections, gives estimates, and finally closes the sale.

Replenish Stock

Once a sale is made, the stock present in all outlets needs to be replenished. Otherwise, the company could see a stock-out (that is, nil or not enough stock), which is not good at all since the company could lose both existing and prospective customers.

Collect Money

The most important task in sales is collecting payment from the customer, on time. Very often companies extend credit and the Sales Team has to track and collect the money on time.

Increase Revenue from Sales

The main purpose of generating a sale is revenue growth. Dr Karsanbhai understood this very well. Whenever he would sell a packet of detergent, he would tell his buyers that in case they liked the product, they could refer it to their friends and relatives. Thanks to the word-of-mouth advertising and his efforts, many more people started buying Nirma washing powder and this helped him build a strong client-base. This increase in sales volume resulted in an increase in revenue. Likewise, it is the responsibility of the Sales Department to make sure that they generate more and more sales in order to continuously increase the revenue of the organization.

CUSTOMER SATISFACTION AND RETENTION

While selling products to customers, Dr Karsanbhai always made it a point to take feedback from them regarding any improvements that needed to be made to the product. If the customer is satisfied and happy, he will refer the product to more and more people and also become loyal towards the product. After a sale is made, surveys should be conducted to take their feedback and make improvements to the product according to their needs and wants.

HOW IS A PRODUCT PROMOTED?

It is very important for products to be promoted in order to catch the attention of customers. The three main objectives of sales promotion are:

- to pre-pone the sale: when you sell a toothpaste with an offer such as 'buy one, get one free', you are actually pre-poning the sale by a month, because you make the customer buy two months' worth of toothpaste;
- to clear stock: sometimes companies offer discounts on various products just to clear out old stock that is not being sold easily; and
- to induce a brand switch: sales promotion is also a way of luring customers to switch from favourite brands to yours, and to achieve this the company offers discounts on its products.

TYPES OF SALES PROMOTIONS

Consumer promotion

The Sales Department finds different ways to attract the attention of the customer by coming up with various offers and displaying them through banners, posters, hoardings, and so on. For example, 'Book a flat, get a car free', 'Buy two soaps, get one free', 'Buy a biscuit packet, get a matchbox free'.

Dealer promotion

This type of promotion is done by keeping the dealer in mind. Organizations can tell dealers that if they sell a product, more than the agreed quantity, they will be offered an extra commission. So it becomes the responsibility of the dealer to sell to consumers and make them buy a particular product over others. This can be done by displaying the product in such a way that it catches the eye of the customer as soon as she/he walks into the outlet.

SECTION 2
ENTRY-LEVEL JOB ROLES

There are four types of sales as discussed in Section 1, and each has an exciting entry-level job role for sales role aspirants. To recap, these are as follows:

CODE	ROLE
SAL 1	B2B Sales Executive

SAL 2	Direct Sales Executive
SAL 3	Channel Sales Executive
SAL 4	Pre-sales Executive

SAL 1 B2B SALES EXECUTIVE

Job Description

A B2B sale, as mentioned earlier, means business to business selling. It involves one company selling its products, goods, or services to another business enterprise. A B2B Sales Executive is someone who helps the company in selling its products or services to other companies.

A B2B Sales Executive is usually involved in the whole sales-cycle, which includes:

- acquiring new customers;
- acquiring new orders from existing customers;
- building and maintaining relationships with customers during delivery of the product/service; and
- collecting payment.

Typical Responsibilities

Understand the products/services and the sales process followed by your company. You can talk to your Manager in case you need clarity about any point. Your day might start with identifying what your action plan for the day is and review of your target achievements till that day. You may need to:

- Collect information about prospective customers.
- Preparing proposals/contracts for selling your product or a service.
- Make a formal presentation about the company and your proposal to customers.
- Make follow-up calls/visits.
- Close the sale and collect payment.

B2B Sales Executive: A Profile

Likely salary with 1–3 years of experience	Rs 150,000–Rs 250,000 per annum.
Targets	Achieving monthly, quarterly, and annual targets for revenue and collections. Acquiring new customers. Retaining existing customers.
Challenges	Attracting new clients by identifying the right prospects and convincing them about how you/your company can deliver. It's not an easy task because initially your customers know more about your product than you do and competitors will be entrenched. You need to know your product and your competition in depth. Negotiating the best price and collecting monies without losing the customer's goodwill. In this field you get to meet a lot of people with different personalities. You cannot impress every prospect by applying the same approach. So you need to know how to effectively communicate and engage with different people.
Skills	Excellent networking and relationship-building skills. Developing a very positive mind-set and coming across with high energy. A highly disciplined work-style. Good communication and presentation skills.
Stress	Moderate to high.
Travel on the job	You will have to travel within the city or tour regularly, depending upon the territory allotted to you.
Impact on stakeholders	The customers are impacted most by this role.
Career prospects	You will initially start off as a Sales Executive. After two/three years, you will be promoted to the post of an Assistant Manager–Sales. Based on how well you perform and the experience/skills you develop, you can become a Territory Sales Manager and then Area Sales Manager over a period of five to eight years.
Future salary with 5–7 years of experience	Rs 400,000–Rs 700,000 per annum.

A Practitioner's View

Sales Executive, Sukumar, Hyderabad

Mr Sukumar has been working as a B2B Sales Executive for the past three years. When we asked him about his experiences and why he would recommend this role to a fresher, he said:

'A B2B sale is very challenging. To make a customer believe in your products or services is not an easy job as they have their own reservations. To be able to make a sale, firstly you should have belief and confidence in what you are selling to a customer. This helps me create a strong impression in the minds of customers. I am an extrovert and like interacting with people. My job complements my personality. That is why I like doing this role. I would recommend this role to any fresher who wishes to make a career in sales, as it helps in understanding the concepts of selling. The career prospects are good, opportunities are immense, competition is high, and the pay is exciting.'

SAL 2 DIRECT SALES EXECUTIVE

Job Description

A direct sale involves selling a product or a service directly to an individual consumer or the end-user. For example: a car showroom or door-to-door sales. Either way the sale happens only if you, as the sales person, is able to convince the customer to buy. The customer often buys due to emotional rather than logical reasons and hence this is the toughest of all sales roles for a fresher.

Typical Responsibilities

- Representing the organization at trade fairs, exhibitions, and other events.
- Cold-calling on prospects for the purpose of building business.
- Demonstrating the product.
- Closing the sale by booking the order.
- Maintaining reports regarding orders and sales, and updating the Sales Department about the same.

- Identifying new and unmet consumer needs during customer interactions.
- Attending team meetings to discuss various aspects of selling and sharing.

Direct Sales Executive: A Profile

Likely salary with 1–3 years of experience	Rs 100,000–Rs 250,000 per annum plus very high sales incentives.
Targets	Weekly and monthly sales targets in a very competitive environment.
Challenges	Meeting sales targets daily and weekly. To keep a positive mind-set in face of customer rejections. Managing a work–life balance, because you have to work as per a customer's timelines. For example, you may have to work on holidays because customers prefer to shop on holidays. Dealing with difficult customers.
Skills	Selling skills. Strong communication and influencing skills. A smart and friendly appearance. A passion for selling. Being self-motivated. Active listening skills. Ability to work under target pressure. Developing a positive attitude.
Travel on the job	Extensive travel within the city is expected. Outstation travel depends upon the territory allotted.
Impact on stakeholders	Customers are directly impacted.
Stress	Initially stress levels are very high. The stress declines once you pickup the tricks of the trade, provided you have a 'sales personality'.
Career prospects	Your career prospects will be very good, if you succeed. You can become a Sales Lead within two years and a Sales Manager within five years.

Future salary with 5–7 years of experience	Rs 400,000–Rs 800,000 per annum plus very high sales incentives.

A Practitioner's View
Direct Sales Executive, Sambit, Patna

Mr Sambit has been working in the field of direct sales for the last eight-plus years. When we asked him about his experiences and why he would recommend this role to a fresher, he said:

'I like working in the field as it is extremely challenging and there are various opportunities to learn and grow. I have a complete understanding about sales and marketing strategies that really work, because I am in touch with the end-consumer and have honed my sales presentation skills. I also have developed a deep understanding about the customer psyche and the business. Personally, it has helped me develop and maintain social contacts, taught me how to manage my time well, and also taught me how to strike a balance between work and personal life. I would strongly recommend this role to a fresher for many reasons. It will help them in completely understanding the business from a customer's perspective. I would say, the more you work the more you get. It's fun if you can do it the right way.'

SAL 3 CHANNEL SALES EXECUTIVE

Job Description

A channel (B2C) sale means selling though a sales channel that is made up of stockists, wholesalers, distributors, and retailers. This involves lesser selling costs when compared to direct selling. Channel sales involve selling a product to a retailer with the help of channel partners—stockists/distributors, wholesalers, retailers. The Channel Sales Executive's job is to sell to the stockist/distributor (this is called primary sales) who in turn will sell it to the wholesalers and retailers (this is called secondary sales) with the help of sales people they employ. It is the retailer who actually sells the product to the end-consumer (this is called tertiary sales). Obviously, unless the consumer buys from the retailer, the retailer will not buy from the distributor and the distributor will not buy from the company. So the Channel Sales Executive's job is not just to manage primary sales, but manage secondary sales through the Distributor Sales Team and through regular visits to the retailer. But she/he normally is not involved in the tertiary sales but is impacted by it.

Therefore, as a Channel Sales Executive, one will need to plan and achieve sales targets, manage the existing channel partners, provide training and motivation to the Distributor Sales Team, explore business opportunities in new territories by acquiring new partners. The Channel Sales Executive reports to the Channel Sales Manager.

Typical Responsibilities

- Meet with stockists/distributors to review stock levels and to push for primary sales.
- Work the market with the Distributor Sales Team for secondary sales order booking and collections.
- Assist in hiring, training, guiding, and motivating the Distributor Sales Team and help them achieve their targets.
- Work closely with the Marketing Team in distributing PoS communication material.
- Appoint new channel partners, including stockists, distributors, and so on, whenever required.
- Track competition activities and recommend corrective action.
- Prepare sales forecasts for your territory.
- Communicate and execute promotion schemes for the channel, as devised by the management.
- Handle existing business partners (channel partners), and retailers to build a strong loyalty for the company.
- Monitor the performance of distributors and retailers and handle their complaints.
- Assist in conducting product sampling, consumer research, and analysing the data procured.
- Propose innovative promotion strategies to increase sales revenues in your territory.
- Review the activities and also zero in an effective plan to meet monthly targets.

Channel Sales Executive: A Profile

Likely salary with 1–3 years of experience	Rs 150,000–Rs 250,000 per annum plus sales incentives and travel and conveyance allowances.
Targets	Meet monthly, quarterly targets for sales, collections, and market share. Increase the number of retail outlets stocking the product.
Challenges	Meeting set targets despite competitive pressures and channel partner issues. Motivating the Distributor Sales Team, who may not be paid well, towards achieving targets. Extracting orders, while still maintaining good relations with distributors and retailers. Forecasting sales in a rapidly changing market.
Skills	Relationship-building and influencing skills. Team management and interpersonal skills. Enormous energy and work discipline. Decent communication skills, especially in the vernacular.
Travel on the job	You will have to travel extensively within your assigned territory.
Impact on stakeholders	The sales channel and customers are impacted by this role.
Stress	Initially, stress levels are high due to targets. Over a period of time, you will get used to the target pressure, if you have the sales personality.
Career prospects	You will initially start off as a Channel Sales Executive. After two years, you will be promoted to the post of Sales Supervisor or Territory Sales In-charge. In five to eight years you can become a Sales Manager (also often called 'Area Sales Manager'), for a large territory like a state, subject to performance.
Future salary with 5–7 years of experience	Rs 350,000–Rs 500,000 per annum plus incentives and travel and conveyance allowances.

A Practitioner's View
Channel Sales Executive, Debarshree Saikia, Guwahati

Mr Saikia has been working as a Channel Sales Executive for a little over one and a half years. When we spoke to him to understand what interested him the most, he said:

'My job involves dealing with various distributors and vendors. The challenges that I face are mostly payment collections, visiting remote areas, and credit dealings. My confidence and communication skills have increased by working in this field as I get to interact with many different types of people. The scope in this job is immense because the FMCG industry, which adopts this sales model, is growing rapidly and many MNCs are there in this field.'

SAL 4: PRE-SALES EXECUTIVE

Job Description

A Pre-sales Executive is someone who assists the Manager in generating new sales leads through phones/the internet.

The primary duty is to identify new customers and engage with existing customers for new business. The Pre-sales Executive is responsible for making phone calls and sending emails to generate sales leads and pass it on to the Sales Team. To do this you have to understand the business of your company, its products and services, and identify the target segments which may be interested in your products.

Typical Responsibilities

You will have lot of activities to accomplish on a daily basis.

- Firstly, you must understand the prospects base of your company.
- Then using various paid and free databases such as the Yellow Pages, association member list, or Google, you need to generate a prospect list, then connect and identify the key people who can decide about buying your products.
- Making outbound sales calls to customers to introduce the

product, assess their preliminary interest and categorize them into, 'hot, warm, or cold' prospects.
- Set up telephonic and face-to-face meetings for the Sales Team with the 'hot' prospects.
- Make follow-up calls to prospects.
- Generate referral leads.
- Track the status of the sales leads generated.
- Assist the Sales Manager in making sales proposals.
- Assist the Sales Team by conducting research on competition
- Prepare sales lead reports to the Manager as and when required.

Pre-sales Sales Executive: A Profile

Likely salary with 1–3 years of experience	Rs 150,000–Rs 250,000 per annum.
Targets	Meeting weekly and monthly targets for 'hot' sales leads. Connecting with a specified number of prospects every day.
Challenges	Generating sale leads through the phone or internet, on a daily basis. Many prospects hate receiving unsolicited tele-sales calls and can be rude and nasty.
Skills	Strong internet research skills. Good communication (written and verbal) and influencing skills. Time management, networking, and interpersonal skills. A very positive mind-set with a learning attitude.
Travel on the job	This is a desk job.
Impact on stakeholders	The Sales Team (employees) and customers are impacted by this role.
Stress	High, especially in the initial stages.
Career prospects	You can become the Pre-sales Lead in two years, and the Pre-sales Manager in five years subject to your performance.
Future salary with 5–7 years of experience	Rs 300,000–Rs 400,000 per annum.

A Practitioner's View
Pre-sales Team Leader, Manjit, Bengaluru

Mr Manjit heads an entire Pre-sales Team. When we asked him about his views on pre-sales as a career option for freshers, he said:

'Having spent six years in the US, four of which were spent in hard-core technology sales roles, it came as a huge surprise when I came back and saw how big pre-sales had become right here in India. For someone to generate a lead and effectively close it, in short end-to-end sales, remotely, was a real eye-opener and speaks volumes of how India has developed its workforce to compete in a global marketplace.

'Someone interested in sales, particularly international sales, should seriously consider looking at getting into pre-sales and look at developing a long and fruitful career within this domain. Pre-sales Teams are typically categorized into Pre-sales, Sales, and Post-sales. I strongly recommend an individual should go through the process of being part of all three and in the sequence listed above.'

Before we close this chapter let us look at somebody who has carved a brilliant and inspiring career in sales.

B. MUTHURAMAN[1]

Each one of us is aware of the Tata Group and its massive business presence. Here is an individual who joined Tata Steel as a Graduate Trainee in 1966 and rose to become the Vice Chairman. Mr B. Muthuraman joined Tata Steel as a Graduate Trainee. On completion of training, he worked in the areas of Iron-making and Engineering Development for ten years and then moved to the Marketing and Sales Division and spent nearly twenty years there, ultimately rising to the position of Vice President.

He was appointed Managing Director of Tata Steel on 22 July 2001 and then became the Company's Vice Chairman and also the Chairman of Tata International. He was conferred the Honorary Fellowship of the All India Management Association on 6 September 2007.

He is also the recipient of a distinguished Alumnus Award from IIT Madras (1997). He bagged the Tata Gold Medal from the Indian Institute of Metals in 2002, CEO of the Year Award from IIMM in 2002, National HRD Network Pathfinders Award 2004 in the CEO Category, Business Standard Award, CEO of the Year 2005, and CEO with HR Orientation Award in 2005, at the World HRD Congress at Mumbai. Further, he was conferred 'Management Man of the Year 2006–2007 Award' by the Bombay Management Association in 2007.

So he truly is a living legend and an inspiration to many.

This case study is an example of how a person can start his career in other functions but later on move to sales and make it to the top. It also highlights the success of a successful B2B sales career.

5

OPERATIONS DEPARTMENT

I have often heard people asking, 'What is an Operations Department? What do its members do? What is their role?' So this chapter is divided into two sections: Section 1 provides basic information about this department—beginning with the manufacturing sector in which operational roles are very critical and common; while Section 2 takes you through some of the entry-level job roles in the Operations Department.

SECTION 1
A BACKGROUND

The manufacturing industry covers industries like textiles, automobiles, aerospace, food processing, consumer products, consumer durables, leather, machinery and equipment.

Manufacturing accounts for 26 per cent of GDP and employs 22 per cent of the total workforce. Post-liberalization, the Indian private sector faced increasing domestic as well as foreign competition, including the threat of cheaper Chinese imports.[2]

Deloitte's Global Manufacturing Competitiveness Index, 2013 ranked India as the fourth most competitive manufacturing nation out of 38 nations.[3] Many global players from sectors such as the automobile, aerospace, and engineering sectors are focusing more on Indian markets and hence are planning to manufacture in India. This has directly increased the employment opportunities in the manufacturing sector.[4] Today this sector generates around 45 million jobs across sectors like the auto industry, textiles, engineering, food processing, and leather sectors. A recent study forecasts an annual growth of 17 per cent for Indian manufacturing and expects it to cross the US$ 300 billion mark by 2015.[5]

OPERATIONS DEPARTMENT IN THE MANUFACTURING SECTOR

The Operations Department is responsible for production and execution of customer orders. It manages the planning, production, and delivery of goods and services. Let us understand the role of the Operations Department in a business through a simple example.

A car dealer sells a car to a customer. The customer wants a particular model, colour, and set of accessories not currently available in the showroom. So the dealer buys some time from the customer to get the car ready according to the customization ordered by him. The dealer updates the car manufacturer regarding the new order and from there on, the Operations Department takes over.

The Operations Team has to plan and procure the raw materials and components required and then get transported to the manufacturing plant. Production is scheduled on the production line as soon as the planning for materials is done. Once the car is ready, it has to be sent for a quality check before it is dispatched to the showroom. Once the quality check is done, the car is carefully transported to the showroom, ensuring that it doesn't get damaged during transit. The Maintenance Department ensures that the manufacturing equipment is operational and productive and hence supports all the above activities. The Administration Department provides administrative support to the Production Team such as managing the canteen, arranging buses, and liaising with local authorities.

Let's look at each of these functions in detail.

Production planning

This department decides which product will be manufactured in each shift. This is called production scheduling.

Material planning and procurement

This department is responsible for planning and procuring raw materials and other items required as per the production schedules. They deal with various vendors to assess their offers in terms of price, capacity, quality, and delivery period and place the order. They also conduct regular follow-ups to ensure that the purchased goods reach the factories on time. The procurement function is covered elaborately in the Supply Chain chapter.

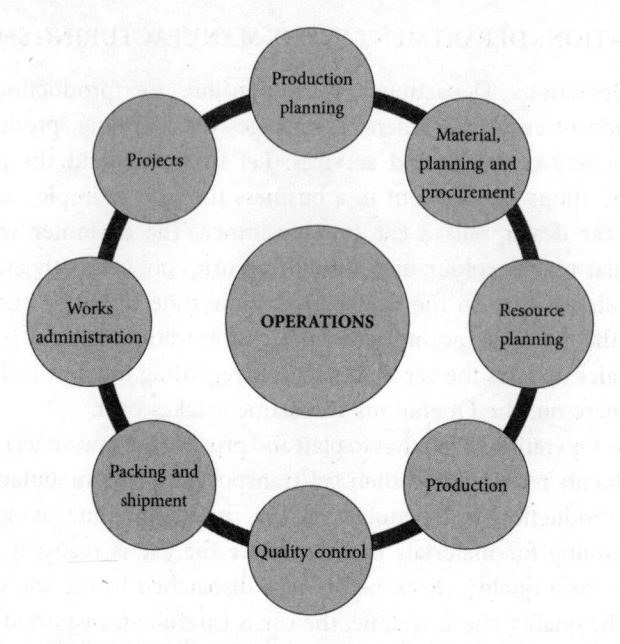

Figure 5.1: Functions of an Operations Department

Resource planning

Machine Planning and Maintenence

The maintenance of machines is also an important part of the production planning process. It is very important to ensure that the machinery used for production is serviced regularly and maintained, so that there is no hindrance in the production process. The primary duty of the Maintenance Department is to ensure that the equipment is running and production is high. If the equipment is down, then the capacity of the machine is not fully utilized. Machines have to be serviced regularly (this is called preventive maintenance), so as to prevent a breakdown in future. Spare parts are required to replace damaged parts and hence have to be stocked.

Manpower Planning

Before production takes place, it is important to plan the manpower required to operate the machines and support the production.

Production

Once the production has been scheduled, the next step is producing or manufacturing the product. It is the responsibility of the Production Department to monitor the production process to ensure that the product is manufactured as per the specifications at the lowest cost and in the shortest possible time.

Quality Control (QC)

Once the product is manufactured/produced, the QC Department conducts a quality check of each and every item produced, to ensure it is in line with the client/customer specifications.

Packing and Shipment

Once the product has undergone a quality check, it has to be shipped to the required location. The Packing and Shipment Department plans and ensures appropriate packaging to minimize damage during transit, and ships the goods with the required documentation, insurance requirements, and so on. The packing and shipment function is covered elaborately in the Supply Chain chapter.

Works Administration

This department supports production and other teams, and is responsible for travel, transportation, security, housekeeping, the canteen, dealing with workplace laws such as the Factories Act.

Projects Department[*]

This specialist department is responsible for the setting up of new projects and the expansion of existing projects. Its responsibilities include design and specifications of new equipment, selection of latest technology, ordering new equipment, receipt and inspection of equipment, commissioning and setting up equipment, training

---

*Note: The Operations Department is also supported by departments such as Finance, Accounts and Personnel Departments—which are covered under the Finance Department and the Human Resources Department sections in this book.

operators, and troubleshooting during the initial stages of commissioning.

SECTION 2
ENTRY-LEVEL JOB ROLES

Since our focus is on graduates, we have identified entry-level job roles with maximum growth potential. Roles in the supply chain, which is part of operations, are covered in a separate chapter.

CODE	ROLE
OPS 1	Production Supervisor
OPS 2	Project Engineer/Trainee
OPS 3	Quality Control Supervisor
OPS 4	Customer Service Engineer

OPS 1 PRODUCTION SUPERVISOR

Job Description

There has to be someone to manage people, and monitor and plan activities in factories where many workmen are involved in manufacturing a product. These tasks are done by Production Supervisors. They are responsible for production output. In smaller companies they may handle the whole factory but in larger organizations, they handle production in a particular department.

Typical Responsibilities

- Planning and scheduling production activities to meet targets.
- Plan for materials and consumables.
- Assign workmen to various tasks.
- Communicate the company's policies and regulations to workers.
- Monitor the workforce.
- Supervise the process of production and solve quality or equipment maintenance issues.
- Ensure that all the safety standards are followed.
- Ensure that activities are carried out in line with the budgets.

- Prepare production reports and communicate the same to the top management.

Production Supervisor: A Profile

Likely salary with 1–3 years of experience	Rs 200,000–Rs 350,000 per annum.
Targets	Ensuring that all production activities take place in a scheduled manner so that goals and targets are met.
Challenges	Ensuring that all workers follow all safety procedures. Since workmen tend to skip safety measures. Managing unionized workmen. Keeping yourself technically updated.
Skills	Good planning skills. Sound technical knowledge of production techniques. Good leadership abilities. Good organizing and problem-solving skills. Being able to work under pressure. Being able to maintain good relations with fellow workers.
Stress	Moderate.
Travel on the job	Very limited travel.
Impact on stakeholders	The customers and workmen (employees) are highly impacted by this role.
Career prospects	Your career prospects are good as you can become a Shift Production In-charge within three to four years and Production Manager in ten years.
Future salary with 5–7 years of experience	Rs 400,000–Rs 600,000 per annum.

A Practitioner's View

Production Supervisor, V.S.R. Anjaneyulu, Hyderabad

Mr Anjaneyulu is working as a Production Supervisor in Indian Immunologicals Ltd, and has around fifteen years' experience. When we asked him about his role and why would he recommend this role to a fresher, he said:

'My job involves planning, implementing, and monitoring production activities. I need to ensure that all activities are taking place as per schedule, in order to avoid any delays in production. Managing the workforce involved is a little challenging as we need to be good to everyone and people must not feel that we are dominating. A lot of coordination is needed between various production units. Therefore, I need to keep myself updated with activities happening across production units to avoid any discrepancies. The learning factor is high in this role as we need to oversee various activities involved in producing a product/drug/vaccine. Candidates who want to join the Production Department are first absorbed as Production Trainees. They need to first attend on-the-job training to understand the process and the standard operating procedures (SOPs). This way the understanding they get regarding the role is also high.'

OPS 2 PROJECT ENGINEER/TRAINEE

Job Description

Project Engineers are responsible for all mechanical, electrical, and instrumentation of the project. In other words, Project Engineers are responsible for erecting and commissioning of all the equipment in a factory and the job also involves drawing specifications of equipment, assisting in identification of equipment vendors, scheduling the installation and ensuring safety of the project site. A Project Engineer Trainee gets exposed and trained to do all the jobs mentioned above.

A Project Engineer is someone who supports the manufacturing team in expanding plant capacity, removing bottlenecks, and carrying out structural and process modifications to improve productivity.

Typical Responsibilities

- Equipment specification.
- Equipment vendor identification.
- Planning and scheduling project activities.
- Commissioning and erection of the equipment.
- Procurement of construction materials.
- Safety at the project site.

Project Engineer/Trainee: A Profile

Likely salary with 1–3 years of experience	Rs 200,000–Rs 400,000 per annum.
Targets	Completion of projects within budgets and on time.
Challenges	Managing the vendors and ensuring that they adhere to their commitments. Monitoring and rescheduling of projects when vendors default. Getting work done from a multi-disciplinary team.
Skills	Sound technical and engineering knowledge. An eye for detail. Good organizing skills.
Stress	Low.
Travel on the job	You will be located at the project site.
Impact on stakeholders	The Project Management Team will be highly impacted by this role.
Career prospects	For the first two years you will be a Trainee and become a full-fledged Project Engineer after that. Within five years you can expect to become a Senior Project Engineer.
Future salary with 5–7 years of experience	Rs 400,000–Rs 700,000 per annum.

A Practitioner's View
Project Executive, Sunil Kumar Krishna, Bengaluru

Mr Sunil Kumar Krishna, has been working as a Project Executive for a little over two years now. When we spoke to him and asked him about his views regarding the job role, he said:

'I joined as a fresher in this field and have gained considerable experience now. My communication and technical skills have improved and I have mastered the art of getting things done. I have learnt to manage my time well and provide solutions to various problems that arise during work. I love my job and will definitely recommend this role to a fresher as the scope is high and so is the learning.'

OPS 3 QUALITY CONTROL SUPERVISOR

Job Description

There has to be someone to inspect the quality of goods being brought into the factory, to see if they are in line with the requirements and quality standards. There has to be someone who finally tests and confirms that the product manufactured is as per standards and specifications laid down. Both these jobs are done by the Quality Control (QC) Supervisor.

Let's understand the importance of a Quality Control Supervisor by this simple example. We all go to departmental stores and buy potato chips. Imagine after you buy it, you find out that the weight of the packet of chips is less than it says? You will not trust the company which manufactured the chips. Therefore, when the Quality Control Department fails to do the job, a customer feels cheated and shifts his brand.

Typical Responsibilities

- Inspect the quality and quantity of the raw materials, consumables, and packaging materials brought into the factory, to ensure they are in accordance with the set quality standards.
- Inspect the quality and quantity of the materials being produced, and ensure that production is taking place in accordance with set quality standards.
- Resolve any issues/complaints from customers regarding finished goods, and prepare reports on findings during inspections and present the same to the management.
- Prepare quality control reports.
- Liaise with the Production Team and share the quality control reports.

Quality Control Supervisor: A Profile

Likely salary with 1–3 years of experience	Rs 200,000–Rs 300,000 per annum.
Targets	Minimize quality complaints from customers. Ensure the integrity of the quality control process.

Challenges	The biggest challenge is resolving conflicts with the Production Team and not succumbing to pressure. Quality control documentation has become very detailed and complex.
Skills	Good technical knowledge in the relevant area. Good data-analysis skills. Good communication and interpersonal skills.
Stress	Moderate.
Travel on the job	There is no travel involved in this role.
Impact on stakeholders	The manufacturing team and customers of an organization are highly impacted by this role.
Career prospects	You join at the level of a Quality Control Trainee. With three years' experience you can become a Quality Control Supervisor/Specialist, and thereafter grow to become a Quality Control Manager after ten years in an organization.
Future salary with 5–7 years of experience	Rs 350,000–Rs 600,000.

A Practitioner's View

Quality Control Supervisor, Leena Madhuri, Hyderabad

Ms Madhuri is working as a Quality Control Supervisor with a big pharmaceutical company. She has almost nine years of experience in the field of quality control. When we spoke to her, she gave us a few insights about the role, how it has helped her personally and professionally and why she would recommend this role to a fresher:

'Quality control testing can be a critical driving force for the success or failure of a product as well as organization.

'While performing the role in a progressive team, I get to learn punctuality, dedication, integrity, time management, problem-solving skills, interacting with other people in a positive way, a better way to handle conflict situations and most importantly, taking decisions that are in line with organizational objectives. I enjoy the working environment, work responsibilities, and involvement of the team members.

There is every opportunity to grow and learn additional skills that I might be interested in. Freshers get the opportunity to advance in their careers and develop professional relationships.'

OPS 4 CUSTOMER SERVICE ENGINEER

Job Description

The Customer Service Engineer is responsible for responding to a customer complaint, assess the problem, repair and fix the problem. He also provides effective and valuable tips to customers on the usage of the product, and clears any doubts that a customer has about the product and its usage. The Customer Service Engineer also takes into account the warranty of the product before billing the customer.

Typical Responsibilities

Typically, the customer complaints are received at a call centre. The customer is either asked to bring the product to a service centre (as in the case of a car) or a Customer Service Engineer is assigned to attend to the complaint. Your activities will thus include the following:

- Receiving calls from the call centre and travelling to customers if needed.
- Meeting and greeting the customer.
- Inspecting the products/vehicles/machines and assessing the problem.
- Informing the customer about the problem and the action plan to solve the problem.
- Checking the warranty status and educating the customer on the costs of servicing.
- Identifying the root cause of the problem.
- If the problem can be fixed immediately, fix it after getting customer concurrence on the costs.
- Doing a quality check of the product before handing over to the customer.
- Providing reports on jobs performed.
- Educating the customer on how to prevent the recurrence of the problem and share tips on preventive maintenance.
- Maintaining a record of the problem and solution.

Customer Service Engineer: A Profile

Likely salary with 1–3 years of experience	Rs 180,000–Rs 300,000 per annum.
Targets	Address the customer complaint within the time limit set, at the lowest cost to the customer without any cost or time escalations.
Challenges	The biggest challenge is in managing angry customers upset with product failure and convincing them on the repair costs. Travelling to multiple customer locations irrespective of the weather and time.
Skills	Problem-solving skills. Good technical and up-to-date knowledge in the area of work. Skill and patience to deal with angry customers and their issues.
Stress	Moderate.
Travel on the job	If you are working in a service centre, travel is minimal. If you are visiting customers at their home/workplace, then you will travel locally, daily.
Impact on stakeholders	The customers and company you work for are highly impacted by this role.
Career prospects	Your career prospects are very good due to the demand for high-quality Customer Service Engineers. If you are technically sound you will be promoted to manage a team of Customer Service Engineers, in three to four years. In ten years you can expect to head a regional Customer Service Engineer Team.
Future salary with 5–7 years of experience	Rs 350,000–Rs 500,000 per annum.

A Practitioner's View
Customer Service Engineer, Srinivas, Hyderabad

Mr Srinivas is an expert in repairing most electrical products manufactured by his company. When we spoke to him about sharing his experiences with us, he said:

'My job is not easy. It involves lot of travel as I have to attend to customer complaints on a daily basis. I cover a particular area in a single day. I am given a sheet with details of the customers along with the complaints raised. I go to the location, check the issue with the appliance. Based on the date of purchase, the Customer Care Department and I evaluate if the customer is eligible for free service or has to be charged and based on which I raise an invoice. Sometimes it can be tiring as we have to travel to different places. Sometimes, in spite of prior information, the customer may not be available due to which I have to visit the place again. Earlier I used to find it tough but as I got used to the routine I have started liking the job. I get to explore new things about appliances and sometimes have to use innovative techniques to make them work. If machines and appliances interest you then this job is for you.'

6

FINANCE AND ACCOUNTS DEPARTMENTS

Before we delve into the job roles we will examine in Section 1, the role and function of the Finance Department and the Accounts Department—both of which manage 'money' in any organization and are interdependent. Section 2 covers the entry-level job roles available in both these departments.

SECTION 1
BACKGROUND: FINANCE

WHEN DOES AN ORGANIZATION MAKE A SURPLUS/PROFIT?

Organizations are said to make a cash surplus only when the cash inflow is greater than the cash outflow, in a given period of time.

Therefore, there has to be someone who can track and forecast all the outflows and inflows in order to analyse if the company has made a cash surplus or deficit. If there is a cash deficit, the company needs to borrow and if it is a cash surplus, the company needs to invest. This is why organizations to have a Finance Department.

WORKING CAPITAL AND ITS MANAGEMENT

Working capital is defined as the current assets (including cash) that the company needs to operate. Current assets include the assets the company has in hand such as the raw material and finished goods inventory, advances, cash and bank balances, investments, as well as the money owed to it by customers who have purchased its goods/services on credit. Customers who have received credit from the company are called 'debtors'.

Similarly, when the company makes purchases, it does not pay its suppliers/vendors immediately, but purchases on credit. Suppliers who sell to the company on credit are called 'creditors'. The amount that the company owes to its creditors is called 'current liabilities'.

The 'working capital gap' is the gap between a company's current assets and its current liabilities.

Now suppose the company's current assets are less than its current liabilities, what will happen? The creditors will not be paid 'on time' and will slowly cut off supplies to the company and the operations will stop. So the Finance Department will have to step in and get a bank loan to cover the working capital gap.

BASIC FUNCTIONS OF A FINANCE DEPARTMENT

The Finance Department of an organization broadly deals with:

1. creating a concrete financial plan;
2. arranging long-term and working capital funds for the business;
3. preparing and monitoring budgets for various departments;
4. investing surplus funds; and
5. managing investors and shareholders.

1. Creating a Concrete Financial Plan

This involves forecasting the revenues and costs and creating a funds flow statement.

2. Arranging Long-term and Working Capital Funds

Funding/financing and investing

The Finance Department deals with financial institutions and banks to see that there is adequacy of funds as and when required.

Forex management

When a company has foreign transactions it may earn in one currency and spend in another. Money will have to be converted from one currency to another at the prevailing exchange rate. The Forex Team's job is to ensure that the company converts currency at the best exchange rates.

3. Preparing and Monitoring Budgets for Various Departments

Maximize profitability by minimizing costs

It is the responsibility of the Finance Department to see that the company controls costs.

Manage budgets and forecasts

It is the duty of the Finance Department to plan, allocate, and manage budgets to various departments.

Conduct regular management audits

The Finance Department is responsible for conducting regular management audits to ensure that the company and its employees are functioning as per the standard financial policies and operating procedures.

4. Investing Surplus Funds

Treasury management

The excess cash that a company has after making all payments is invested by the Treasury Team.

5. Managing Investors and Shareholders

Maximize shareholder value

Shareholders* are a company's most important stakeholders. The Finance Executive makes sure that the shareholder interests are taken care of.

Shareholder relations

Shareholders, and other investors like banks, have the right to know each and every development that is taking place in the company financially. Their requests and complaints need to be redressed very quickly and this is the duty of the Shareholder Relations Team.

---

*This category of investors has been discussed in Chapter 1.

BACKGROUND: ACCOUNTS

Organizations have to maintain a record of all financial transactions and this is done by the Accounts Department.

ACCOUNTS RECEIVABLE/DEBTOR MANAGEMENT

Every company offers credit to its trusted customers, and customers who owe money to the company are called debtors. The outstanding amounts owed by them are called 'accounts receivables'. The accounts receivables list must be monitored regularly and money collected should be accounted for properly.

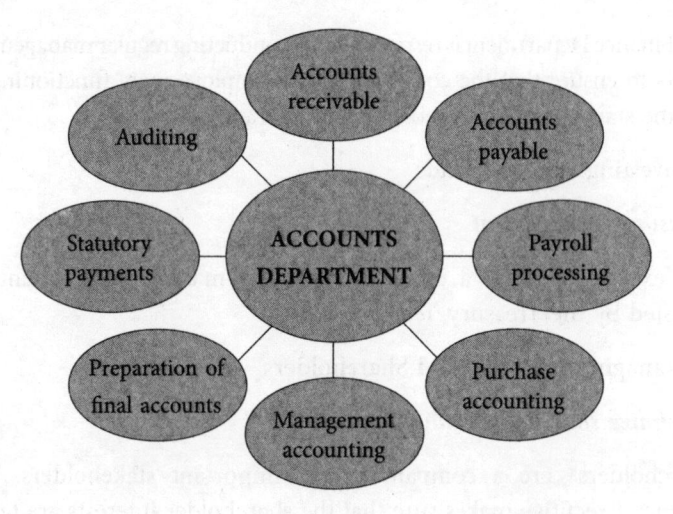

Figure 6.1: Functions of an Accounts Department

ACCOUNTS PAYABLE/CREDITOR MANAGEMENT

Every company has a list of suppliers/vendors who supply first and are paid after a credit period. The list of suppliers/vendors to whom the company owes money are called creditors and the outstanding amounts are called 'accounts payable'. The supplier bills must be processed for payment and accounted for properly.

PAYROLL PROCESSING

When you take services of people, you need to pay them a salary for the work done. While paying salaries, there are some deductions like income tax, Provident Fund, and so on that must be made. The salaries are processed monthly—this is called payroll processing, and ensures that the payments are made and accounted properly.

PURCHASE ACCOUNTING

Companies make a lot of purchases of raw materials, consumables, and capital assets like machinery. These purchases have to be accounted for properly.

PREPARATION OF FINAL ACCOUNTS

The most important function of the Accounts Department is to prepare final accounts. The Accounting Department records all the financial transactions of revenues and expenses. They need to make provisions for expenses like depreciation. They prepare a profit and loss account based on these entries. In most companies all these entries are made using an accounting software. Once a profit and loss account is prepared, the next step is the preparation of a balance sheet and cash-flow statements.

AUDITING

Auditors cross-check all transactions recorded in the accounts books to check that there are no discrepancies. This is done on a periodical basis (monthly, quarterly, or annually) depending on the decision taken by the top management of the company. Annually, all companies have to get their accounts audited and signed by an external Chartered Accountant.

STATUTORY PAYMENTS

Organizations and their clients need to make regular payments (income tax, service tax, PF, ESI) to the government. There are different deadlines for payment and someone has to calculate, track, and remit the government dues on time to avoid legal complications.

MANAGEMENT ACCOUNTING AND INFORMATION SYSTEMS (MIS)

Management accounting systems help organizations take strategic business decisions to improve a company's performance based on real data. For example, to arrive at the right price for the various products and services of the company, a lot of cost data has to be analysed which is done by an MIS Executive.

SECTION 2
ENTRY-LEVEL JOB ROLES IN FINANCE AND ACCOUNTS

Roles in Finance

CODE	ROLE
FIN 1	Finance Executive
FIN 2	Chartered Accountant
FIN 3	Investor Relations Associate
FIN 4	Budget Analyst
FIN 5	Treasury Officer/Executive
FIN 6	Forex Officer

Roles in Accounts

CODE	ROLE
ACC 1	Accountant/Accounting Executive
ACC 2	MIS Executive

FIN 1 FINANCE EXECUTIVE

Job Description

A Finance Executive's job is to fund the operations of the organization. For example, an organization needs cash to pay salaries on the first of every month, irrespective of whether its customers pay their dues or not. The only way to deal with this is to get a working capital loan against the dues from customers (called debtors) and pay salaries on time.

A Finance Executive's job is to keep track of the cash position of the company.

Let us also differentiate between the role of a Finance Executive and an Accountant Executive. The Finance Executive funds the operations, whereas an Accountant Executive's primary job is to keep the books of accounts of the organization—how much income has been generated, what is the current profit and loss, what is the current cash balance, and so on. In other words, an Accountant Executive tracks the financial health of the organization.

Typical Responsibilities

Your activities/responsibilities include:

- Creating and managing a budget plan for the company and providing periodical reports on whether the budgets are being met.
- Conducting a daily cash-flow analysis.
- Evaluating various opportunities for unlocking cash. (For example, it may be advisable to sell the non-moving inventory at a discounted price to generate cash).
- Liaising with the accounting team to see that the book-keeping is up-to-date to generate timely MIS reports.
- Building and maintaining strong relationships with financial institutions such as banks and state financial corporations, and submitting periodic reports to them.
- Attending frequent review meetings.

Finance Executive: A Profile

Likely salary with 1–3 years of experience	Rs 250,000–Rs 500,000 per annum.
Targets	Ensure company has enough cash to fund its operations. Minimize interest rates when borrowing, and maximize interest rates when you invest. Manage risk when you invest. Suggest long-term options to raise capital.
Challenges	Timeliness and accuracy of data is a challenge. Raising money when the company is not doing well is tough.
Skills	Excellent MS Excel skills. Good negotiation skills. Sound domain knowledge in finance.
Stress	Low to moderate.
Travel on the job	Very rarely.
Impact on stakeholders	Management and investors—including banks/financial institutions—are the key stakeholders impacted by this role.

Career prospects	Competent Finance Executives are in short supply. Typically, after two years you would become a Senior Executive (Finance), and become Deputy Manager Finance within three years thereafter.
Future salary with 5–7 years of experience	Rs 500,000–Rs 800,000 per annum.

A Practitioner's View
Finance Executive, Suresh, Vijayawada

Mr Suresh has been working as a Finance Executive for the past two and a half years. He says:

'I am excited about my job because without cash, any company will come to a standstill. In today's environment, customers do not pay on time and often delay. The only way to manage is to borrow working capital from our bankers. To borrow, we need to apply and get working capital limits from the banks. To apply for limits, we need to project the company's profit and loss accounts and balance sheets for the next three years.

'So not only do I know what the current financial health of the company is, I also get to know the future of the company. The business leaders are always in touch with me, share information, and seek my help to tide over a financial crisis. So every day is a new day and every day there is a new problem to be solved.'

FIN 2 CHARTERED ACCOUNTANT

Job Description

Many Indian companies are raising equity by listing with the New York Stock Exchange (NYSE) and London Stock Exchange (LSE), and therefore, have global investors. These global investors will have to understand and interpret an Indian company's balance sheet and profit and loss statements in exactly the same way as they interpret those of a company from the United States (US) or the United Kingdom (UK). So, the Indian company has to prepare the company's accounts as per the Indian Accounting Standards (IAS), which are the Indian rules and regulations; the US Generally Accepted Accounting Principles or USGAAP, which are the US regulations; or, as per other global accounting standards called International Financial Reporting Standards or IFRS.

A Chartered Accountant (CA) is a professional authorized by the Indian law to sign a balance sheet, thereby certifying that the information it contains is accurate and is prepared as per the approved accounting standards. Without a CA's certification of accounts, no banker will give loans and no investor will put money into a company.

A CA normally has a graduation in business, accounting, or finance. She/he must pass the CA exams—Inter and Final—to become a member of the Institute of Chartered Accountants of India (ICAI). Details of the course are available on the ICAI website.

The course is available in various countries under different names; in the US it is called the Certified Public Accountant (CPA) course, and in the UK it is called the Association of Certified Chartered Accountants (ACCA) course.

Typical Responsibilities

You may function as an independent entity or work in an organization. A CA performs a variety of functions.[6]

- Accountancy: Reviewing accounts and the preparation of financial statements, whether they are the simple accounts of a small NGO or the complex and detailed accounts of large public listed companies.
- Auditing: The purpose of auditing is to satisfy the users of the financial statements you prepare, that the accounts presented to them are drawn up as per the correct and latest accounting principles, and that they represent a true and fair view of the financial state of affairs.
- Taxation: The assessment of taxes is closely linked to financial accounts. The CA, with experience in accounts, is in an advantageous position to prepare returns for tax purposes, represent assesses before the income tax authorities, and render general advice on taxes to his clients. The services of

a CA may be requisitioned by the Income Tax Department for auditing taxation cases with large revenue potential.
- Cost Accountancy: A CA is equipped to provide information on costing for the guidance of management, introduce cost control methods, and assist the management in determining appropriate selling prices.
- Special Company Work: A CA's services or advice is frequently sought in connection with matters such as the formation, financial structure, and liquidation of limited companies.
- Investigation: CAs are often called upon to carry out investigations to ascertain the financial position of business houses for the purpose of issue of new shares, purchase, or sale or financing of business, finding out reasons for increase or decrease of profits, reconstruction, and amalgamations.
- Executors and Trustees: A CA is also often appointed as an executor of a Will or Trust, in order to carry on the administration of the estate or settlement.
- Directorship: Many CAs hold senior positions in industry and commerce and as directors of their companies.
- Secretarial Work: The CA is an important link in the management chain and works with the Company Secretary (CS).
- Management Accounting: The CAs service is utilized in a variety of ways such as in formulation of policies, control, and performance evaluation.
- Share Valuation Work: A CA undertakes the valuation of shares of public and private companies at the time of amalgamation or reorganization.
- Other Activities: CAs also act as Arbitrators to settle disputes, especially those connected with insolvency work such as the preparation of statements of affairs, and the duties of a trustee in bankruptcy or under a deed of arrangement.

Chartered Accountant: A Profile

Likely salary with 1–3 years of experience	Rs 400,000–Rs 800,000 per annum.
Targets	Ensure that the company and its management function ethically in accordance with the standard

	financial and accounting principles and procedures. Assist the management in assessing and improving the financial viability of the business/es.
Challenges	Meeting compliance guidelines: New guidelines are published every day. These have to be interpreted and communicated to the management, as CAs are supposed to be experts in their domain. Meeting deadlines: There are daily deadlines for various MIS reports and statutory reports. So every day there will be some key tasks to finish. Many CAs have to work 12-hour schedules to meet deadlines and also learn on the job. Auditing financial reports and providing business advice. For example: When you conduct audits and find discrepancies in accounts, you may be pressurized not to disclose the discrepancies. But you will have to be diligent in your work and report every key finding and take corrective actions. Minimizing financial leakage by establishing internal controls. Keeping information confidential.
Skills	High domain skills. Expert in multi-tasking and delegating work. Excellent skills in MS Excel and computer-based accounting systems. Excellent analytical skills. Strong supervisory skills.
Stress	Moderate to high.
Travel on the job	You do not have to travel except for audit purposes to offices/factories/branches.
Impact on stakeholders	Investors, management, and government agencies are impacted the most by this role.
Career prospects	A CA after two years can expect to be promoted to an Assistant Manager and after five years can become Head of the Accounts Department of a mid-size company.
Future salary with 5–7 years of experience	Rs 700,000–Rs 1,000,000 per annum.

A Practitioner's View

Chartered Accountant, Y. Swarnasiva, Chennai

Mr Y. Swarnasiva has completed one and a half years as a CA. When we asked him about his experiences, he said:

'This is a very challenging role. I get to interact with the top management, bank officials, and statutory bodies. Personally, it has helped me a lot. Professionally, it helped me gain recognition among my colleagues, friends, and society. I have been promoted from the executive level to managerial level.

'Chartered Accountants are entrusted with substantial responsibility under various legislations such as compulsory audit of all companies, banks, stock brokers, big Income Tax assessees, and large bank borrowers. This shows the confidence and trust reposed by the government and society in the profession. Society has increasingly recognized the services of CAs across the entire gamut of management consultancy services—including management accounting, management information and control systems, international finance, information technology, and the financial services sector. The scope is extremely high and I would recommend that those interested must attempt the CA exams. If they clear it they can enjoy a secured future.'

INVESTOR RELATIONS

FIN 3 INVESTOR RELATIONS ASSOCIATE

Job Description

An Investor Relations Associate is responsible for handling all communication that has to be passed on to investors on a periodic basis, and also handle their grievances regarding share transfer, dividend payment, and so on.

Typical Responsibilities

- Providing services to investors by passing on relevant information regarding operations.

- Handling investor queries and grievances regarding share transfer and dividends.
- Assisting in organizing shareholder meetings, such as the Annual General Meeting.
- Preparing investor transaction reports on share delivery to Accountants and the management body of funds.
- Updating the investor records like shareholder lists.
- Liaising with Share Transfer Agents on shareholder communications.
- Liaising with the banks on dividend returns.

Investor Relations Associate: A Profile

Likely salary with 1–3 years of experience	Rs 200,000–Rs 300,000 per annum.
Targets	On-time handling of investor complaints, and timely despatch of relevant information/reports to investors.
Challenges	Every investor expects exceptional investor service. Ensuring accuracy of transactions outsourced to share transfer agents.
Skills	You must have excellent knowledge about capital market regulations. Must have excellent communication and networking skills. Must have problem-solving skills.
Stress	Low.
Travel on the job	There is no travel involved in this role.
Impact on stakeholders	The investors and the shareholders are impacted by this role.
Career prospects	You will start off as an Associate and then move on to become an Investor Relations Manager over a period of five to eight years.
Future salary with 5–7 years of experience	Rs 300,000–Rs 500,000 per annum.

A Practitioner's View
Investor Relations Manager, Hitesh, Mumbai

Mr Hitesh is working as an Investor Relations Manager in a leading company. When we asked him about his role and experiences, he said:

'Investor relations is like dealing with the cream of intellectual people who are well-to-do in terms of financial matters. I need to be very careful in communicating with them because the company's future is at stake. They have every right to know about the financial status of the company, any new deals that the company has signed, and so on. This information has to reach them as per the stock market rules. The growth aspects are very high in this role. Therefore, I would recommend this role to freshers.'

FIN 4 BUDGET ANALYST

Job Description

A Budget Analyst (also known as a Financial Analyst) is responsible for preparing and examining budget estimates and reporting any variances to the top management. This person will directly report to the Finance Manager but works with Managers from all departments to help them plan departmental budgets.

Typical Responsibilities

- Work with Operating Managers to develop their budget.
- Analyse budget estimates received from various departments.
- Preparing budget reports and monitoring cash outflow reports.
- Preparing a standard budget manual for policies and procedures.
- Bench-marking the company with its competitors and creating analytical reports.
- Advising management to take proper decisions on financial planning.
- Performing a cost-benefit analysis to compare various operating programmes and explore innovative solutions.
- Coming up with novel ideas to improve organizational efficiency.

Budget Analyst: A Profile

Likely salary with 1–3 years of experience	Rs 200,000–Rs 350,000 per annum.
Targets	Completing the budgeting process on time, and ensuring timely and accurate budget analysis reports.
Challenges	Getting data on time from various Operating Managers. Synchronizing data across the organization.
Skills	Must have analytical and MS Excel skills.
Stress	Moderate.
Travel on the job	Very little.
Impact on stakeholders	Employees of the organization, investors, financial institutions, and shareholders are impacted by this role.
Career prospects	You will start off as a Budget Analyst and then move on to become a Team Leader/Manager and manage a team of Analysts. Many will move into finance roles after two to three years.
Future salary with 5–7 years of experience	Rs 300,000–Rs 500,000 per annum.

A Practitioner's View
Budget Analyst, Manish, Delhi

Mr Manish has been working as a Budget Analyst in a consulting firm for the past three years. When we asked him about his experiences and why he would recommend this role to a fresher, he said:

'The role of a Budget Analyst is very crucial in an organization. I am given access to all the important financial information regarding the company. I get to deal with Business Managers and top management to put forward my views after I have done my homework. I am asked to verify as to why the X amount has been allocated as the budget for a project, when should one consider revising the budget, and other factors. It gives me a lot of exposure, and the learning and growth prospects are also very good. This is why I would recommend this role to any fresher who wants to develop a career in business management.'

TREASURY MANAGEMENT

FIN 5 TREASURY OFFICER/EXECUTIVE

Job Description

Every company needs short-term money, or has cash which it can invest for the short-term. A Back Office Treasury Officer/Executive works under the supervision of the Treasury Manager, to ensure that money is borrowed or invested as per company policies and procedures. This is called, 'the back office work of money market operations.' Controls are established by the management to ensure that the Treasury Team does not take unnecessary trading risks. As a Treasury Officer, you will update trading records and manage the documentation to assist the Treasury Team.

Typical Responsibilities

- Gathering information on the trades made by the Treasury Team.
- Updating cash position and bank reconciliations.
- Completing all the back office records and maintaining required documentation.
- Maintaining general ledger integrity and ensuring an efficient monthly book-closure process.
- Tracking investments and preparing cash-flow statements.

Treasury Officer/Executive: A Profile

Likely salary with 1–3 years of experience	Rs 200,000–Rs 350,000 per annum.
Targets	Ensuring accurate and timely documentation of market operations.
Challenges	Ensuring documents are executed as per the complex legal requirements.

Skills	Time management skills.
	Good communication skills.
	Keen eye for detail.
Stress	Low to moderate.
Travel on the job	None.
Impact on stakeholders	The management is impacted most by this role.
Career prospects	You will start off as a Treasury Officer; after five or more years you could be selected to head the Treasury Back Office.
Future salary with 5–7 years of experience	Rs 400,000–Rs 600,000 per annum.

A Practitioner's View
Treasury Officer, Lakshmi Prasad, Hyderabad

Mr Lakshmi Prasad is working as a Treasury Officer. When we asked him about his experiences, he said:

'Working in this role has personally helped me manage my own expenses and cash inflow in a better way, as I have become more organized and cautious while dealing with monetary transactions. In the company we have set policies and procedures to manage cash. So ensuring all transactions take place in accordance with these set rules is what we do. The prospects are bright and that would be one reason I would recommend this role to a fresher.'

FOREX MANAGEMENT

FIN 6 FOREX OFFICER

Job Description

Companies require a Forex (short for Foreign Exchange) expert, who can advise them on the best time to convert from one currency to another. Unfortunately, it is very difficult to predict the exchange rates because the Forex market, just like the equity market, fluctuates daily. The Forex Officer's job is to assist companies, individuals, banks, and so on in understanding Forex markets. She/he contacts various Forex experts, studies the forecasts made by them and then advises the company when to convert, or when to take a Forex cover. A Forex Officer is hired by large corporates, banks, insurance companies, and hedge fund companies.

Typical Responsibilities

- Gathering information and conducting detailed research on foreign exchange markets.
- Preparing guidelines on Forex for the business.
- Assisting and training people regarding effective Forex management.
- Preparing exchange rate forecasts and giving trade recommendations.

Forex Officer: A Profile

Likely salary with 1–3 years of experience	Rs 300,000–Rs 500,000 per annum.
Targets	Minimizing Forex risks, while maximizing Forex gains.
Challenges	Providing right recommendations when you get conflicting opinions from experts. Reacting very quickly to Forex market changes.
Skills	Excellent research and analytical skills. Sound knowledge in the area of work (Forex markets and international markets).
Stress	High.
Travel on the job	Minimum travel involved.
Impact on stakeholders	The management of the company you work for will be impacted the most.
Career prospects	Career progression in this role depends on gaining expertise. One option is to become a Forex dealer in a financial institution like a bank.
Future salary with 5–7 years of experience	Rs 600,000–Rs 1,200,000 per annum.

A PRACTITIONER'S VIEW
Forex Professional, Vivek Malviya, Delhi

Mr Malviya is pursuing a career in Forex Management. He shared:

'I did my MBA in 2008. Financial Engineering and Derivatives was the only subject that attracted me. I finally found my dream job as a derivative and risk professional. I found four strengths that could make me a risk professional—quantitative ability (working with numbers), knowledge of financial markets, decision-making, and strategy development.

'I found my interest lay in Forex risk management because I could utilize my analytical ability and financial knowledge. I was very familiar with trade finance and Forex derivatives. It's truly a very dynamic profile to work and you always live with the market that operates 24 hours.

'I would certainly recommend this as a promising career choice, but for that you need to prepare a road map. In short, you cannot ignore academic knowledge—in the financial industry, valuation models and methodologies are used at each step. Along with sound academics you must be aware about the current economic scenario, financial markets and products, and try to adopt an innovative way of thinking.'

ACC 1 ACCOUNTANT/ACCOUNTING EXECUTIVE

Job Description

Organizations have to prepare important accounting statements such as cash statements, profit and loss statements, and balance sheets. There are many people involved in preparing the above statements. One of them is an Accountant. These statements have to comply with the standard accounting principles and procedures and hence accounts are computerized. Every individual does not have expertise in this area. That is why Accountants are becoming specialists.

Typical Responsibilities

- Preparing documents for the issue of cheques, cash withdrawals, and so on.

- Answering queries of employers/vendors on various accounting issues.
- Making petty cash payments to employees.
- Preparing bank reconciliation statements.
- Book-keeping: reviewing various accounting documents and posting the same on the computer.
- Preparing of daily MIS and discussing it with superiors.

Accountant/Accounting Executive: A Profile

Likely salary with 1–3 years of experience	Rs 150,000–Rs 300,000 per annum. A candidate with an MCom degree can expect at least 15 per cent more salary than a BCom graduate.
Targets	Ensuring minimal discrepancies in accounts. Accurate and timely recording of all accounting transactions.
Challenges	Preparing accurate reports on profit and loss and final accounts. Maintaining data secrecy by establishing internal controls and keeping information confidential.
Skills	Excellent grip over accounting softwares such as Tally, Wings, and others. Having a certification on Enterprise Resource Planning (ERP) softwares such as SAP or Oracle Apps will be a big advantage. Must have analytical and MS Excel skills. Above average communication skills.
Stress	Moderate.
Travel on the job	Minimum travel involved.
Impact on stakeholders	The management of the organization, suppliers, and investors are impacted by this role.
Career prospects	The career prospects are bright. You can become a Senior Accounting Executive and then manage a team of Accountants by becoming an Assistant Manager–Accounts in five years.
Future salary with 5–7 years of experience	Rs 300,000–Rs 500,000 per annum.

A Practitioner's View
Accountant, A. Phanindra, Nizamabad

Mr Phanindra has been working in the field of accounting over the past seven years. He started his career as a Junior Accounting Executive and has become an expert in the areas of taxation, statutory dealings, accounts receivable and payable, and bank reconciliation statements. He says:

'When I started working as a Junior Accounting Executive, I had very limited knowledge about preparation of profit and loss statements, final accounts of organizations, processing payrolls, and so on. But after working for almost seven years in this field, I have been able to plan, manage, organize, and analyse the revenues and costs that are associated with carrying out a business and also on how to reduce costs and increase savings without affecting the daily operations. The most interesting part is dealing directly with vendors regarding their payments and also attending to queries raised by employees. There is so much one can learn by working as an Accountant.'

ACC 2 MIS EXECUTIVE

Job Description

MIS stands for Management Information System. Every management wants analytical reports on operations. Assisting the senior management in business analysis, coordinating, preparing, presenting, and reviewing reports are the activities that an MIS Executive performs.

Typical Responsibilities

- Assisting top management in business analysis.
- Consolidating data and generating reports.
- Preparing and automating routine reports.
- Monitoring and evaluating data accuracy by performing trend analysis of data.

MIS Executive: A Profile

Likely salary with 1–3 years of experience	Rs 120,000–Rs 250,000 per annum.
Targets	Providing error-free data analysis and reports to the top management as and when required.
Challenges	Meeting targets and deadlines. Dealing with, and organizing, large chunks of data.
Skills	Apart from basic common skills, an MIS Executive has to be extremely proficient in MS Excel. Written communication skills. An analytical mind.
Stress	Moderate.
Travel on the job	There is no travel involved in this role.
Impact on stakeholders	The employees of the organization and of the Finance Department in particular, are impacted by this role.
Career prospects	This role has become very popular in organizations and hence career prospects are very bright. You can become a Senior MIS Executive and then an MIS Manager once you gain experience and manage a team of MIS Executives.
Future salary with 5–7 years of experience	Rs 300,000–Rs 500,000 per annum.

A Practitioner's View

MIS Executive, M. Shiva Krishna, Vijayawada

Mr Shiva Krishna has been working as an MIS Executive for the past two and a half years. He has hands-on expertise in areas of data management and MS Office applications. He shares:

'The reason why I like my job is because I love working with numbers. Preparing daily reports for the management without making any mistakes is one of the most important functions in my role. The challenging part is that there is no scope for making even a slightest error. Therefore, one needs to be extra careful and vigilant while preparing reports.'

7
INFORMATION TECHNOLOGY DEPARTMENT

We cannot do without computers or laptops in most of our homes and offices. Communicating electronically has become a necessity. Accounting, Operations, Human Resources (HR) and various other departments use software to ensure that their business runs smoothly.

Section 1 provides a brief background on the important role information technology (IT) plays in any organization, while Section 2 details entry-level job roles in the IT Department.

SECTION 1
BACKGROUND

Though companies like Tata Consultancy Services (TCS) were providing IT professional services around the world from the 1980s, IT started in a big way in India only in the late 1990s with the increased use of PCs and email. IT took off after the internet revolution. Today companies use computers for many things—email, e-conferences, web phones, presentations, e-documents and of course, for a variety of software applications (Enterprise Resource Planning [ERP], e-HR, Customer Relations Management [CRM], and many customized softwares).

ROLE OF AN IT DEPARTMENT IN AN ORGANIZATION

Companies need setting up of secured computer servers and drivers, configuring networks, setting up employee workstations, developing software, helping people use the software, and providing access control as per the role and level of employees. A normal man/layman who does not understand technology cannot do these jobs. We need individuals with specialized skills to perform these activities. This is why the concept of having a full-fledged IT Department came into the picture.

Automating processes

In modern times computers have taken over repetitive tasks. For example, salaries used to be processed manually. Today almost every company uses salary processing software.

Accuracy of data

However perfect an individual is, there is always scope for error, but with computers there is very little margin for error. The person who is entering the data into a computer can make mistakes but the computer has mechanisms to detect it and correct it.

Speed

Every company uses computers to generate quick and reliable reports.

Management of data

Secured servers, e-rooms, and databases store data. Companies have a lot of confidential data that need not be shared with all the employees. Information Technology helps companies keep confidential data secure by controlling access to data through passwords.

Communications made easy

Today computers have made communications between people very easy with web phones, teleconferences, web meetings, and instant chats in addition to emails.

WHERE TO LOOK FOR ENTRY-LEVEL JOBS IN THE IT DEPARTMENT?

Most companies outsource software development to IT companies. In addition, IT infra-management is also outsourced. So the bulk of IT jobs are in IT companies and these are covered separately in Chapter 17. Here we cover only those few jobs that are not outsourced.

It is now very clear that every company needs an IT Department which is organized through many sub-departments. Let us briefly look at these.

IT Procurement

An IT Department negotiates with various vendors and buys IT products and services at a competitive price.

Network Infrastructure

Designing and setting up email communication, internal chat systems, audio and video conferencing, Voice Over Internet Protocol (VOIP) phones for calling, recording and storing messages, all must be done. All these activities are performed by the Network Infrastructure Team. This team also maintains and upgrades these systems, trains users, and handles complaints.

Instructional Design

Training is an important function in any organization. Today companies have shifted to online training. There are various mandatory e-learning/online courses and training courses that employees need to take. The process of designing these online courses is very different from a classroom course because there is no instructor and, therefore, is designed by an Instructional Designer.

Web and Multimedia

The creation of websites and other multimedia programs by using various web application tools and technologies, forms an integral part of the Web and Multimedia Department.

SECTION 2
ENTRY-LEVEL JOB ROLES

CODE	ROLE
IT 1	Network Executive
IT 2	Instructional Designer
IT 3	Junior Web Designer

IT 1 IT NETWORK EXECUTIVE

Job Description

An IT Network Executive, also known as an IT Infrastructure Executive, is an expert responsible for managing the computer hardware network—PCs, laptops, servers, routers, switches; and helping computer users access the software and hardware.

Typical Responsibilities

- Establishing and adding to the IT network—both hardware and software.
- Adding authorized users with access control.
- Installing software systems.
- Provide trainings for users.
- Configuring the servers and databases.
- Setting up Local Area Network (LAN) and the Wide Area Network (WAN).
- Ensuring uptime of the network and its users.
- Troubleshooting, and fixing user complaints.
- Setting up internet connectivity—broadband and dedicated lines.
- Setting up email services.
- Installing cyber security software, such as 'firewalls'.
- Optimizing the network so that users do not complain of 'slow' response.
- Periodically backing up data.

IT Network Executive: A Profile

Likely salary with 1–3 years of experience	Rs 200,000–Rs 300,000 per annum.
Targets	Close to 99 per cent uptime of the network. Response time and turn-around time (TAT) for user complaints. Network security: monitor and eliminate security issues.
Challenges	Hardware and software are continuously evolving with new versions. But users are not evolving as fast. Hence users are always complaining and have to be handled tactfully. Users want super-fast resolution of their problems. This is very difficult especially if the hardware and software are old and not compatible.

	Each server platform (like Windows, Linux), is unique and different and practical knowledge is not easy to acquire.
Skills	Excellent domain knowledge: usually a Network Certification like CISCO Certified Network Associate (CCNA) is essential. Strong analytical and problem-solving skills. Above average communication skills.
Stress	Moderate.
Travel on the job	Travel is normally only by exception and hence is low.
Impact on stakeholders	The employees of an organization are impacted most by this role.
Career prospects	Your career prospects will also be good because you can become a Network Team Leader in three years and Network Manager in five to seven years.
Future salary with 5–7 years of experience	Rs 350,000–Rs 600,000 per annum.

A Practitioner's View

IT Network Manager, Madan Kumar, Bengaluru

Mr Kumar is working as an IT Network Consultant. He has nine-plus years of experience in IT. He is an expert in infrastructure management. When we asked him to share his experiences with us, he said:

'My job is complex, at the same time interesting. It is a white collar job. I like working on various technologies and systems. I would recommend this role to a fresher because the scope in this job is extremely high. The demand for this role is also high and depending on the company, candidates can expect a decent pay as well.'

IT 2 INSTRUCTIONAL DESIGNER (FOR E-LEARNING)

Job Description

Today, learning/training has gone online and are called e-learning courses. These courses do not have a teacher or instructor. The learner will interact only with the computer and it is also a form of computer-based training (CBT). Someone called an Instructional Designer designs these courses to make them very interesting and engaging, based on the science and psychology of learning.

In e-learning, the teacher's role of creating the interactivity and making the class interesting, creating the assessment at the right time, and so on, has to be programmed or designed. The learning is delivered to the learner as a series of instructions, called instructional design (ID), to get the student completely absorbed and engaged in the course.

The Instructional Designer works with Subject Matter Experts (called SMEs) who decide on the course coverage, Content Writers who actually write content as per the ID, and Web Designers who will visualize the content and create the course.

Typical Responsibilities

- Connect with the Course Director to understand the purpose of the course and learner profile.
- Connect with prospective learners to understand the way they learn and the technology environment.
- Connect with SMEs to understand the subject on which the course is to be designed.
- Design and develop the ID for the course, based on the above and brief the Content Writer.
- Review course content to check if it is as per the instructional design.
- Work with the web design, graphic artists, and so on, to make e-learning more interactive and interesting.
- Develop an instruction-materials library.
- Constantly update one's knowledge and skills related to the instructional design field.

Instructional Designer: A Profile

Likely salary with 1–3 years of experience	Rs 200,000–Rs 400,000 per annum.
Targets	E-learning course durations are measured as 'learner hours'. The Instructional Designer's first target is to

		deliver the e-learning course in the shortest duration with maximum learner engagement. The second target to deliver the instructional design for the maximum number of learner hours every month.
Challenges		There are many types of learners. Some learn well visually, some learn well by listening, and some learn by doing. The Instruction Designer's challenge is to design courses that will deliver the learning, irrespective of the type of learner. The Instructional Designer must be able to work on courses in various domains, including unfamiliar domains, and work with a variety of stakeholders such as Subject Matter Experts and Content Writers.
Skills		Having a deep knowledge about learning psychology. Develop a creative mind. Ability to understand any complicated subject by reading and talking to experts.
Stress		Moderate.
Travel on the job		There is no travel involved in this role.
Impact on stakeholders		The learners are highly impacted by this role.
Career prospects		Typically, after two years an Instructional Designer becomes a Senior Instructional Designer, and thereafter can also become a Content Project Manager leading a team of Instructional Designers, Content Writers, and Web Designers. Since there is a shortage of Instructional Designers, growth prospects are very bright.
Future salary with 5-7 years of experience		Rs 600,000–Rs 900,000 per annum.

A Practitioner's View

Instructional Designer, Rachna, Mumbai

Ms Rachna has around fifteen years of experience in IT with over ten years of experience in Instructional Design. When we asked her to share her experiences with us, she said:

'My job is to enhance the learning of the students who

take my e-learning course by adapting the latest techniques in instructional design. I have learned to think creatively, look for innovation, blend my technical and language skills, and have an eye for detail. It gives me the scope of doing so many different things.

'The compensation received is good. It is a good career option because this e-learning industry is growing rapidly in India and there is a huge demand for Instructional Designers.'

IT 3 JUNIOR WEB DESIGNER

Job Description

A Junior Web Designer's responsibility is to create web pages that attract website visitors and make them stay and explore the entire website. She/he will work on the layout, visual appearance, and navigation of the website.

Typical Responsibilities

- Meet customers/stakeholders to take their brief for web properties like company websites; email campaigns, social media pages, and so on.
- Think and ideate on various design options by using contemporary technology and the latest research.
- Review designs that you have created with clients and end-users, and work on software to create the websites.
- Test the web properties for ease of navigation (also called usability), completeness, and so on, and publish them on the web.

Junior Web Designer: A Profile

Likely salary with 1–3 years of experience	Rs 100,000–Rs 250,000 per annum.
Targets	Creation of websites and web properties in the shortest time, with least file sizes and ensure that the website visitor stays in the web property.
Challenges	Staying abreast of web technology which changes every day.

	Blending web technology with visual creativity. A good Web Designer attains the right balance between creativity and customer specifications and overcomes the frustration of seeing her/his best design rejected by the customer.
Skills	Command over web technology and tools. Should have excellent knowledge in software applications like Photoshop, HTML, Adobe Dreamweaver, and Flash.
Stress	Low to moderate.
Travel on the job	This job does not require outstation travel.
Impact on stakeholders	The visitors to the website and the customers who pay for the website will benefit the most by your work.
Career prospects	You can become a Senior Web Designer with two-plus years of experience and thereafter, become a Team Leader and manage a team of Web Designers with five years of experience.
Future salary with 5–7 years of experience	Rs 350,000–Rs 600,000 per annum.

A Practitioner's View

Web and Multimedia Designer, Manoj Deshmukh, Mumbai

Mr Deshmukh is working as a Senior Multimedia Designer and has four years of work experience in this field. When we asked him to share his experiences with us, he said:

'Web designing is an upcoming field. We get to implement new designs and are given a free hand when it comes to designing of concepts and websites. Working in this role, I learnt how to communicate with internal clients and understand their requirements and expectations. I have also learnt how to make my work more and more creative and manage my work based on priorities. Since this is a creative field, it makes an exciting career for freshers.'

8
HUMAN RESOURCES DEPARTMENT

One of the most important departments in any organization, the Human Resources (HR) Department, is responsible for managing every employee's entry into any organization till her/his exit, and ensuring that the employee stays productive till the last day at work.

Section 1 looks at the role and functions of the HR Department and Section 2 at the entry-level job roles.

SECTION 1
BACKGROUND

The HR department must efficiently manage the employee lifecycle from entry to exit, through the following functions which are organized into sub-departments.

- Recruitment
- Training
- On boarding
- Performance management
- Compensation management
- HR services
- Industrial relations
- Strategic HR

Every employee is recruited with a purpose at the right salary. She/he needs to know what is expected from her/him, and needs to be trained. She/he must engage in various tasks that are required. In case the employee has any issues within the organization, her/his issues need to be taken care of. Lastly, if the employee has to leave the organization, then the final settlement also needs to be made amicably. Each of these functions in the lifecycle of an employee are interdependent and work towards achieving the big picture, that is, employee productivity.

SUB-DEPARTMENTS IN THE HR DEPARTMENT

Recruitment

The Recruitment Department's job is to ensure that the right people are selected, at the right time, and at the right pay scale.

We can divide recruitment into the following sub-roles.

Talent Sourcing

Talent sourcing is about identifying and connecting with the right prospect and has become a specialist function. There are many new sourcing methodologies that have come into the picture, such as sourcing through job boards, recruitment advertisements, social media, and referral programmes. So some of the entry-level roles that we will cover in this book, based on the above sourcing methodologies, include:

- E-recruiter
- Functional Recruiter
- Headhunter
- Tele-recruiter

Data Management

All this recruitment data has to be entered, stored, and managed. This job is basically performed by a Recruitment Data Analyst.

Training

The main responsibility of this sub-department is to train employees as per organizational needs. The business leaders, Operations Managers, Line Managers determine the training needs for their teams and it is the duty of this department is to create training programmes, deliver training programmes, and coordinate all the training activities in the organization. To cater to these training needs, organizations need:

- Content Specialists
- Trainers
- Training Coordinators

Performance Management

The employee performance against goals and objectives (also called Key Result Areas [KRAs]) is monitored by the boss and is measured on a quarterly, half-yearly, and annual basis. The Performance Management Executive in the HR team helps the boss conduct the performance review in a scientific manner.

Compensation Management

Here, the primary objective is to ensure that employees are paid salaries in alignment with the talent-market scenario, by conducting compensation surveys. Employees should neither be underpaid (as that would lead to employee dissatisfaction), nor overpaid (as that would make the company uncompetitive). When a new employee joins the company, the Compensation Sub-department must ensure parity by making sure that she/he is paid the right salary, by taking into account the salaries of other employees in the company doing similar jobs. The HR Compensation Management Executive manages all these aspects.

Employee Engagement and HR Operations

The primary duty of this sub-department is to ensure that employees are active and are fully engaged with their jobs. Employee engagement means that the employee is motivated to do the job, knows what to do, how to do it, and has the resources to deliver the results. Organizations conduct activities like the celebration of festivals, birthdays, family events, sports events, communication workshops, and so on, to boost employee morale and motivation. This is the job of the HR Operations Executive.

The HR Operations Executive is also responsible for maintaining employee databases, record-keeping, identifying training needs, managing their attendance system, managing the code of conduct and discipline, protect employees against sexual harassment, resolve employee conflicts, resolve boss-employee issues, and many more such duties.

Industrial Relations (IR)

In large companies, especially in the manufacturing industry, employees form trade unions (also called labour unions). A trade union is an organization of employees, working for the benefit of employees. It seeks higher pay and benefits, better working conditions, and better safety at work for all members of the union. The trade union, through its leadership, bargains with the employers, negotiates labour contracts (collective bargaining), and signs an agreement known as the 'Union Settlement'. It is the responsibility of the union to ensure that employees work as per the agreed productivity norms, without causing any hindrance. Typically, the IR Department's role is to maintain industrial harmony by interacting with employee unions, and this department is often located in the factory premises.

Strategic HR

The primary duty of Strategic HR is to ensure that the skills and competencies of employees are in alignment with the changing business strategies of the company and its competitors. They conduct research to benchmark the company's HR strategies against the competition's, to improve the effectiveness of the HR function. For example, during the research conducted, if Strategic HR finds out that the company is overstaffed, they provide valuable suggestions to the top management on 'right sizing' via Voluntary Retirement Schemes (VRS) where the non-productive employees are asked to leave with adequate compensation.

There are various roles in top and middle management in the HR function but our main focus is only on the following entry-level job roles.

SECTION 2
ENTRY-LEVEL JOB ROLES

CODE	ROLE
HR 1	E-recruiter
HR 2	Headhunter
HR 3	International Tele-recruiter
HR 4	Recruitment Data Analyst
HR 5	Content Specialist
HR 6	Corporate Trainer

HR 7	Training Coordinator
HR 8	Compensation Management Executive
HR 9	Operations Executive
HR 10	Industrial Relations Executive (Trainee)

RECRUITMENT DEPARTMENT

HR 1 E-RECRUITER

Job Description

E-recruiting is the process of hiring candidates using electronic resources like job boards and the internet, and the person who does this job is called an E-recruiter.

Typical Responsibilities

- Visiting popular job board databases to shortlist candidates for interviews.
- Understanding the requirements of the position and presenting your company, and the vacancy to a prospective candidate through attractive job postings.
- Developing and executing online recruitment campaigns—by emails, banner advertisements, and so on.
- Connecting with job prospects through social media and networking sites such as Facebook and LinkedIn.
- Calling up prospective candidates and briefing them about the job opportunity and convincing them to apply.
- Follow-up calls with active candidates during various stages of the recruitment process.
- Preparing status reports for various stakeholders/departments.
- Coming up with creative and innovative ideas for sourcing candidates through the internet.
- Must have a clear understanding about the talent market and must be able to close positions successfully.

E-recruiter: A Profile

Likely salary with 1–3 years of experience	Rs 100,000–Rs 250,000 per annum.
Targets	Closing maximum number of positions within the given time-frame. Sourcing the right candidates—those who will stay and perform in the company.
Challenges	Convincing the passive job-seekers (those who are not looking for a change) to apply. Hiring despite your company's recruitment challenges. For example, your company may not pay the highest salary in the industry. Closing positions quickly when the candidate is not in a hurry.
Skills	As an E-recruiter, you need to know everything about job boards, networking sites, internet technologies like video CVs, and stay updated with regard to these technologies. Excellent convincing skills.
Stress	Low to moderate.
Travel on the job	There is no travel involved in this job.
Impact on stakeholders	The prospective employees and the Hiring Managers are directly influenced by this role.
Career prospects	The career prospects are also very bright as you can become a Senior Recruiter and then manage a team of E-recruiters.
Future salary with 5–7 years of experience	Rs 250,000–Rs 400,000 per annum.

A Practitioner's View
E-recruiter, Sri Lakshmi, Bengaluru

Ms Sri Lakshmi has three years of experience in this field. When we asked her to share her experiences with us, she said:

'This job gives me a fair exposure to communicate with people across various levels and industries. I not only enjoy the exposure but also get a chance to hone my interaction and networking skills. I would recommend this job to freshers because it gives them a chance to get extensive knowledge about the job market, boost their confidence, and also improve their communication skills.'

HR 2 HEADHUNTER

Job Description

There are two types of job-seekers: active job-seekers and passive job-seekers. An active job-seeker is someone who is seriously looking for a job and constantly knocks on the doors of employers. A passive job-seeker is someone who is satisfied with the existing job, and is not very keen on changing.

A Headhunter has a very unique role created with the sole purpose of connecting with passive job-seekers and get them interested enough to apply.

Headhunters belong to the Talent Sourcing Sub-department within Recruiting.

Typical Responsibilities

- Studying job requirements and preparing a source plan (where the prospect is currently working).
- Visiting job boards and social media sites like LinkedIn to identify prospects.
- Making telephone calls to various people to find contact details of target candidates.
- Preparing a game plan to convince each prospect.
- Preparing a powerful write-up on job opportunities and sending it to prospects.
- Calling up prospective candidates and convincing them to send their current résumés.
- Following up till the résumés are received.
- Providing updates to candidates.
- Networking with candidates through social media, email.
- Attending technical conferences to network with prospects.

Headhunter: A Profile

Likely salary with 1–3 years of experience	Rs 200,000–Rs 350,000 per annum.
Targets	To basically get a fixed number of quality résumés within a given timeline. Staying connected with a large number of prospects.
Challenges	Passive candidates are difficult to reach and are often rude. They also expect high pay increases for switching jobs. So convincing them to consider a job at a lower pay increase is a challenge.
Skills	Exceptional communication skills, both written and oral. No fear of rejection (refer to 'An Exceptional Case' given below). Persuading and convincing skills. Networking skills.
Stress	Moderate to high.
Travel on the job	Limited travel within the city may be required to meet candidates.
Impact on stakeholders	Hiring Managers will be impacted the most.
Career prospects	In three years you will become a Senior Headhunter, sourcing only top management profiles. In five years you will manage a team of Headhunters.
Salary with 5–7 years of experience	Rs 400,000–Rs 800,000 per annum.

An Exceptional Case

Mr K.S. Reddy worked with us as a Headhunter. A client of ours wanted to hire electrical engineers with experience in Transformer Operations. I called Reddy, and gave him a brief that we needed the résumés of a few electrical engineers within two days. He said he would do the needful and left the office. To my surprise, he came back to my cabin the next day and placed eight résumés on my table.

I asked him what he had done in order to source the résumés and his answer took me by surprise.

He said, 'Sir, I went to the industrial area and said that I had come from APSEB (the Andhra Pradesh State Electricity Board) and would like to meet the Electrical Engineer. The management called the Electrical Engineer and he took me for a factory tour thinking that I had come to inspect their transformer. After some time, I gave him my card and told him that in case he was looking for a change of job, he could call me as I had an exciting offer for him. Like that I went to few factories and collected résumés of interested candidates.'

I was very impressed by the way he took up the challenge and delivered the required number of résumés. For me, this is how a typical Headhunter should be. He should not have any fear of being rejected by a candidate.

A Practitioner's View
Headhunter, Jayasree Pavani, Hyderabad

Ms Pavani is working with a recruitment consulting firm. She has seven years of experience in recruitment, executive search, and leadership hiring. She is also a senior member of the Executive Search Division in that firm. Says she:

'Headhunting is my major area of focus and expertise, which involves industry research, mapping various sources including professional and social networks, the web, and so on to find out suitable professionals, quickly reaching them with a subtle and confidential approach. It is important that you approach the candidate with a good amount of information on the job requirement, create the interest and take the discussions forward, have a well-rounded view of the profiles of candidates, and present their professional credentials, to the client in the right light. I enjoy doing this job as it gives me a lot of confidence to deal with various passive job-seekers and convincing them to take up the new offer is a great experience.'

HR 3 INTERNATIONAL TELE-RECRUITER

Job Description

A Tele-recruiter uses a telephone to source new prospects for various roles in organizations. This role is common in the India offices of the US-based IT staffing companies. The US-based IT staffing company will get manpower indents for jobs in the US and pass it on to the India office. A Tele-recruiter in the India office will identify candidates living in the US, talk to them, get them interested, assess and pass on the shortlist to the US office to process them further. Since the candidates are in the US, the Indian Tele-recruiter will work in night shifts.

This person is responsible for sourcing candidates from various portals, referrals, job-seeker databases. He/she will have to shortlist candidates, conduct telephonic interviews, screen candidates and if they are eligible, schedule a detailed personal interview for them. The Tele-recruiter will have to maintain a database of the work they do—based on the number of calls, leads, and prospects—and report to seniors.

Typical Responsibilities

- Understanding the manpower requirements.
- Sourcing candidates through portals, social networking sites, and databases.
- Shortlisting eligible candidates.
- Making telephone calls to candidates and setting up teleconference timings.
- Presenting the job opportunity and the employer to a prospective candidate effectively over the phone and email.
- Following up with the prospect and getting them interested in the job opportunity.
- Preparing status reports for various stakeholders/departments.
- Follow-up calls with active candidates during various stages of the recruitment process.

International Tele-recruiter: A Profile

Likely salary with 1–3 years of experience	Rs 200,000–Rs 300,000 per annum.
Targets	Sourcing and convincing a given number of eligible candidates to apply every day.
Challenges	Working in night shifts. Assessing candidates over the phone, especially their seriousness in pursuing the job opportunity quickly, without irritating the prospect. It is important not to get intimidated or overwhelmed.
Skills	Exposure to the domain in which candidates are being hired, for example, software roles. Excellent English communication (oral) skills and active listening skills.
Stress	Low to moderate.
Travel on the job	None, this is a desk job.
Impact on stakeholders	Candidates seeking jobs and employers are directly impacted by this role.
Career prospects	With two years of experience you will be a Senior Tele-recruiter but as you gain experience and skills you will be promoted as a Team Lead managing a team of Tele-recruiters after four years.
Future salary with 5–7 years of experience	Rs 350,000–Rs 500,000 per annum.

A Practitioner's View

Tele-recruiter, Prarthana Roy, Mumbai

Ms Roy has been in the recruitment industry for the past two years. When we asked her to share her experiences with us, she said:

'Being a part of the recruitment industry, I have learnt a lot. Interacting with different types of people across the industry has given a good exposure and improved my interpersonal skills. Personally, I have improved my communication (oral and written), decision-making, time- and task-management skills. Professionally, I have improved my business communication, and convincing skills. Working in this role has also helped me understand a professional's mind-set.

'I really enjoy recruitment. It is a difficult job and you never get bored. I do feel sometimes as if I am a babysitter or the mother hen. Working with diverse individuals and various personalities is challenging. Getting heard and understood is a very difficult challenge that I face on the job. You do not go into this job just because you like people. You need common sense, must be able to control your emotions, and have a strong disposition in order to handle the tough parts of the job, and must be able to handle various situations.

'I would recommend this job to a fresher since they enter the industry with fresh minds and high expectations, they will get a very good exposure in terms of knowledge about various roles. Apart from this, they can polish their communication skills and confidence level.'

HR 4 RECRUITMENT DATA ANALYST

Job Description

Recruiters generate large volumes of data and often use recruitment software (called the Applicant Tracking System).

A Data Analyst is responsible for collecting, analysing, interpreting and presenting the data and trends through graphs, reports, charts, and so on.

Typical Responsibilities

- Analysing and reporting on the status of recruitment.
- Analysing and reporting on the performance of the recruiting teams and identifying the top and poor performers.
- Recommending incentive schemes to improve performance.
- Analysing quality issues and recommending action plans.
- Presenting insightful reports.

- Updating one's knowledge in the current field by attending training sessions and seminars.
- Analysing recruitment market patterns/trends and educating the internal teams.

Recruitment Data Analyst: A Profile

Likely salary with 1–3 years of experience	Rs 150,000–Rs 250,000 per annum.
Targets	Generating accurate and timely reports. Improving the quality of the reports continuously.
Challenges	Data accuracy: Many times the data input may be wrong, leading to wrong conclusions. Check if data is complete: Sometimes data is analysed even when there are gaps in the data.
Skills	Excellent grip over MS Excel and other business analytics software. Strong analytical skills and data visualization skills.
Stress	Moderate.
Travel on the job	This job does not involve travel.
Impact on stakeholders	This role will directly impact the Recruiting Team and Hiring Managers.
Career prospects	Very bright, because this is a new field within recruiting and you may become a Senior Data Analyst in two years and then be made Head of Department in five years. A few can move into the Business Analytics Team of the company, which analyses the whole company.
Future salary with 5–7 years of experience	Rs 300,000–Rs 500,000 per annum.

A Practitioner's View

Recruitment Data Analyst, B. Srinivasa Rao, Hyderabad

Mr Srinivasa Rao has been working as a Data Analyst for the past two and a half years. He has seven years of experience in data management, MIS, and data analysis. He shares:

'The most important aspects that interest me while doing data analysis are handling huge raw data, understanding the market and working on Excel. Analysing, formatting, and merging data by doing workflow analysis forms an integral part of my role. I have gained immense expertise in Microsoft Excel after working in this role.'

TRAINING DEPARTMENT

HR 5 CONTENT SPECIALIST

Job Description

Content Specialists are people who possess specialized writing skills and are responsible for delivering content based on the topic. Content Specialists specialize in particular fields like business, politics, science, medicine, education, arts, advertising, and marketing. In training, they are required to develop training material for classroom training and for e-learning courses.

As a Content Specialist, you will usually work in a team of Subject Matter Experts (SMEs) and Instructional Designers.

Typical Responsibilities

- Understanding purpose (called the 'learning objective') for which content is required.
- Identifying reliable and genuine sources for referencing.
- Conducting research in the required area and gathering and analysing basic information.
- Discussing with Subject Matter Experts to understand the content domain and arrive at the content outline.
- Developing detailed curriculum for training programmes.
- Compiling researched data, tables, pictures, and so on.
- Verifying and validating information from multiple sources.
- Keeping detailed track of information sources.
- Ensuring that content is written keeping the target audience in mind.
- Reviewing the content regularly to see that there are no gaps.
- Writing and editing content in line with the copyright laws.

- Identifying visuals like pictures, diagrams, and symbols, to increase impact.
- Creating interactive learning elements like quizzes to verify recall of the content.
- Assess and review the published content.
- Work as per the time plan agreed with the team.

Content Specialist: A Profile

Likely salary with 1–3 years of experience	Rs 200,000–Rs 350,000 per annum.
Targets	Meeting the productivity norms for various types of content. Ensuring that the content is reader-friendly, error-free, and contemporary.
Challenges	Comprehending a variety of topics in which content is required, quickly. To ensure that there are no violations of copyright laws.
Skills	Excellent comprehension and written skills, with a flair for words. A passion for reading and developing content. A creative mind.
Stress	Moderate.
Travel on the job	There is no travel involved in this job.
Impact on stakeholders	Learners who read the content are directly impacted.
Career prospects	Very bright because this is an emerging field. In three years you could become a Senior Content Writer and become a Content Lead in five years.
Future salary with 5–7 years of experience	Rs 400,000–Rs 600,000 per annum.

A Practitioner's View
Content Writer, Sunitha Sambaraju, Hyderabad

Ms Sambaraju has thirteen years of experience in content development, training, and sales. She has handled various Training and Content Teams. When we spoke to her regarding her views on content development as a career option for freshers, she said:

'Content development is a career which requires a person to be creative, come out with interesting ideas and methodologies to deal with concepts. It is a good career option which has immense growth potential. It gives me the exposure to work across different sectors and learner segments. Personally, I have learnt to manage people, projects, and tough situations. I enjoy doing this role and feel that it is certainly a good career option to consider.'

HR 6 CORPORATE TRAINER

Job Description

Why do corporates train their employees? Without effective training, employees under-perform and invariably quit the company.

Training must be conducted in a scientific and learner-centric way by experts, called Corporate Trainers, trained in the art and science of training.

To be a Corporate Trainer, you need to be a graduate from any field. Having a postgraduate degree and relevant certification in training will be helpful. In addition, every training company conducts training for trainers (called Training the Trainers Programme, or TTT).

Boot Camp

Here the Trainer is given five to ten days of classroom training on effective training techniques, the science of learning, and the art of managing different types of learners.

Course Training

Before the Trainer conducts a specific course, he/she is given a TTT on that specific course by an experienced Master Trainer and is also given a training guide to follow.

Typical Responsibilities

- Identify the training need—the area in which employees need to be trained.

- Prepare a curriculum in consultation with experts.
- Work with Instructional Designers to develop a training design appropriate for the learners.
- Work with the Content Writer to plan the entire course content including games and quizzes to be conducted during the classroom session and learner hand-outs
- Undergo TTT programmes to master the training delivery.
- Conduct training sessions as per training design.
- Evaluate the training session by taking feedback and making necessary improvements.

Corporate Trainer: A Profile

Likely salary with 1–3 years of experience	Rs 250,000–Rs 350,000 per annum.
Targets	Every day and in every training session, the Trainer has to ensure that the takeaways for the Trainee are met as per the training design.
Challenges	Sticking to a course design and delivering training as per the trainer manual, every day and every time. Managing different types of learners.
Skills	Excellent leadership and people-management skills. Good story-telling skills in addition to excellent public-speaking skills. A keen and genuine interest in the learner is essential.
Stress	Medium.
Travel on the job	Extent of travel depends upon the amount of outstation training.
Impact on stakeholders	The employees of the organization (learners) are impacted by this role.
Career prospects	In three years you can become a Senior Trainer and in five years become a Master Trainer or a Training Lead managing a team of Trainers.
Future salary with 5–7 years of experience	Rs 350,000–Rs 500,000 per annum.

A Practitioner's View
Corporate Trainer, D. Harsha Vardhan Reddy, Hyderabad

Mr Reddy has been working as a Corporate Trainer for the past eight years. When we spoke to him, he shared some very interesting aspects of being a Corporate Trainer. He said:

'As a Trainer, I face new challenges every single day. I get to interact with new sets of students/employees who have different personalities and attitudes. Understanding them and ensuring that everyone present in the classroom is able to get some value-addition from the training session is a challenge in itself. Working as a Trainer has personally helped me increase my memory, sense of humour, and also my communication and interaction skills. Above all, we get to learn something new from every candidate.'

HR 7 TRAINING COORDINATOR

Job Description

Trainers are responsible for ensuring the success of the classroom training sessions but do you know who organizes the training programme? Who finalizes the date and venue, ensures that the classroom is fully equipped with all the facilities required to make the training session successful, invites participants, makes sure of the hotel bookings for the participants' stay, ensures that the trainer reaches the venue on time? It is the Training Coordinator.

Typical Responsibilities

Training Coordinators usually need to:

- Check with the internal stakeholders of the organization to know their training plan.
- Check with Trainers regarding their schedules.
- Assign respective Trainers to take training sessions according to their area of expertise and specialization.
- Publish training calendars.
- Identify and invite training course participants.

- Plan and arrange for training resources like training venues, projectors, learner guides, hotels for stay, finalizing the lunch menus.
- Take feedback from the students/employees on the Trainer, training venues, and so on by conducting surveys at the end of every training session.
- Keep a track of the expenses incurred to organize a training session, ensuring that the cost does not overshoot the budget.
- Collect feedback from Trainers, Trainees, supervisors of Trainees and suggest improvements.

Training Coordinator: A Profile

Likely salary with 1–3 years of experience	Rs 150,000–Rs 300,000 per annum.
Targets	To ensure zero rescheduling of training sessions. To ensure training budgets are not exceeded. To ensure participant satisfaction on training arrangements.
Challenges	To be able to multi-task, as you will be handling multiple training sessions at different locations. Accepting last minute changes due to unexpected developments.
Skills	Ability to handle tough situations and act calmly. Excellent planning and coordination skills. Ability to multi-task.
Stress	Medium.
Travel on the job	Yes, locally and possibly outstation too.
Impact on stakeholders	The employees of the organization (Trainees) and the Trainers are impacted most by this role.
Career prospects	You can become a Senior Training Coordinator in three years, and head the Training Support Department in five years.
Future salary with 5–7 years of experience	Rs 350,000–Rs 500,000 per annum.

A Practitioner's View

Training Coordinator, Shalini Rao, Hyderabad

Ms Rao has been working as a Training Coordinator for the past two and half years. When we asked her why she likes doing this job, she said:

'My job involves coordination with Training Managers, Trainers, Content Specialists, vendors and others, regarding training sessions. I find my role interesting and challenging, because if I miss out on any single aspect the whole process gets delayed. Which means I have to be alert at all times. Personally, I get to learn a lot of things while working in this role.'

HR 8 COMPENSATION MANAGEMENT EXECUTIVE

Job Description

Any employee has one key expectation that she/he is paid a fair salary, in proportion to skills, experience, qualification, and expertise. Who determines fair compensation? It is the Compensation and Benefits Team. Every company has its own compensation and benefits policy, which determines how the new employee will be paid compared to the existing employee, and how employees will be rewarded for performance.

The next important issue is the break-up of salary. Every employee wants the income tax to be minimized. So the breaking of total compensation into basic salary, house rent allowance, medical reimbursement, and so on, is again determined by the compensation policy which again, is set up by the Compensation and Benefits Team.

Compensation Management Executives are specialists in researching, developing, and establishing a pay system for employees. They develop and implement compensation strategies and policies to retain the performing employees and also help Operating Managers determine their team bonuses.

Typical Responsibilities

- Monthly salaries are processed and pay slips are generated for every employee.

- Design and implement tax-friendly compensation policies.
- Developing and implementing the performance pay and incentives system.
- Handling employee queries on salaries and benefits.
- Ensuring that income tax is deducted correctly and remitted to the income tax authorities.
- Ensuring that employees receive 'Tax Deducted at Source' (TDS) certificates at the end of the year.
- Conducting salary surveys to determine market compensation.
- Benchmark compensation with competition.

Compensation Management Executive: A Profile

Likely salary with 1–3 years of experience	Rs 200,000–Rs 400,000 per annum.
Targets	Design and implement a compensation policy that promotes a performance culture and is in line with the talent market. There is no daily target except ensuring that employee queries are quickly addressed.
Challenges	Coming up with innovative compensation strategies despite limited compensation data. Handling confidentiality of compensation data. You will have to handle data personally and cannot delegate the job.
Skills	MS Excel skills to analyse data. Analytical skills. Adequate knowledge of income tax.
Stress	Low.
Travel on the job	None.
Impact on stakeholders	The employees of the organization are impacted by this role.
Career prospects	In three years you can become a Senior Executive and in seven years become the Compensation Manager at the corporate office.
Future salary with 5–7 years of experience	Rs 500,000–Rs 850,000 per annum.

A Practitioner's View
Compensation and Benefits Executive, Vidyasagar, Hyderabad

Mr Vidyasagar has nearly five years of experience in the field of HR and compensation management. When we asked him why he would refer this role to a fresher, he said:

'Salary is not the biggest motivator but is the biggest de-motivator. It is my job to ensure that employees pay the right amount of income tax, save money for a rainy day by investing in Provident Fund schemes; employees are differentiated from other employees through performance-linked pay, and employees get the best advice for tax-saving investments. In short, my job is to ensure that the salary and benefits are designed to benefit the employee.'

Mr Vidyasagar shared with us a challenging situation that he had faced. His company was looking for a candidate to fill a certain position. Even though the candidate did not have any master's degree, the level of experience and expertise he had was on par or even better than those who had a master's degree. So he had to convince the management regarding the same as they were not ready to accept paying him as much as they were paying candidates who had a master's degree. He said that convincing them was not at all easy as he had to collect various data to prove the candidate's ability.

HR 9 OPERATIONS EXECUTIVE

Job Description

Every organization has an HR manual which spells out the various employee-related policies and benefits like leave, office timings, housing loans, conveyance reimbursements, and performance appraisals. An HR Operations Executive's job is to help each employee understand the HR manual and abide by it. If the employee has any grievances in the implementation of the HR manual, the HR Operations Executive will have to resolve them. In short, the Operations Executive's job is to implement the HR manual.

Typical Responsibilities

- Handle/organize joining formalities.
- Leaves and attendance management.
- Providing attendance data for monthly payroll.
- Managing advance salary, ad hoc bonuses, loans.
- Confirmations, performance appraisals, resignations.
- Handle/organize exit interviews.
- Handle/organize full and final settlements.
- Handling employee database records (both in soft form and files management) and submit reports.

Operations Executive: A Profile

Likely salary with 1–3 years of experience	Rs 120,000–Rs 250,000 per annum.
Targets	Ensuring all reports and records are up-to-date. Ensuring that salaries and settlements are processed on time. Resolving employee grievances on time.
Challenges	Resolving employee grievances is a difficult job since it involves other departments like Finance, and these departments may not cooperate. Job is repetitive and can be monotonous. Documentation management is tedious work.
Skills	Excellent grip of MS Excel. Attention to detail.
Stress	Moderate.
Travel on the job	None.
Impact on stakeholders	The employees of the organization will be impacted by this role.
Career prospects	You can become a Senior Operations Executive in three years and become an HR Operations Manager in eight to ten years.
Future salary with 5–7 years of experience	Rs 350,000–Rs 550,000 per annum.

A Practitioner's View
Senior HR Operations Staffing Executive, G. Neelima, Hyderabad

Ms Neelima is working as a Senior HR Operations Staffing Executive with a recruitment consulting firm. She has seven years of experience in the field of HR Operations. She says:

'I have been a part of the HR Operations function, ever since I started my career. This job has not only helped me build my confidence, but has also made me an organized individual. You get to understand different personalities. I get motivated when I resolve employee issues on time and get their appreciation.'

She shared a recent experience. She was handling 10 clients. When payrolls were processed, some of the candidates did not give their correct account numbers. Due to this the money got credited into someone else's account. So she had to call the candidates, inform them about the same, coordinate with the bank, and again credit the money into the correct accounts. She also had to deal with the bank to find out in whose account they had wrongly credited the money; speak to the bank staff regarding the same and find out a way by which she could get the money back, because if she did not do so, the company would hold her liable for the loss. Therefore, when things go wrong, stress levels go up, but one has to manage it.

HR 10 INDUSTRIAL RELATIONS EXECUTIVE (TRAINEE)

Job Description

In any large manufacturing company, workers are organized and form unions to protect their interests. The management and the union have to work together to ensure that the workmen are productive and there is industrial peace.

So in order to deal with unions, organizations have an Industrial Relations (IR) Department which is an important link between the workmen and the management of the company. The IR Executive is a junior member of the IR Department.

Typical Responsibilities

- Assist management in ensuring peace and harmony at the workplace.
- Assist supervisors in ensuring work discipline.
- Guide supervisors in adoption of applicable labour laws.
- Receive, process, and resolve grievances.
- Ensure orderly employee entry and exit through the Time Office.
- Document and bring to the attention of the management, any disputes raised by the union.
- Arrange meetings between management and the union to resolve the disputes.
- Constantly update management on the latest amendments to labour laws and its impact.

Industrial Relations Executive (Trainee): A Profile

Likely salary with 1–3 years of experience	Rs 200,000–Rs 350,000 per annum.
Targets	Ensure workmen productivity as per agreed norms. Minimal work stoppages due to labour issues. Compliance with labour laws. Timely resolution of grievances.
Challenges	Staying updated on labour laws. Managing multiple unions with multiple agendas. Engaging with politicized unions.
Skills	Active listening skills and communication skills. Good negotiation skills. Relationship-building skills.
Stress	Stress in this role in normal times will be moderate. During times of labour dispute, stress will be high.
Travel on the job	Minimal.
Impact on stakeholders	The workmen and their supervisors and the unions are impacted the most by this role.
Career prospects	Once you join as an IR Executive, you can move up the ladder to become an Assistant Manager after three years, Deputy Manager in five years, and Industrial Relations Manager in ten years.

| Salary with 5–7 years of experience | Rs 350,000–Rs 500,000 per annum. |

A Practitioner's View
Industrial Relations Executive, Samuel M., Hyderabad

Mr Samuel is working as an Industrial Relations Executive with India's leading manufacturer of vaccines. He has almost seven years of work experience in this field. When we spoke to him and asked him to share his experience, he said:

'I had two years of experience in HR concepts but was a fresher in the field of industrial relations. Initially I was worried whether I could handle this job but with the support of superiors and management, I have successfully completed five years of handling the industrial relations and payroll aspect of HR.

'My role requires interaction with employees regarding their issues. Every employee in this organization knows me in person. It gives me immense satisfaction when I am able to solve employee issues and concerns. I believe that we learn many things when problems are more. Working in this role helped me develop my personality and also understand how to deal with a variety of issues that employees and management face. As years passed, my remuneration increased, but so have my responsibilities. I would say that the opportunities for freshers in the manufacturing sector are high and so if anyone wants to pursue a career in industrial relations, I strongly recommend this career option.'

9
LEGAL DEPARTMENT

One of my friends wanted to buy a house. When he found a property that he liked, he asked the seller for copies of various documents related to the house, such as the Draft Sale Deed and Encumbrance Certificate, and took them to his Legal Adviser to verify that all the documents were legally acceptable and that the property was not under any litigation.

In the same way, organizations also have a Legal Department to ensure that they are able to comply with all necessary laws, manage litigations, and also prevent litigations.

SECTION 1
BACKGROUND

All organizations operate within a legal system. There are over 30 key laws and regulations that affect a business in India. Some of these are the Companies Act (1956), Central Board of Revenue Act (1963), Income Tax Act (1961), Direct Taxes Code Act (2010), Indian Partnership Act (1932), Income Tax Act (1922), Customs Act (1962), Shops and Establishments Act (1953), Indian Contract Act (1872), Factories Act (1948), Foreign Trade Act (1992), Indian Trade Unions Act (1926), Sales Promotion (Conditions of Service) Act (1976), Industries (Regulation & Development) Act (1951), Mines Act (1952), Foreign Exchange Management Act, and many more.[7]

Every organization has to comply with these laws, as applicable. Many large organizations have in-house Legal Departments to ensure compliance, though small- and medium-sized companies prefer to seek legal advice from external consultants.

The cost of running an illegal set-up can be very high—from fines, imprisonment of directors, and even shutting down and declaring bankruptcy.

Every Indian company is run by a Board of Directors in compliance with the Companies Act (1956) which sets out the responsibilities of companies and their directors. The primary duty of the Company Secretary is to assist the Board of Directors in conducting board meetings and ensuring the company is run as per the prevailing Company Law framework and corporate governance guidelines. The Company Secretary prepares briefs, pleadings, documents, memorandums, and also helps in filing information with various statutory authorities such as the stock exchanges.

While there is a difference in the job roles of a Legal Department and Company Secretary, in many smaller companies, the Company Secretary may also play the additional role of the Legal Officer.

Section 2 looks at two popular entry-level job roles in the Legal and Secretarial Department.

SECTION 2
ENTRY-LEVEL JOB ROLES

CODE	ROLE
LEGAL 1	Corporate Legal Assistant/Secretarial Assistant
LEGAL 2	Company Secretary (Trainee)

LEGAL 1 CORPORATE LEGAL ASSISTANT/SECRETARIAL ASSISTANT

Job Description

Providing appropriate legal advice to the management of the company and its employees is one of the most important functions of the Legal Department. Another important function of this department is to make sure that the company and its employees follow workplace laws without any deviations, by providing them timely updates and training. They also report deviations, if any, to the top management.

The Legal Department is responsible for all legal transactions, dealing with statutory bodies, filing of legal documents, communicating changes in laws and regulations, contract drafting and negotiations, handling real estate documentation for the company, employment laws, deal with employee discrimination cases, litigation management, and so on, to make sure that the company is getting the best possible legal advice. They also handle cases filed by, and cases filed against, the company. They handle the preliminary filings in a dispute but actual court representation is done by an outside expert. They also conduct legal searches on cases to answer legal questions and doubts raised. They are basically supported by Paralegals, Legal Assistants, and Legal Secretaries. The Legal Department also provides regular updates to the top management on any ongoing legal proceedings.

There is usually a lot of documentation that has to be prepared and filed. Some of this data may also need to be edited time and again after various hearings, discussions between Lawyers, Senior Legal Executives, among others. A Corporate Legal Assistant is responsible for assisting the Head of the Legal Department in all activities, including documentation. A lot of research activity is involved in this role.

A Corporate Legal Assistant needs to have a clear understanding of standard business operating procedures laid down by the regulators. Smaller companies cannot afford to maintain legal teams in-house and hence outsource them. So this role is also available in legal firms.

Typical Responsibilities

- Meeting business Managers and legal experts to discuss and understand various legal issues.
- Researching, collating, and organizing information for legal documents.
- Conducting research on law regarding any changes/amendments, case studies.
- Giving status updates of the previous day's proceedings and arriving at a plan of action on how to take matters ahead.

Corporate Legal Assistant/Secretarial Assistant: A Profile

Likely salary with 1–3 years of experience	Rs 200,000–Rs 350,000 per annum.
Targets	Timely legal scrutiny of documents. Comprehensive and relevant research.

Challenges	Each case being unique, requires working long hours and the study of voluminous documentation. Key information often arrives very late. Despite all this, timelines have to be met because missing a legal deadline can be very costly to the company. Staying updated on amendments to the law. Being practical and being familiar with the way law is practised.
Skills	Good domain knowledge about legal documents and laws. Excellent written communication and comprehension skills. Time management skills.
Stress	Moderate.
Travel on the job	There is limited travel involved in this role.
Impact on stakeholders	Business Managers are highly impacted by this role.
Career prospects	In five years you can become a Legal Officer and in ten years you can lead the Legal Department in a mid-sized company.
Future salary with 5–7 years of experience	Rs 400,000–Rs 700,000 per annum.

A Practitioner's View
Legal Assistant, M. Nagaraju, Hyderabad

M. Nagaraju was working as a Legal Clerk (Legal Assistant) in a Senior Lawyer's office. We asked him to share his experiences with us and why would he recommend this role to a fresher. He said:

'Dealing with legal matters needs a lot of detailing, as one mistake can change the client's future. Therefore, we need to be very careful in arranging all the required documents and forms. We do a lot of research in order to gain complete and comprehensive knowledge about various aspects related to the case. If any fresher wishes to start a career in this field it is certainly a very good starting point and the learning is also very high.'

LEGAL 2 COMPANY SECRETARY (TRAINEE)

Job Description

One of the key stakeholders in any organization is the investor—in equity or in loans. The investor's key expectation is 'corporate governance', which means that the company is run professionally and transparently as per the guidelines set by regulatory bodies and prevailing laws. A Company Secretary's function is to ensure compliance or conformity with the above expectations and be the intermediary between the company management and its board representing shareholders and investors.

In addition, a Company Secretary is a liaison officer between the company board and shareholders. A good example of the importance of the role is when a company decides to go in for a public issue. The Company Secretary is involved in drafting the various documents to be submitted to the Securities Exchange Board of India (SEBI), investment bankers, and so on. The Company Secretary is involved in allotment of shares to various applicants and ensuring that the share allotment is made transparently and in line with the regulations.

A Company Secretary is responsible for answering the shareholders' questions about any developments in the company. Even if the Company Secretary does not need to provide legal advisory services, it is very important to have complete knowledge of the laws that might affect his/her areas of work if he/she seeks to play a bigger role in the company.

Typical Responsibilities

- Initiating process-driven policies and monitoring compliance with all prevailing corporate governance laws—the Companies Act, stock exchange regulations, SEBI Act and other related laws.
- Liaising with statutory bodies in India—such as the SEBI and RBI—and making sure that the organization is in compliance with the requirements of the regulators.
- Preparing agendas for conducting board meetings, shareholder meetings, and also recording and circulating the minutes, developing action plans to implement the board decisions and implementing the action plans.

- Monitoring changes in legislation and regulatory requirements, and advising the board.
- Providing support to the Legal Team as and when required.

Company Secretary (Trainee): A Profile

Likely salary with 1-3 years of experience	Rs 240,000-Rs 350,000 per annum.
Targets	Maximum compliance with all regulations. Ensuring minimum litigation/penalty. Meeting shareholder expectations through timely distribution of information, dividend, and quick redressal of issues.
Challenges	Too many regulations to comply, too many amendments, and too many court judgments to study. Effective administration to see that the decisions taken by the Board of Directors are implemented.
Skills	Thorough knowledge of the law, especially Company Law, and the Company Secretary qualification. Good communication skills. Ability to work under pressure. Attention to detail.
Stress	Moderate.
Travel on the job	Very limited.
Impact on stakeholders	The shareholders of the company and the regulators are impacted the most by this role.
Career prospects	A Company Secretary (Trainee) can become an Assistant Company Secretary in three years and can grow to become a Company Secretary in a mid-sized company in ten to fifteen years.
Salary with 5-7 years of experience	Rs 400,000-Rs 700,000 per annum.

A Practitioner's View

Company Secretary, Karishma Mahesh Joshi, Mumbai

Ms Joshi has over two years of work experience in this field. When we spoke to her asking her why she would recommend this career to a fresher, she said:

'A Company Secretary is a governance professional, who advises the boards of companies on strategy formulation, compliances, and governance matters. By virtue of integrated knowledge of multiple disciplines of law, management, finance and corporate governance, a Company Secretary is the vital link between the company, its shareholders, and regulatory bodies. She/he scrutinizes and advises the board on good governance practices and systems in the company.

'I have handled various matters relating to corporate restructuring, like mergers, takeovers in the organization; specialized in documentation and compliance with Listing Agreements, Reserve Bank of India (RBI) and SEBI guidelines, due diligence, conducting board meetings, shareholders' meetings and all legalities involved with inter-corporate investments and loans, regulatory compliances, and so on.

'The educational background, knowledge, training, and exposure that a Company Secretary acquires makes him/her a versatile professional capable of providing a wide range of services to companies of all sizes, cooperatives, other corporate bodies, firms. A qualified Company Secretary has good employment opportunities and can also be a Practising Professional. I strongly recommend this as a career option to students who are looking to pursue this course.'

10
SUPPLY CHAIN DEPARTMENT

In every supermarket in India, you find products manufactured in many parts of India, China, Korea, Japan, and even other far-flung nations across the world. Have you ever wondered how goods manufactured in different countries, by different manufacturers, reach supermarkets and are still affordable? It is through effective supply chain management.

SECTION 1
BACKGROUND

Corporate organizations deliver goods from their manufacturing plants to customers through various stocking points set up at different locations. Finished goods are distributed from these stocking points to retailers or dealers closest to the customers (called 'outbound logistics') at an economical cost. Raw materials and consumables have to be procured and shipped to the manufacturing plants, economically (which is called 'inbound logistics'). Let's look at the various functions involved in a typical supply chain in a soap manufacturing company, for instance.

Procuring materials

When companies have to manufacture a product, they first need to procure raw materials. For example, to manufacture a soap you need to procure fatty acids, alkali, additives to enhance the colour, texture, and scent of soap, packaging materials, and other items.

Inbound logistics/transportation

Once you identify from where you need to procure materials, you will have to make arrangements to get all the raw materials transported from different locations to the place of production, that is, the factory where they will be processed to make a finished product. For example, fatty acid from Maharashtra, alkali imported from China, perfumery chemicals from France, packaging materials from Delhi may be shipped to a soap manufacturing plant in Chennai.

Production

Once the raw materials are brought to the factory, the production takes place.

Outbound logistics/transportation

Once the soaps are ready, they need to be packed and transported from the place of production to the place of sale. This process involves a lot of transportation as the goods need to be transported to various company stock points or warehouses from where the goods are transported to a distributor godown. These distributors sell the goods to wholesalers who in turn sell the goods to retailers in bulk. Finally, the retailer sells them to customers who walk into their store. This is how a manufactured soap reaches the end-user—the customer.

Supply chain networks are used by almost all organizations, big or small. Products should be available to consumers at the right place, right time, and right price. Effective supply chain management helps organizations to:

- reduce logistics cost; and
- increase revenue and customer loyalty by ensuring stock availability.

SECTION 2
ENTRY-LEVEL JOB ROLES

CODE	ROLE
SC 1	Supply Chain Officer (Outbound)
SC 2	Purchase Officer

SC 1 SUPPLY CHAIN OFFICER (OUTBOUND)

Job Description

A Supply Chain Officer's role is very common in a Fast Moving

Consumer Goods (FMCG) company like Colgate or Unilever with the key responsibility of moving goods from the production centre, to the retail store. A single company like Colgate produces many varieties of toothpastes and sells these in different pack sizes (also called SKU or stocking units). You may want to buy the toothpaste of your choice, in the pack size of your choice, at a retailer of your choice. The price of the toothpaste must be same in all outlets. If you do not get what you want, which is called the 'stock-out' situation, you may even buy some other brand and never return to the earlier brand. So the biggest challenge here is to transport packs of toothpastes of different sizes, across India, at the lowest cost, without the 'stock-out' situation happening even in one among a million retail outlets. You must also ensure that there is no overstocking of the inventory to minimize working capital. You will be involved in planning delivery timings, ensuring that there is enough stock of goods, monitoring the order and packaging process, tracking transactions and maintaining a record for the same. It is a very vital and important role.

Typical Responsibilities

- Appointment and management of warehouses and stock points.
- Inventory management at warehouses.
- Contracts and payments to all transporters.
- Executing the documentation required for transportation of goods, including invoicing.
- Handling transport bottlenecks.
- Performing stock checks at regular intervals.
- Providing SKU-wise forecasts of demand.

Supply Chain Officer (Outbound): A Profile

Likely salary with 1–3 years of experience	Rs 180,000–Rs 300,000 per annum.
Targets	Minimize the gap between the order received from a distributor and the order fulfilled, through proper inventory management. In other words, ensure maximum order fulfilment.

Challenges	Minimize the cycle time for order delivery. Minimize obsolete inventory. Minimize the cost of distribution. Forecasting demand in a competitive scenario at the SKU level. Achieving the right amount of inventory to prevent 'stock-outs' and also minimize excess inventory. Crisis management: keeping goods safe and moving even when the city shuts down for a 'bandh'.
Skills	Sound planning. Self-confidence and a high level of integrity.
Stress	Moderate.
Travel on the job	Limited.
Impact on stakeholders	The customers and the Sales Team are highly impacted by this role.
Career prospects	You can become a Senior Supply Chain Executive after three years. After about ten years, you can become a Supply Chain Manager of a mid-sized company.
Future salary with 5–7 years of experience	Rs 350,000–Rs 450,000 per annum.

A Practitioner's View

Supply Chain Executive, Y.P. Giri, Hyderabad

Mr Giri has over three years of experience as a Supply Chain Executive with a big pharmaceutical company. When we asked him his views about this role and why he would recommend this role to a fresher, he said:

'Working as a Supply Chain Executive, I come across different kinds of problems and every time I solve a problem, it teaches me something new. My job is not monotonous. It has helped me personally and professionally. The role is very challenging as it deals with different kinds of individuals, skilled/unskilled; requires strong interpersonal relationships; you need to be proactive in foreseeing logistics issues and preparing to handle tough situations.'

'As I work in a bio-pharmaceutical (vaccine) company I have learnt the importance of planning, which is very important in the distribution of vaccines and the maintenance of a proper cold chain till it reaches the consumer. In the process I have learnt the importance of different modes of transport used in moving vaccines through various channels. I have now learnt the entire process of the supply chain and I am very confidently handling the tasks independently. If you like challenges then this is a role you must consider.'

SC 2 PURCHASE OFFICER

Job Description

A Purchase Officer is responsible for timely procurement of goods and services at minimal cost, by selecting the right vendors. You will work very closely with the Finance and Production Planning Departments of the company. To be a good Purchase/Procurement Analyst:

- you must be able to negotiate with vendors while making purchases so that they give you the best possible deal; and
- you should strictly follow the company's policies and procedures while dealing with vendors.

Typical Responsibilities

- Conducting research to identify new vendors.
- Inviting quotes from vendors.
- Negotiating with the vendors along with the Finance Department and placing orders.
- Following-up with vendors for timely delivery.
- Preparing purchase budgets.
- Handle various vendor issues like payment, tax forms.

Purchase Officer: A Profile

Likely salary with 1–3 years of experience	Rs 150,000–Rs 300,000 per annum.
Targets	Buying at lower than the budgeted price without compromising on the quality. Ordering on time. Compliance with the procurement manual.

Challenges	Mastering procurement of all types of goods and services, including raw materials, consumables, and project items. Maintaining healthy and professional relations with vendors, especially when vendors try to influence your decision.
Skills	Analytical skills. Good research skills. Good commercial acumen.
Stress	Moderate.
Travel on the job	Travel will be minimum.
Impact on stakeholders	Manufacturing Team is impacted the most.
Career prospects	In three years you can become a Senior Purchase Officer. In ten years, can head the Purchase Department.
Future salary with 5–7 years of experience	Rs 350,000–Rs 600,000 per annum.

A Practitioner's View
Purchase Officer, Naveen, Hyderabad

Mr Naveen is working as a Purchase Manager. He has 10 years of work experience. When we asked him to share his experiences with us, he said:

'My job involves dealing with matters relating to procurement of raw materials, packaging, and capital items. This is a complex role as you need to have good knowledge about taxation, imports, exports and their implications on delivery of goods.

'My activities differ on a day-to-day basis. The career growth for freshers is also extremely good as the learning is really high. You get to learn a lot of aspects of procuring materials, tax percentages, import and export regulations, different packaging materials, and quality inspection methods. Therefore, I strongly recommend this as a good career option for freshers.'

SECTION 3

ENTRY-LEVEL JOB ROLES IN INDUSTRIES

11

AUTOMOTIVE SECTOR

SECTION 1
BACKGROUND

Vehicles have become a necessity in every household. Do you know that the total number of registered motor vehicles on Indian roads reached 172 million in March 2013?[8]

The following statistics establish the importance of the automotive industry in India.[9]

- India was the largest manufacturer of three-wheelers in 2014–15 and the eighth largest commercial vehicle manufacturer in 2014–15.
- India is the biggest two-wheeler market on this planet.
- The Indian two-wheeler manufacturing industry is the second largest (after China), in the world. Indian two-wheeler production reached 18.5 million units in 2014–15.
- India is the largest tractor manufacturing country (around one-third of the total world output) in 2011–12.
- The industry accounts for around 22 per cent of the country's manufacturing GDP.
- Seven Japanese (Suzuki, Honda, Toyota, Nissan, Isuzu, Mitsubishi, Datsun), five German (BMW, Mercedes Benz, Audi, Skoda, Volkswagen), four other European (Fiat, Jaguar, Renault, Lamborghini), two American (Ford, General Motors), and one Korean (Hyundai) manufacturer, compete with three big Indian (Tata, Mahindra, Maruti) manufacturers in the passenger car segment, making India one of the world's most competitive markets.
- Indian car manufacturers are becoming global players. Tata

Motors has acquired Jaguar, a leading UK car manufacturer.
- Hero MotoCorp Ltd (Formerly Hero Honda Motors Ltd), the world's largest manufacturer of two-wheelers, is based in India and manufactures more two-wheelers than its erstwhile partner, Honda Motors.

AUTOMOTIVE SECTOR

Growth Scenario in Coming Years

A report published by Deloitte states that 'India is expected to become a major automobile manufacturing hub and the third largest market for automobiles by 2020'.[10]

Employment Scenario

Two-wheeler production at 76 per cent dominates the Indian automotive industry, followed by passenger cars at 16 per cent.

Automotive manufacturing in India is currently concentrated in three major clusters, in the cities of Chennai and Pune, and in Gurgaon/Manesar in the National Capital Region. The state of Gujarat is the emerging new cluster.

Educational Qualifications for Jobs in This Sector

The bulk of the jobs are for people who have completed class 12, or have an Industrial Training Institute (ITI) or other diploma, in both the auto and the auto-components industries.

Interesting Facts About Jobs in the Auto Sector[11]

- The jobs are mainly in the private sector.
- The jobs in the auto sector are in automobile (OEM or Original Equipment Manufacturing) where the vehicles are assembled; the auto-components industry which supply components to the OEM and lastly, the auto service industry where the vehicles are bought and serviced.
- Automotive components manufactured in India include components for engines, the body, transmission, suspension, electrical parts, and other equipment.
- While automobile manufacturing (OEM) is dominated by the large

Indian companies and MNCs, auto-component manufacturing is largely in the small and medium (SME) sector.
- In the OEM industry, the bulk of the jobs (two out of three jobs) are for ITI/diploma holders while 27 per cent of the jobs are for graduate and postgraduate engineers who take up design and managerial jobs; 75 per cent of the jobs in OEM are in manufacturing or research and development (R&D).
- In the auto-component industry, the bulk of the jobs (three out of four jobs) are for class 12 or below and ITIs. Diploma-holders (18 per cent) and graduate/postgraduates (7 per cent) have the rest of the jobs; 87 per cent of the jobs in the auto-component industry are in manufacturing or R&D.
- The bulk of manufacturing or R&D jobs in OEM and the auto-component industry are for mechanical engineering and automobile engineering technicians.
- Salaries in the auto-component industry are low compared to OEM.
- Direct employment in the auto sector will reach 15 million by 2022. See Table below:

Table 11.1

Sub-sector	Direct employment in million		
	2013	2017	2022
Auto manufacturers (OEM)	1.87	2.04	2.33
Auto-component manufacturers	4.81	5.99	7.26
Service centres	2.8	3.1	3.44
Dealerships	1.5	1.68	1.95
Total Sector	**10.98**	**12.81**	**14.88**

- As mentioned earlier, most of the roles in automobile or auto-component manufacturing are common for all manufacturing companies and have been covered extensively in Chapters 3 to 10.
- The Auto Dealership Sub-sector is a very crucial segment in this industry. There are around 369,000 service centres in India. Around 300,000 are in the organized sector. The key job roles in this sub-segment is that of mechanics and dent removers.

- 78 per cent of the jobs in the service centres are for mechanics and Spare Parts/Service Supervisors.
- 60 per cent of the jobs in dealership are for new vehicle sales.
- If you further drill down to entry-level jobs for graduates in dealership and service centres, the roles available are mainly Salesmen and Service Supervisors. Only these two roles are covered in this chapter.

Before moving on to the job roles in this chapter, we would like to share the success story of a great personality from the auto sector.

DR BRIJMOHAN LALL MUNJAL

Late Dr Brijmohan Lall Munjal was the Founder, Director and Chairman Emeritus of the $3.2 billion Hero Group. He was the President of the Confederation of Indian Industry (CII), Society of Indian Automobile Manufacturers (SIAM), and was a Member of the Board of the Reserve Bank of India (RBI). Dr Munjal enriched the Hero Group with his vision of sound business governance and value-driven management practices.

His foresight made the Hero Group a leader in its field. Dr Munjal is a role model for Indian industry in corporate governance and ethical and value-driven management practices. His principle-based leadership has led the Group companies to receive the best industrial governance and safety awards and acquire stringent value certifications. Dr Munjal was also amongst the first Indian industrialists to effectively implement backward integration and is acknowledged as the trendsetter in that area. Apart from the promotion of Indian industry, he was actively involved in many national associations such as CII, SIAM, ASSOCHAM, and PHD, and was a member of the Regional Board of RBI. He was an Honorary Fellow of the Indian Institute of Industrial Engineering.

SECTION 2
ENTRY-LEVEL JOB ROLES

CODE	ROLE
AUTO 1	Showroom Sales Executive
AUTO 2	Service Supervisor

AUTO 1 SHOWROOM SALES EXECUTIVE

Job Description

When you visit a showroom to buy a car or a motorcycle, a Showroom Sales Executive greets you and enquires about your interests. Based on your interests, she/he shows you various models that are available, explains the features of different vehicles to you in detail, and helps you to pick the right one for your budget.

Typical Responsibilities

- Responding promptly to customer queries.
- Providing factual, detailed information as to why the vehicles are better than those of competitors.
- Understanding customer interests and suggesting the best buy.
- Guiding customers to also buy vehicle insurance.
- Explaining about the additional accessories that the company will provide in case the customer buys the car.
- Arranging for test drives.
- Negotiating with customers and arriving at a price that is mutually acceptable.
- Filling up all the required paperwork and other formalities, in case the customer buys the vehicle.
- Updating stock registers and informing the manufacturer about orders.
- Providing sales reports to the management.
- In case of exchanges, getting the old car assessed and informing the customer about the value she/he may get.

Showroom Sales Executive: A Profile

Likely salary with 1–3 years of experience	Rs 150,000–Rs 300,000 per annum, including sales incentives.
Targets	Number of vehicles sold. Conversion ratio: number of customers per hundred walk-ins. Value of accessories sold per vehicle.
Challenges	Customers don't easily trust a car Salesman who comes across as pushy and selfish. So be careful to not seem over-eager or pushy.

	Working late nights and on weekends to suit customer convenience, is commonplace.
Skills	Good networking and communication skills. Excellent listening skills. Direct selling skills. A very positive attitude.
Stress	Moderate to high.
Travel on the job	None.
Impact on stakeholders	The company you work for, and the customers are impacted by your work.
Career prospects	You join as a Sales Executive and can thereafter, become a Sales Manager.
Future salary with 5–7 years of experience	Rs 350,000–Rs 500,000 per annum, depending on the company you work for.

A Practitioner's View
Showroom Sales Executive,
Sridhar (name changed), Hyderabad

Mr Sridhar has been working as a Showroom Sales Manager for the past five years. When we spoke to him and asked him about his views regarding the job, he said:

'I joined the automobile industry as a Showroom Sales Executive. I found the role challenging but later, as I built experience, I started loving the job. Interacting with customers, developing knowledge about the auto industry in general have been the best experiences. Sometimes one may face tough situations like not meeting sales targets, dealing with unruly customers and fake customers, but that is how one evolves in the job. It's an exciting career and I would certainly recommend it to freshers.'

AUTO 2 SERVICE SUPERVISOR[12]

Job Description

Let us assume that your car is giving you trouble while driving. You decide to take it to the service station to get it fixed. When you reach the service station, the Service Supervisor is assigned to examine your car and identify the real issue. He also informs you about the approximate time it would take to complete the repair, the estimated cost, and so on.

For customers who cannot afford or do not want the recommended repairs, he can offer alternatives and explain the consequences of those options. He then coordinates with the mechanic and prepares a work order. He supervises the work done by mechanics on vehicles. He ensures that the vehicles that have come for servicing, are given back to customers in a perfect condition.

He is the link between a customer and a mechanic, who effectively communicates with both parties to eliminate issues.

Typical Responsibilities

- Supervises a group of skilled craftsmen and service employees.
- Troubleshoots problems in vehicles by performing relevant tests and interpreting the results.
- Assists in overseeing and supervising the insurance inspection of vehicles, and helps in preparing documentation for the insurance claims.
- Reads, understands, and uses manuals, CD-ROM based diagnostic applications, diagrams.
- Prepares preliminary estimates on work orders and repairs.
- Schedules the maintenance and assigns tasks to the Servicing Team.
- Requisitions supplies, parts, and materials necessary for the maintenance, repair, and servicing of vehicles.
- Plans, holds, and documents safety meetings.
- Maintains open communication with supervisors and subordinates.
- Performs related duties and responsibilities as assigned.

Service Supervisor: A Profile

Likely salary with 1–3 years of experience	Rs 200,000–Rs 300,000 per annum.
Targets	Maximize the service revenues. Maximize spare parts sales. Minimize turnaround time for the customer. Minimize customer quality complaint.

Challenges	Continuously staying updated on the latest models. Customers will never be totally satisfied with the service done; therefore, dealing with unhappy customers is a major challenge. Managing mechanics' productivity is tough.
Skills	Mechanical and technical skills. Attention to detail. Problem-solving skills. Good influencing skills.
Stress	Moderate to high.
Travel on the job	None.
Impact on stakeholders	The company you work for, the mechanics, and the customers are impacted by your work.
Career prospects	You join as a Service Supervisor and can thereafter grow into a role managing multiple workshops.
Future salary with 5–7 years of experience	Rs 300,000–Rs 400,000 per annum, depending on the company you work for.

A Practitioner's View

Service Supervisor,
Praveen (name changed), Hyderabad

Mr Praveen has been working as a Service Manager for the last five years. When we spoke to him and asked him about his views regarding the job, he said:

'A Service Supervisor's job calls for a lot of patience with decent mechanical skills. Customers who come to service stations have minimum knowledge about mechanical terms for car parts. Explaining the same to them and coordinating with mechanics is very challenging. The more experience we have, the more knowledge we absorb. This will help us in doing our job more efficiently. My interests were always inclined towards automobiles and learning more and more about them. If a fresher is looking for a career in the auto sector, then I will definitely recommend this role as a starting point as the career prospects are bright.'

12

CIVIL AVIATION

According to Wikipedia, aviation is the practical aspect or art of aeronautics, being the design, development, production, operation, and use of aircraft, especially heavier-than-air aircraft. There are two broad sectors in aviation—military and civil. Civil aviation is further sub-divided into scheduled flying and general aviation. Scheduled flying is what we normally do—going to an airport and taking a scheduled flight. General aviation includes all non-scheduled civil flying, both private (like corporate jet flights) and commercial (like chartered cargo flights). General aviation may include business flights, air charter, private aviation, flight training, ballooning, parachuting, gliding, hang gliding, aerial photography, foot-launched powered hang gliders, air ambulances, crop dusting, charter flights, traffic reporting, police air patrols, and forest fire fighting.

The bulk of jobs for fresh graduates are in the scheduled commercial domain and hence this is the focus in this book.

SECTION 1
BACKGROUND

HISTORY OF AVIATION[13]

Orville and Wilbur Wright, two American brothers, inventors and aviation pioneers, are credited with inventing and building the world's first successful 'heavier-than-air' vehicle—the airplane.

Since the aircraft had to take off from and land on some place, airports were built. Like any other machine/automobile, aircraft also require service and maintenance. Therefore, we have airfields where planes are parked, serviced, and maintained. When people travel via planes, they reach airports at least a couple of hours early. Therefore, to keep travellers occupied till the time they board the aircraft, duty-free shops, food joints, relaxation centres have opened up within the airports. This has opened up lot of business and employment opportunities. Air tickets had to be booked. Check-in counters had to manned. Luggage had to be handled. As air travel became affordable, more people travelled by air, which meant more airports had to be built. Planes could also carry cargo and so the air cargo business opened up. On an average about 4.5 million people worldwide travel every day by planes. To cater to their needs there were about 43,794 airports by the end of 2012, across the world.[14]

THE INDIAN SCENARIO

The Airports Authority of India (AAI) manages a total of 125 airports (excluding the five privatized airports at Bengaluru, Cochin, Hyderabad, Mumbai, and Delhi), which include 11 international airports, 81 domestic airports, 25 civil enclaves at defence airfields and eight customs airports.

Apart from these airports, according to an article on dnaindia.com, AAI is planning to set up 50 new low-cost airports across 11 states. The passenger traffic has also increased to support 19 private airlines operating in India, alongside Air India. Today, the airlines business in India contributes around 0.5 per cent to the national GDP.

Indian Airport Passenger Traffic

There are many domestic and international airlines operating from India. The passenger traffic reached 169 million in the financial year (FY) 2012–13.

Employment in the Aviation Sector

The sector at present employs around 1.7 million individuals. Aviation industry employees are better paid than people employed in the other sectors of the transportation industry such as the railways and roadways, despite an extremely competitive market and low profitability. As most of us know, the aviation industry is going through a tough phase and has not been doing well—with many big airlines such as Kingfisher forced to shut down after making huge losses due to the high cost of aviation fuel, among other things. In the year 2010–11, this industry saw many job cuts and a dip of around 15 per cent in hiring as well.

But with the entry of new players, the domestic aviation and foreign aviation sectors recovered partly with the Aviation Sector creating the highest number of new jobs at over 72 per cent in 2012–13.

The last six months have been particularly good for the sector, say industry experts.[15]

The industry has opened up various avenues for students who want to pursue a career as a Pilot, Ground Staff, Cabin Crew, Aircraft Maintenance Engineer, or other airlines' jobs. There are professional courses for most of the jobs on offer. These courses are expensive but student loans make it possible to enrol.

Before we move on to entry-level job roles for graduates we would like to briefly profile one of India's reputed aviation entrepreneurs, Captain Gorur Ramaswamy Gopinath.

CAPTAIN G.R. GOPINATH

Captain G.R. Gopinath only dreamt big, but also made it big in the aviation industry. Within four years of its inception, the airline he launched—Air Deccan—became India's largest low-cost airline.

Captain Gopinath was born on 13 November 1951 in Karnataka. He served the Indian Army for eight years, retiring as a Captain and also fought the Bangladesh Liberation War in 1971. After taking early retirement, he established an ecologically sustainable sericulture farm. His innovative methods earned him the Rolex Laureate Award in 1996. In 1997, he co-founded Deccan Aviation, a charter helicopter service. Later, in 2003, he founded Air Deccan, a low-cost airlines, the main aim of which was to connect various towns and cities in the country at a rate affordable to the common man. When Captain Gopinath was asked by *Headlines Today* what people thought about him and his endeavours, he said:

'I think perception is important and the truth is always somewhere in between. This company, for example, whose hangar you are sitting in, was incorporated in 1995. It took me three years to get the licence. I started here with a tent and one helicopter as a small company, but today it is the largest general aviation company in India to cater to infrastructure, high networth individuals, and corporate houses. We also maintain 60 third-party aircraft. We have been here for a very long time. I am a dreamer, as you said. But as I dream, I design. It has also sometimes led me to failures. There is also a burning optimism in me.'

Captain Gopinath has received various awards for Air Deccan. Air Deccan merged with Kingfisher in the year 2007. Before the merger, Air Deccan connected 69 cities around India. He also founded Deccan 360, a freight flight business in 2009.

One lesson that each and every one can learn from him is to never stop dreaming! Don't just dream but also work towards realizing your dream.

SECTION 2
ENTRY-LEVEL JOB ROLES

CODE	ROLE
AVA 1	Trainee Co-pilot
AVA 2	Cabin Crew
AVA 3	Ground Staff

AVA 1 TRAINEE CO-PILOT (TRAINEE FIRST OFFICER)

Job Description

A Pilot is someone who flies an aircraft to transfer passengers and/or cargo from one location to another for leisure or business purposes. A Pilot's job is highly technical and requires lot of training. While 12th Class pass qualification is adequate to be a pilot, graduates can also succeed.

Aircrafts are generally operated by two individuals, a Pilot and a Co-pilot. The Pilot is in command of the aircraft and is assisted by the Co-pilot, so that neither is fatigued.

Typical Responsibilities

- Reporting for the pre-flight briefing, where you decide the route to the destination, most fuel-efficient cruising altitudes, and take into cognisance all weather reports en route to the destination.
- Making sure there is additional fuel for alternate choice of airport in case of an emergency.
- Head for the aircraft, do a 'walk-around' to do an external check and assure yourself that all is as it should be.
- Get into the flight deck, begin pre-flight checks.

ENTRY-LEVEL JOB ROLES IN INDUSTRIES / 153

- Communicate effectively and accurately with air traffic control throughout the flight as needed, giving them clear read-backs. Respond to the flight control instructions.
- Communicate with passengers before take-off, during the flight, and before landing.
- Keep alert, keep cool, maintain a pleasant working environment on flight deck.
- Handle in-flight emergencies if any occur.
- Ensure that the flight takes off, stays on course, and lands safely and on time.
- Report any engineering/other significant untoward issues that occur during the flight.
- Submit flight reports, as required, at the end of flight.

Trainee Co-pilot: A Profile

Likely salary with 1–3 years of experience	Rs 600,000–Rs 1,200,000 per annum. The salary of a Co-pilot is low in the initial years and picks up as she/he picks up experience measured by flying hours. In addition to the salary, flying allowances up to 85 per cent of the basic salary may be paid, linked to the actual flying hours. In addition, Pilots/Co-pilots are entitled to a free stay at hotels at various overnight or longer stops, get lunch/dinner allowances, insurance, pick-up/drop from the airport, among other facilities.
Targets	Number of flying hours per month, which can go up to 120 hours per month. On-time departure and arrival of flights. Adherence without deviation to the airline's Standard Operating Procedures (SOPs).
Challenges	Working odd hours can cause sleep deprivation. Making sure you know your emergency drills and routines well enough.
Skills	Must pass the Pilot Aptitude Test and must be physically fit to be a Trainee Co-pilot. Good analytical skills. Good communication skills. Ability to keep calm under pressure.

Stress	Moderate to high.
Travel on the job	Plenty.
Impact on stakeholders	The passengers and the airline are directly impacted by this role.
Career prospects	You will initially start of as a Trainee First Officer (Co-pilot) flying on the right seat before eventually qualifying as the Captain and moving into the prized left seat. All this depends on how well you perform in your role, the economic status of the airlines, and the demand–supply gap of Pilots.
Future salary with 5–7 years of experience	Rs 2,400,000–Rs 3,600,000 per year depending on the airline you are working with.[16]

A Practitioner's View
Captain Bavicca Bharti, Indigo Airlines

Many individuals dream about becoming a Pilot, but there are very few who realize their dream. One such person is Bavicca Bharti. She is the youngest commercial Pilot in India and works for Indigo Airlines. While travelling with Indigo, I found her story in their inflight magazine and thought that I should share it.

'At an age when most teens are more than a little dazed and confused, this girl was more than sure of what she wanted. Ten days out of school, she packed her bags and moved to the middle of Maharashtra, to get her Pilot's licence. Moving from bustling Mumbai to small town Shripur was tough but Bavicca was so crazy about airplanes she even bunked with one! And so, despite all the changes, Bavicca raced through her training and was certified as a commercial Pilot at the age of just 18! That is the youngest in India, ever! It doesn't end there. She also became India's youngest Flight Commander and interestingly, she and her mother are one of the few mother and daughter Pilot duos in the whole country. Bavicca has clocked over 2500 hours of commercial flying!!'

AVA 2 CABIN CREW

Job Description

Members of the Cabin Crew (an Airhostess/or a Flight Attendant) are those responsible for the safety and comfort of passengers on board. They assist passengers during boarding and explain to them how to use the safety equipment that is available on flight. They also serve refreshments to passengers, making their flight a pleasant one.

During emergencies, their main task is to prepare the cabin for an emergency landing and evacuate passengers safely once the aircraft comes to a stop. They are also first-aid trained and ensure that passengers get medical attention during times of need.

The Cabin Crew members are provided extensive training to ensure that passengers are provided with safety services during emergency situations. Emergency training includes rejected take-offs, emergency landings (including landing on water called 'ditching'), emergency evacuations, cardiac and other in-flight medical situations (including on-board births and deaths), smoke in the cabin, fires, depressurization, dangerous goods and spills in the cabin, and hijackings.

Typical Responsibilities

- Assisting the passengers during boarding, seating, and deplaning.
- Informing the flight deck in case of any suspicious/dangerous behaviour/actions by any passenger.
- Ensuring that all the safety equipment on the flight is functioning properly and conducting safety demonstrations.
- Ensuring that all supplies like food and water are sufficient according to passenger strength.
- Securing the aircraft doors during a flight.
- Serving passengers and Pilots with refreshments.
- Explaining the usage of safety equipment to passengers.
- Answering any queries/questions raised by passengers.
- Attending to passengers in times of medical emergency and providing them necessary first aid.
- Dealing calmly during emergency situations.
- Selling duty free items on board to interested passengers.
- Following the instructions of the flying crew during the flight.

Cabin Crew: A Profile

Likely salary with 1-3 years of experience	Rs 200,000–Rs 400,000 per annum, plus flying bonus/allowances based on the flying hours. This amount can touch up to Rs 500,000 per annum. In addition, free pick-up and drop from airports, free overnight stay, food allowance, medical and life insurance.
Targets	Zero passenger complaints. Handling on-board situations calmly and pleasantly.
Challenges	Dealing with unruly passengers. Handling emergency situations. During such situations, many passengers tend to get very panicky. Looking fresh and cheerful at the end of every flight—even if it is 12 hours or more.
Skills	Excellent communication skills. Self-assured and pleasing personality.
Stress	Moderate during normal flight conditions and high during emergency situations.
Travel on the job	Plenty.
Impact on stakeholders	The passengers and airlines you work for are impacted by this role.
Career prospects	You can become a Senior Crew Member (called a Purser in some airlines), and thereafter, Chief Cabin Crew Member. Side-stepping to Cabin Crew training within the company is also possible.
Future salary with 5-7 years of experience	Rs 500,000–Rs 800,000 per annum.

A Practitioner's View

Cabin Crew, Neha (name changed), Mumbai

Ms Neha was working as an Air Hostess with one of the biggest international airlines. When we spoke to her about her job and experiences, she said:

'Working as a Cabin Crew member was very challenging, interesting, and exciting. There are many aspects to the job that one should look at while choosing it as a career. Of course you get to fly around the world and visit new places, but at the same time, you often encounter tough situations while performing the role. One has to remain strong and composed. Sometimes flights can be very exhausting, but once you get into the curve, you get used to this change in lifestyle. It certainly pays very well and has many incentives. I would certainly recommend this as a career for freshers who are looking to make their career in this field, but they should make the choice after a good amount of research and guidance.'

AVA 3: GROUND STAFF

Job Description

When a passenger reaches the airport she/he is often guided by people belonging to the Airport or Airline Ground Staff to the check-in counter. There other Ground Staff members seated behind the counter to issue boarding passes, check the baggage in and other duties.

Ground Staff also help to make special arrangements to transfer passengers who require special assistance—those with disabilities, pregnant ladies, people travelling with small infants and kids, and so on. They manage the check-in process by checking passenger ID cards, allocating seats, weighing the baggage, tagging and transferring the baggage to be loaded on to the flight.

Typical Responsibilities

- Reaching the airport according to the shift time.
- Activities include:
  - assisting the passengers while boarding and disembarkation;
  - ensuring that all the baggage is securely checked and loaded into the correct carrier;
  - helping passengers who require special assistance; and
  - reporting any issues related to baggage and flight delays to superiors.

Ground Staff: A Profile

Likely salary with 1–3 years of experience	Rs 150,000–Rs 250,000 per annum.
Targets	Quick and efficient check-in. Friendly passenger service.
Challenges	Quick transit of passengers arriving by delayed flights. Handling angry passengers affected by delayed flights or lost baggage.
Skills	Excellent communication skills. Calm demeanour.
Stress	Moderate.
Travel on the job	There is no travel involved in this role.
Impact on stakeholders	The passengers and the airlines/airport company for whom you work are directly impacted by this role.
Career prospects	You can become a Supervisor and then a Manager once you gain experience.
Future salary with 5–7 years of experience	Rs 300,000–Rs 400,000 per annum.

A Practitioner's View
Ground Staff Executive, Philips, Hyderabad

Mr Philips has been working as a Ground Staff Executive for the past three years. When we spoke to him and asked him his experiences, he said:

'My job is to see that everything is organized and that there is no chaos at the airport. Many people are flying for the first time and are new to the boarding system. I explain the process to them and guide them to the right counter to check-in and collect their boarding passes. Then I guide them on how to board the flight without any problem. Our job is to basically serve customers and I like doing my job.'

13

BANKING

SECTION 1
BACKGROUND

A bank is an intermediary between depositors who have surplus money and borrowers who are in need of money. They collect money from depositors by paying them interest and lend the same to people at a higher rate of interest. On the whole, they deal with finances of companies, individual customers, or group of customers.

BANKS CAN BE CLASSIFIED INTO VARIOUS TYPES

Public Sector Banks/Nationalized Banks (PSB or PSU Banks)

These are organizations owned by the government. In addition to profit objectives, they also meet social objectives.

Private Banks

These are not owned by the government. Since they have limited social objectives, they focus more on the urban areas, and customers from the middle class and above.

Foreign Banks

These banks operate in India, but the ownership is largely held overseas.

Retail Banks

They deal with individuals and small businesses. They lend money to individuals in the form of loans such as personal loans, car loans, home loans, as well as to small firms to start up their business.

Investment Banks

They assist individuals, corporations, and governments in raising financial capital.

Corporate Banks

They serve big corporates. They provide long-term funds and short-term funds in large amounts.

Co-operative Banks

These are owned by a group of individuals/institutions on a co-operative basis set up to help each other. They mostly serve the financial needs of their own community.

Regional Rural Banks

They are banking organizations set up in different states of the country to serve rural citizens residing in various towns and villages. They might operate in urban areas too, but their main focus is to serve rural areas.

As of 2013, there were 209 banks providing credit to customers (consumer banks), and 82 investment banks (these are banks that help consumers raise money from others). There were 26 public sector banks, 23 private sector banks, 43 foreign banks, 35 cooperative banks, and 82 regional rural banks providing credit.

NON-BANKING FINANCIAL COMPANIES

The NBFCs do what the banks do—raise money from depositors and others and lend to borrowers. A good example of an NBFC is the 'chit fund'.

EMPLOYMENT OPPORTUNITIES IN THE BANKING SECTOR[17]

For the year ending 31 March 2013, Indian banks did business worth over 2 trillion USD.

As of 2013, 26 public sector undertaking (PSU) banks were the largest employers in banking with 73 per cent of the workforce and all of them need fresh talent. The 23 private sector banks are growing very rapidly and require fresh talent. So jobs are available in the PSU sector as well as the private sector.

As per the NSDC Human Resource and Skill Requirements reports, the banking and NBFC sectors will hire 67 per cent more manpower between 2013 and 2022 (as shown in Table 13.1). This is a dream opportunity for fresh graduates.

Table 13.1: Total Employment in the Banking and NBFC Sector as per NSDC

Total employment			Employment growth	
2013	2017	2022	2013–17	2017–22
All figures in million				
1.89	2.38	3.16	0.49	0.78

Sales and business development roles are expected to witness a large increase—from 5 per cent of the total workforce to 35 per cent of the work force in 2020 (as per NSDC reports). This again is a great opportunity for fresh graduates in PSBs, because current employees are generalists not well-trained in, nor keen on, sales and business development roles.

Private banks hire largely on merit. Even the PSU banks hire candidates (both the reserved and open categories) on merit, based on competitive examinations. This is a great opportunity for graduates without the 'right' connections to help them get the job.

The banking sector has recorded 15 per cent growth in the last five years. This growth will continue because banks are working to bridge the under-penetration of banking (only 59 per cent of households had bank accounts in 2014, before the launch of the Prime Minister's Jan Dhan Yojana or PMDJY, in August 2014). The target therefore, is to reach 100 per cent households. This in turn will create a lot of business and jobs in the banking sector. This has never happened before in the recent history of India.

Employee costs make up about 62 per cent of the costs of the PSBs, as against 37 per cent in the private sector. Globally, this ratio is about 50 per cent for most banks. Thus, alternative channels such as Banking Correspondents* (BCs) would be essential. This again means that PSU

---

*Banking Correspondents are local people living in areas that banks have not yet reached or find hard to reach (away from national highways, in the

contd.

banks will outsource some of their activities to private companies and this means more jobs for graduates in the private sector where hiring is faster and easier.

Technology-led services, such as the ATM, have changed the way banking is done. This has reduced the number of lower-grade jobs of staff involved in transaction processing, especially in PSU banks. This means more officer jobs, more people who are technology savvy, and both these factors favour young graduates.

Table 13.2: Composition of Employees in Banking (2001 and 2013)

Item	% total employees (2001)	% total employees (2013)	Remarks
Officers	28.1%	51.3%	Huge increase in officer cadre.
Clerks	50.0%	34.4%	Big decline in clerical roles due to automation.
Sub-staff	21.9%	14.3%	A decline, but not as large as with clerks.

The number of bank branches is expected to double, while the number of ATMs is expected to increase five times during 2010–20. There are aggressive expansion plans from the NBFCs as well. This means more jobs for graduates.

According to the NSDC report, Tier I and Tier II cities are the biggest opportunity centres for business and so more bank branches have opened in these towns. Now you can start your career closer to your home town.

The largest freeze after 1985, on hiring in PSBs for more than a decade, resulted in a shortfall of experienced workforce at the middle-management level and led to high expectations from entry-level employees. This means that banking sector will have a severe

---

interiors/in hilly, or heavily forested terrain, or in remote desert hamlets). The nearest bank branch hires BCs from among the locals and these BCs take basic banking services doorstep to doorstep in a bid to increase banking outreach and free people from generational debts to the moneylender, encourage savings, and so on.

shortage of middle Managers. This means graduates who join now, perform and stay will have excellent growth prospects due to this shortage of talent.

The recent RBI decision to allow new players and specialist players in the banking sector is also expected to generate tremendous employment opportunities, both at entry- and middle-management levels.

WHERE ARE THE LARGEST NUMBERS OF ENTRY-LEVEL JOBS IN BANKING?

Every retail bank has five sets of people.

1. The first set markets the liabilities—fixed deposits, current and savings accounts, recurring deposits.
2. The second set markets the assets—car loans, housing loans, personal loans, gold loans, credit cards, working capital loans, long-term loans.
3. The third set conducts customer transactions, including resolving customer complaints, opening new accounts. This staff is called the Operations Staff.
4. The fourth set is composed of banking specialists who provide foreign exchange services, corporate credit, treasury, Letters of Credit (LCs), among other services.
5. The fifth set is made up of the Back Office Team which does the accounting and provides back office support like administration and IT for the above transactions.

By far the largest and the most important people in a large private sector retail bank are the first three sets of people. However a PSB's focus has been on operations and the bulk of its employees are clerks and officers operating from a branch.

WHY ARE BANKING JOBS IN DEMAND? WHY SHOULD ANYONE JOIN THE BANKING INDUSTRY?

Many graduates prefer a PSB job as it offers more job security than a job in the private sector, and the pay and perks are also decent. There is a mistaken notion that the PSU banks will retain everyone irrespective of performance. This may be true of the past, but it is not true anymore. Despite this, PSU bank jobs are very popular because the salary and benefits are very attractive.

Many private sector banks offer salaries and perks that are more attractive, but job security depends mainly on performance.

The most interesting part is that students from any field can pursue a career in banking. Private sector banks often focus on hiring management graduates, Chartered Accountants, and certified Financial Accountants, but any student with a good academic background who passes the all-India banking examinations conducted by them, can get a decent job in a PSB.[18]

HOW DO BANKS HIRE?

Passing the Common Written Examination (CWE) and common interviews conducted by the Institute of Banking Personnel Selection (IBPS) is a prerequisite for selection as a Probationary Officer (Scale 1), Specialist Officer posts, Clerical Cadre posts in 20 PSU banks (excluding, the State Bank of India [SBI], and its subsidiaries), and regional rural banks. Since 2014, only those who have a university degree are eligibile for taking these tests. You also have to be within the specified age limit.

The CWE syllabus and general instructions on filling in the IBPS online application are provided in the exam notification. Each candidate is intimated the date and venue of the exam via a call letter that becomes available for download a few days after they register at the IBPS website. The IBPS CWE is one among the most competitive and popular examinations in India. In the year 2013–14, alone more than 22 lakh youth took the CWE III exam.

Table 13.3: Exams Conducted at PSU banks for Officer and Clerical Cadres[19]

Exam conducted for	Registered candidates	Exam takers	Vacancies in 2013	Exam takers per vacancy
PSU Bank Clerk	1.424 million	0.997 million	32,453	1:30
PSU Bank Officers	1.319 million	0,917 million	22,415	1:40

| PSU Bank Special Officers | 0.410 million | 0.302 million | 4,400 | 1:68 |
| Total | 3.153 million | 2.216 million | 59,268 | 1:37 |

A large number of coaching institutes provide coaching to the thousands of bank aspirants. Now you would understand the popularity of PSU bank jobs.

Coming back to the IBPS CWE, it is an objective type online exam, with negative marking for false answers. Based on the CWE scores, the IBPS invites candidates for common interviews at various centres. Based on the combined scores of the written test and interview, and based on the bank preferences given by the candidate and the vacancies available, the candidates receive offer letters from a bank.

The SBI and its associate banks conduct separate exams, not through IBPS, periodically for recruitment to fill clerk and officer posts. Cooperative banks also conduct their own recruitment drives for these posts. The private sector banks conduct individual recruitment drives directly in campuses, through advertisements and through recruitment consultants. The PSU banks train their new employees extensively, while private sector banks train as per the role.

Before moving on to Section 2 on entry-level job roles we would like to briefly profile a high-achiever from the banking sector.

MS RANJANA KUMAR[20]

Ms Kumar started her career with the Bank of India (BOI) in the year 1966 as a Probationary Officer, and held several senior positions with BOI within the country until 1995, when she was sent on posting to the United States as BOI's Chief Executive Officer of US operations, based out of New York.

In 1995 she became Executive Director holding concurrent charge as Chairperson and Managing Director of Canara Bank. In 2000 she was elected Chairperson and Managing Director of the Indian Bank. By 2003 Mrs Kumar held the following posts: Chairperson, National Bank for Agriculture and Rural Development (NABARD); Director, National Commodity & Derivatives Exchange (NCDEX) Ltd; Chairperson, Governing Council, Bankers' Institute of Rural Development (BIRD),

Lucknow; Member, Governing Council, Jawaharlal Nehru Institute of Development Banking, JNIDBI, Hyderabad; Honorary Visiting Professor of Administrative Staff College of India, Hyderabad; Member, Board of Trustees, Indian School of Microfinance for Women, Ahmedabad; and, Member, Governing Council, National Innovation Foundation, Ahmedabad. In December 2005 she was made Central Vigilance Commissioner at the Central Vigilance Commission (CVC).

She has been Non-executive Independent Director at GVK Power & Infrastructure Ltd since November 2011. She has been an Independent Director of SKS Microfinance Limited since 8 March 2013. She has been a Director of Andhra Pradesh Paper Mills Ltd since 6 December 2011 and serves as a Director of the National Stock Exchange (NSE) of India Ltd. Mrs Kumar has been an Independent Director of Tata Global Beverages Limited since 29 January 2010 and Coromandel International Ltd since 19 March 2010.

She has given lectures at various forums in India and abroad including at IITs, Indian Institutes of Management (IIMs), Wharton School, Stanford University, World Bank, and Asia Society New York. She has also authored a book, *A New Beginning—the Turnaround Story of Indian Bank*, with a foreword by Dr A.P.J. Abdul Kalam, former President of India.[21]

So, you see what is possible when you join a bank!

SECTION 2
ENTRY-LEVEL JOB ROLES

CODE	ROLE
BANK 1	CASA Executive
BANK 2	Recovery Officer
BANK 3	Probationary Officer
BANK 4	Branch Customer Relationship Executive
BANK 5	Branch Operations Clerk

BANK 1 CASA EXECUTIVE

Job Description

A CASA Executive works towards promoting and acquiring Current Accounts (CA) and Savings Accounts (SA) of a bank. S/he needs to meet targets on a monthly basis, by meeting prospective clients and convincing them to open a CA or a SA.

Typical Responsibilities

As a CASA Executive, you will be attached to a specific branch and will work in a team of CASA Executives and report to a Manager. Your typical activities will include the following.

- Mapping the territory around the branch.
- Interacting with the walk-in customers to the branch to generate leads.
- Conducting special drives for lead generation in offices, housing colonies, and so on.
- Meeting prospects and promoting CASA (Current Account, Sales Account).
- Complete the customer documentation for becoming an account-holder.
- Cross-selling of other financial products.

CASA Executive: A Profile

Likely salary with 1–3 years of experience	Rs 100,000–Rs 200,000 per annum.
Targets	Number of accounts opened in a month.
Challenges	Most prospects may already have a bank account and hence selling a second bank account is the main challenge. Completing the customer documentation without error or gaps in information.
Skills	Excellent communication and persuasion skills. Good networking skills. Good knowledge about banking products and services.
Stress	Initially, the stress levels are high. Once the sales technique is mastered, stress levels drop significantly.
Travel on the job	None.
Impact on stakeholders	The customers who visit the bank are highly impacted by this role.

Career prospects	Successful CASA Executives have a fast-track career. In two years you can become a Team Lead and in three to four years become a CASA Manager.
Future salary with 5–7 years of experience	Rs 500,000–Rs 900,000 per annum.

A Practitioner's View
CASA Executive, Ramesh, Hyderabad

Mr Ramesh has been working as a CASA Executive for the last one and a half years. When we asked him to share his experiences with us, he said:

'Persuading people to open a Savings Account/Current Account is not an easy task, because there are numerous banks available. You need to explain to the prospect why she/he should open an account with your bank only and what are the benefits being offered compared to competitors. I like challenges, hence I like this role.'

BANK 2 RECOVERY OFFICER
Job Description

A Recovery Officer (also known as a Collections Officer) is responsible for performing recovery activities according to bank policies and legal guidelines. For example, when a housing loan borrower loses his/her job, then repayment of loan instalments becomes very difficult. The Recovery Officer's job is to assess the reason behind the delayed payment, and negotiate with the borrower for part payment and/or reschedule the instalments. In some cases, the borrower intentionally defaults and the Recovery Officer may have to recommend the use of legal methods for full recovery of the loan. Some banks appoint recovery agencies and the Recovery Officer has to work with these agencies.

Typical Responsibilities

Your role is very important as you will be helping recover money from defaulters. As a Recovery Officer, you will typically undertake the following activities:

- Contacting defaulters.
- Assessing the reasons for default and intention to pay.
- Conducting checks and securing payments.
- Recommending re-scheduling of loans.
- Working with debt collection agencies.
- Reviewing reports and participating in special collection drives.

Recovery Officer: A Profile

Likely salary with 1–3 years of experience	Rs 120,000–Rs 180,000 per annum.
Targets	Maximize recoveries and reduce the number of written-off accounts.
Challenges	Managing defaulters who have no intention to pay. Working with aggressive customers.
Skills	A strong personality. Good communication and negotiation skills.
Stress	Low to moderate.
Travel on the job	The job involves only local travel.
Impact on stakeholders	The customers and clients of the bank are directly impacted by this role.
Career prospects	Prospects are bright as you can move into the lead role in three years and become a Manager in seven years.
Future salary with 5–7 years of experience	Rs 250,000–Rs 350,000 per annum.

A Practitioner's View
Recovery Officer, Sudhakar, Hyderabad

Mr Sudhakar is working as a Recovery Officer in a bank. He has three years of experience in this field. When we asked him about his experiences regarding this role, he said:

'People often have an impression that Recovery Officers are rough individuals. But that is not the fact. We Recovery Officers often try to resolve issues amicably with clients of the bank in case of any issues. But sometimes some customers are not cooperative. It is not an easy job, but I like doing my job as it gives me satisfaction that in a way, I am helping the bank recover its money.'

BANK 3 PROBATIONARY OFFICER

Job Description

A Probationary Officer (PO) is the starting level for anyone who wishes to reach the top levels of any large bank. Many PSU bank Chairmen joined as POs and grew up the ladder. A PO performs all banking and administrative duties. You will be trained in giving credit to companies, handling retail loans, seeking deposits, issuing demand drafts (DDs), LCs, and so on. Monitoring and solving customer issues is the main responsibility of a bank PO.

Typical Responsibilities

- Managing cash transactions under the supervision of seniors.
- Supervising clerical staff present in the bank and ensuring that they are performing their duties.
- Taking decisions regarding customer credit issues.
- Processing loans under the supervision of senior officers.
- Monitoring accounts of corporate borrowers.
- Assisting customers to fill up the right documentation.
- Issuing cheque books to customers.
- Handling demand drafts, ATM cards, LCs to be issued to customers.

Probationary Officer: A Profile

Likely salary with 1–3 years of experience	Rs 350,000–Rs 500,000 per annum.
Targets	Your main target will be accomplishing all the tasks assigned to you successfully within the specified time-frame as per bank guidelines. Adding profitable accounts to the branch.

Challenges	Understanding customer issues. Each customer has a unique set of problems. So you have to probe, identify the real problem and guide them to the right department/person. Banking guidelines are complex and have to be followed in toto, to avoid audit queries later on. Bank Clerks working under you may have more experience and knowledge than you and getting work out of them can be a big challenge. Meeting targets and deadlines every day, means you will work late very often.
Skills	Sound domain knowledge of bank procedures. People-management skills. Active listening and learning skills. Relationship-building skills, specially with regard to customers. Communication and influencing skills.
Stress	Moderate to high.
Travel on the job	A PO will be posted in a branch and travel will be only local.
Impact on stakeholders	The customers and the Managers in the bank are directly impacted by this role.
Career prospects	After successfully completing your probation, you will be absorbed as an Assistant Manager. Thereafter you can become a Branch Manager and based on your performance and potential, you can even become the Chairman of the bank.
Future salary with 5–7 years of experience	Rs 700,000–Rs 1,000,000 per annum.

A Practitioner's View

Probationary Officer, Vamsee Naresh, Hyderabad

Mr Vamsee Naresh has been working as a Probationary Officer for nearly two years. When we spoke to him regarding his role and why he would recommend the role to a fresher, he said:

'I like doing my job. It is a good starting point for anyone who wants to pursue a career in banking. I get to learn a lot of things since I perform different activities. More than anything else, it has helped me become financially independent as I do not have to depend on anyone for my living and I can also support my family financially. Disbursing loans, dealing with customers, providing support to seniors at the bank are some of the activities that I like the most. I would recommend the role to a fresher because the exposure is really high and so are the opportunities.'

BANK 4 BRANCH CUSTOMER RELATIONSHIP EXECUTIVE

Job Description

When you go to your branch, you are greeted by a person who finds out the purpose of your visit and assigns you to a Customer Relationship Executive (CRE). She/he takes you to her/his cubicle, makes an arrangement for your seating, speaks to the concerned department regarding your issue, and tries to get it resolved. If there are any further formalities that you need to fulfil, the Branch CRE guides you. Therefore, the main responsibility of a Branch CRE is to ensure that she/he builds strong relations with customers and helps them out in every possible way when they are facing any issues.

The second task of the Branch CRE is to cross-sell the bank's products. Cross-selling is when a CRE tries to sell a product of the bank when a person walks in for some other reason. For instance, after solving your problem, the CRE may ask you whether you are planning to buy a house and may give you details of housing loan schemes of the bank.

Typical Responsibilities

- Reaching the branch early before it opens for customers.
- Understanding customer complaints and solving them.
- Guiding customers to appropriate officers.
- Building relationships with customers and understanding their banking needs.
- Identifying cross-selling opportunities while interacting with customers.

- Delivering quality service to achieve customer satisfaction.
- Keeping abreast of the latest bank's products/services and regulations.
- Complying with bank policies and procedures.
- Ensuring security of customer information.

Branch Customer Relationship Executive: A Profile

Likely salary with 1–3 years of experience	Rs 200,000–Rs 350,000 per annum.
Targets	High customer feedback rating. Activating dormant accounts. Cross-selling.
Challenges	You need an in-depth knowledge of the bank and its products. The job is very demanding with a continuous flow of customers. Working late is common in PSBs.
Skills	Customer relationship management skills. Communication skills. Problem-solving skills.
Stress	Moderate, once you master the role.
Travel on the job	You will be stationed at a bank branch.
Impact on Stakeholders	The customers are directly impacted by this role.
Career Prospects	You will join as a CRE and the move up the ladder to become an Assistant Customer Relationship Manager in two to three years. Once you gain considerable experience, you will become a Customer Relationship Manager, in five to seven years. Other career options also exist in retail banking.
Future Salary with 5–7 years of experience	Rs 400,000–Rs 700,000 per annum.

A Practitioner's View
Branch Customer Relationship Executive,
Syed Mehtaj, Chennai

Mr Mehtaj from Chennai is a Customer Relationship Executive with a large private bank. When we asked him to share his experiences about the role and why he would recommend this job to a fresher, he said:

'For a fresher and for someone in his/her first job, any learning should be substantial. In my current role I have learnt to handle both internal and external customers and also to optimize the output from both ends. Working for such a huge organization definitely gives a lot of exposure to industry and understanding the psychology of the people and hence every day is a great learning experience. Career opportunities, domain knowledge, excellent corporate exposure are some of the many reasons I like my role and I would recommend this role to anyone who wants to make a career in corporate banking.'

BANK 5 BRANCH OPERATIONS CLERK

Job Description

Branch Operations Clerks perform varied functions like opening and closing accounts, keeping a track of interests, receipts, data entry, handling files, and also recording day-to-day transactions that take place in the bank.

Typical Responsibilities

This position is probably the most important in the bank as Clerks are responsible for handling activities and organizing things. Your typical activities will include:

- Ensuring that activities in your area are running smoothly.
- Opening new accounts for individuals as well as companies.
- Clarifying doubts of customers regarding, finances, loans, interest.
- Help in currency exchange.
- Taking care of records of clients for future references.
- Focus on meeting departmental goals and objectives.
- Processing closure of accounts.
- Dealing with external collection agencies to handle unsatisfactory accounts and individuals.
- Responding to staff queries and the top management regarding activities of the department.

Branch Operations Clerk: A Profile

Likely salary with 1–3 years of experience	Rs 100,000–Rs 120,000 per annum.
Targets	Ensuring that all activities in the bank are running smoothly. Finishing the assigned tasks on time.
Challenges	Maintaining good relations with fellow workers. Updating reports on a daily basis. Understanding what exactly a customer needs and guiding him/her to the right department.
Skills	Multi-tasking. Decent communication skills. Attention to detail.
Stress	Moderate to high.
Travel on the job	Very limited.
Impact on stakeholders	The employees of the bank are directly influenced by this role.
Career prospects	A Clerk can slowly grow to become a Bank Officer or a Supervisor after gaining considerable experience.
Salary with 5–7 years of experience	Rs 200,000–Rs 350,000 per annum.

A Practitioner's View

Branch Operations Clerk,
Suresh (name changed), Hyderabad

Mr Suresh has been working as a Branch Operations Clerk in a bank for nearly two years. When we spoke to him regarding his role and why he would recommend the role to a fresher, he said:

'To actually understand what activities take place in a bank and how various internal departments function, it is extremely important to perform this role. I get to work and understand a lot of new things about the functioning of a bank as I get to deal with almost all departments. It is a very exciting and challenging role and a good starting stage for anyone who wishes to make a career in banking. For freshers, it is a great opportunity to grab on to.'

14

EDUCATION

Education plays an important role in the progress of an individual, society, and the country. So every child born in India should have the opportunity to get an education and this is the primary reason for education becoming a fundamental right of everyone and education becoming compulsory for children between six and fourteen in India.

SECTION 1
BACKGROUND

The education system in India is multi-layered: pre-primary (nursery, P1 and P2), primary (class 1 to class 5), upper primary (class 6 to class 8), secondary (class 9 and class 10), higher secondary (class 11 and class 12), graduation (engineering, arts, fine arts, science, commerce, medicine), and postgraduation (MBA and master's) and doctoral (MPhil, PhD) are the various sub-sectors. The skill sub-sector deals with school drop-outs and is typically linked with certification, diploma, and integrated courses.

DID YOU KNOW THIS?

- That 24 million children are born every year in India and almost every child is enrolled into one of the 800,000 primary schools spread across India? That 259 million children go to one of the 1.4 million schools every day? That even though 27.1 million children join class 1 (including older children) only 13.2 million children pass out of class 10 and 8.3 million children pass out of class 12, every year? That two out of three children will not complete class 12?
- That the literacy rate went up four-fold in sixty years, from 18 per cent in 1951 to 73 per cent in 2011? Despite this, only 48 per cent

of the class 5 students can read class 2 text (ACER 2015 study).
- That the Indian market size of primary, secondary, and higher education is estimated at Rs 282,000 crores in the year 2014?[22]
- That there are 33 different school educational boards in the country, including the Central Board of Secondary Education (CBSE), Council for the Indian School Certificate Examinations (CISCE) which is the umbrella for ICSE and ISC and the various State Educational Boards.
- That the University Grants Commission (UGC) and the All-India Council for Technical Education (AICTE) were formed to ensure quality of technical and higher education. The 12th Five Year Plan (2012–17) approved a budget of Rs 19,800 crore for UGC for these five years. AICTE spent Rs 330 crore in plan and non-plan expenditure in 2011–12 (as per the AICTE Annual Report). Despite spending approximately Rs 5,000 crore every year in these two institutions, only 10 to 25 per cent of our graduates are employable.

Table 14.1: School and College Statistics at a Glance

Sl no.	Level	Definition	No. of students enrolled in 2013–14 (in million)	Annual pass-outs to next level estimated in 2012–13 (in million)
1.	Primary	Classes 1,2,3,4,5	132.4	
2.	Upper primary	Classes 6,7,8	66.5	
3.	Secondary	Classes 9,10	37.3	13.2
4.	Higher secondary	Classes 11,12	22.3	8.3
5.	Certificate, diploma, integrated courses	Skill sector	2.4	0.68
6.	Graduation	BA, BSc, BTech, BCom, BEd, BPharm, MBBS, diploma courses	23.6	5.92

7.	Postgraduation	All master's courses	3.7	1.33
8.	Total school	Sl no. 1 to 4	258.5	
9.	Total college	Sl no. 5 to 7	29.7	8.03

Enrolment in private sector primary and secondary schools are increasing despite much higher costs.

> The Hindu, based upon the findings of a 2011–12 survey carried out by the National Council for Applied Economic Research (NCAER), reported that enrolment in private schools rose from 28 per cent in 2004–05 to 35 per cent in 2011–12. Private school enrolment is increasing even though it is five times as expensive as going to a government-run school. Per month household expenditure on private schooling ranges from over Rs 18,000 in Delhi, to just over Rs 3,500 in Uttar Pradesh.

THE MARKET FOR EDUCATION SECTOR IN INDIA

According to the Deloitte Education Sector Team, the Indian Education Sector has been recognized as a 'Sunrise Sector' for investment in the recent past.[23] According to NSDC Human Resource and Skill Requirements reports, the sector grew at 13 per cent per annum from 2008 to 2012 to reach Rs 228,000 crore, which makes it one of the fastest growing sectors in India. In 2013–14, the sector further grew to Rs 292,000 crore. The school segment is the biggest market, accounting for 70 per cent of the total market in 2013–14 with the college segment being the second largest at 20 per cent of the market.

EMPLOYMENT SCENARIO IN THE EDUCATION AND SKILLS SECTOR

Interesting facts about employment in the Education Sector[24]

- Employment in the Education Sector includes employment as Teachers and as Non-teaching staff in schools and colleges, private coaching and tutoring, Teacher training, the development, provision of multimedia content and e-learning, IT training in schools, educational software development, skill enhancement training, and so on.

ENTRY-LEVEL JOB ROLES IN INDUSTRIES / 179

- But the bulk of the jobs are in teaching institutions only and hence is the focus in this chapter. Some of the roles in e-learning, IT, software development are covered in other relevant chapters in this book.
- The government sets norms for Teacher training, Teacher hiring, and Teacher's salaries both at the school and college levels.
- The government pays better salaries than the private sector in schools and colleges because many of the private sector institutions tend to pay less than the norm set by the government.
- According to the NSSO 66 Round, in 2011–12, 13.92 million people were employed in this sector of which only 7.31 million (53 per cent) were teaching staff and the balance (47 per cent) were non-teaching staff. So this sector provides non-teaching jobs in plenty. The largest number of non-teaching staff were in primary schools at 4.06 million followed by 0.63 million in colleges in 2011–12.
- In 2013–14, 6.7 million were teaching in schools. A BEd qualification is essential for teaching staff in schools.
- In 2012–13, over 815,000 professionals were teaching in colleges—over 54 per cent in Arts/Science/Commerce colleges and 27 per cent in Engineering colleges. A PhD qualification is preferred for teaching jobs in colleges.

EMPLOYMENT FORECAST IN THE EDUCATION SECTOR

- Please see Table 14.2 below for employment forecasts.

Table 14.2: Employment in the Education Sector[25]

Sub-sector	Employment in million		
	2013	2017	2022
School teaching staff	7.0	7.5	8.9
School non-teaching staff	4.9	5.0	5.0
College teaching staff	0.9	1.1	1.7
College non-teaching staff	0.6	0.9	1.3
Skill training institutes	0.2	0.2	0.3
Total Sector	13.5	14.7	17.3

- The growth will be in school teaching staff due to the lower student–Teacher ratio of 35:1 required as per the new RTE (Right to Education) Act.
- There will be a growth in college teaching staff due to the lower student faculty ratio of 10:1 recommended by UGC and higher enrolment expected.
- Graduates are not suitable for teaching staff in colleges because PhDs are preferred and hence this role is not covered in this book.
- BEd graduates and diplomas in school education are suitable for teaching staff in schools.
- Graduates are suitable for non-teaching staff in colleges, which will almost double to 1.34 million by 2022.
- Employment in the skills sector will also double by 2022 and the Skill Trainer role is covered in this chapter.

Before moving on to the entry-level job roles, we briefly spotlight an outstanding Indian Teacher who went on to become the President of India.

DR SARVEPALLI RADHAKRISHNAN

The first Vice President of India and the second President of India, Dr Sarvepalli Radhakrishnan was a brilliant student and most of his studies were covered through scholarships. At the age of 17, he joined Madras Christian College and attained his bachelor's and master's in the field of philosophy. The 21 year-old graduated with good marks, was selected as an Assistant Lecturer at Presidency College in Madras (now Chennai), and chose to work there.

His salary was just Rs 17 per month. His hard work, intelligence, and innovative, famous ways of teaching paid him back and he was chosen as the Vice Chancellor of Andhra University when he was around forty years of age. After three years, he was appointed as the Vice Chancellor of Banaras Hindu University.

The Bharat Ratna Awardee (1954), held the position of the Vice President of India from May 1952 to May 1962. He was then made the President of India from May 1962 to May 1967. India celebrates Teacher's Day on the birth anniversary of Dr Radhakrishnan, that is on 5 September.

SECTION 2
ENTRY-LEVEL JOB ROLES

As stated earlier, graduate jobs at the entry-level in this sector are limited to the following.

CODE	ROLE
EDU 1	School Teacher
EDU 2	School Student Counsellor
EDU 3	Student Mobilizer
EDU 4	Skill Trainer

EDU 1 SCHOOL TEACHER

Job Description

Teachers are coaches, mentors, and guides and play a very important role in a student's life. As a Teacher, you will be responsible for instilling quality education in students based on a particular curriculum decided and adopted by the school.

Typical Responsibilities

- Creating and completing lesson plans on a daily basis.
- Monitoring the performance of the whole class and each student.
- Helping weak students by providing them special classes and tuitions.
- Conducting regular tests to assess student performance.
- Making the class interesting by making it interactive.
- Conducting extracurricular activities and outings once in a while.
- Guiding students who participate in inter-school competitions.
- Interacting with parents and giving feedback on their child.
- Complying with the school's policies and procedures.
- Instilling a passion in students for the subject and encouraging them to excel.

School Teacher: A Profile

Likely salary with 1–3 years of experience	Rs 200,000–Rs 350,000 per annum. The salary is better in government schools and large corporate schools. The salary also depends upon the subjects you teach; there is a premium on science and maths Teachers.

Targets	Completion of the syllabus on time. Class attendance must be above the norm set. Pass percentage of the class to be maximum.
Challenges	Dealing with student lethargy: Enormous patience and a strong passion to teach is required to overcome student lethargy. Dealing with parents, expectations. Dealing with the latest technology: Many schools are migrating to computer-assisted learning and Teachers have to become tech-savvy. Understanding various careers: There are more than 100 popular careers on which you as the Teacher must acquire knowledge of and insights into, and stay updated continuously.
Skills	Apart from excellent communication skills, a Teacher is supposed to have a lot of patience in dealing with students. Teachers must also possess class management, planning, and persuasion skills.
Stress	Moderate.
Travel on the job	None.
Impact on stakeholders	The children, parents, and the school management are highly impacted by this role.
Career prospects	Career progression is slow in the teaching profession. After several years, you can become a Senior Teacher teaching higher classes at school. A few Teachers make it to the school administration level of Vice Principal or Principal.
Future salary with 5–7 years of experience	Rs 300,000–Rs 500,000 per annum.

A Practitioner's View

School Teacher, Madhavi Bhagawan, Hyderabad

Mrs Madhavi Bhagawan was working as a Teacher. She has around fifteen years of experience in this field. When we sought her views about the teaching profession being a career option for students, she said:

'Teaching is definitely a very good profession. I love teaching as it helps me remain a lifelong learner. Personally, I have learnt to be more patient and empathetic, and professionally, I have learnt to be up-to-date with regard to knowledge and information. This role gives me immense satisfaction. It helps one to be thorough in gaining knowledge and mastering the subject.'

EDU 2 SCHOOL STUDENT COUNSELLOR

Job Description

A Student Counsellor is someone who guides, educates, and helps students and their parents to take decisions regarding their careers. Student Counsellors also help students build confidence levels by constantly motivating them to take up the right career path without any fear. They take care of any special requirements and difficulties that a student is facing. A Student Counsellor demonstrates high levels of maturity in dealing with a variety of student issues.

Typical Responsibilities

- Interacting with students to establish a bond so that they open up with their issues.
- Talking to them in such a way that they develop trust in you.
- Listening to their issues with attention.
- Motivating and encouraging them to take the right decision.
- Guiding them to the right channels, in case they are facing financial or emotional problems.
- Maintaining a detailed record of student details and interactions with them.

School Student Counsellor: A Profile

Likely salary with 1–3 years of experience	Rs 200,000–Rs 300,000 per annum.
Targets	Number of students counselled. Number of students successfully completing the counselling.

Challenges	Empathizing with the student: The Counsellor should listen to student problems without a preconceived mind-set, or judgement, but at the same time not get too involved.
	Dealing with emotionally disturbed students requires a lot of care, so that they do not develop dependence on the Counsellor.
	There are more than 100 popular careers which you as the Counsellor must acquire knowledge of and insights into, and stay updated continuously.
Skills	Apart from excellent communication skills, a Counsellor is supposed to have a lot of patience in dealing with students. They must also possess strong persuasion skills. They require training in counselling.
Stress	Moderate.
Travel on the job	None.
Impact on stakeholders	Students are highly impacted by this role.
Career prospects	Career progression is limited. After some time, you can set up an independent practice and work with many schools.
Future salary with 5–7 years of experience	Rs 350,000–Rs 450,000 per annum.

A Practitioner's View
School Student Counsellor, Sasi, Hyderabad

Ms Sasi was working with a leading counselling organization. When we asked her about her experiences and why she would recommend the role to a fresher, she said:

'These days, due to various options present, students are often confused as to what to choose as a career. Even parents are equally confused—the mother wants the child to be a doctor, the father wants the child to be a pilot and the child herself/himself wants to become something else!

'A Career Counsellor/Student Counsellor, met a very bright student whose parents wanted him to go abroad for higher education, while he did not. She asked to speak to him alone and it emerged that he was afraid he would face racism since he was dark and that people would make fun of him. So the Counsellor had to convince him that only talent is valued all over the world and not skin colour. After a lot of persuasion, he finally agreed to go ahead. This is how a Counsellor helps students in making the right career choices by solving their issues and concerns. Therefore, my job is to assess the strengths and weaknesses of students and guide them towards choosing the right career path. It is very satisfying to be able to give the right advice to someone. I would recommend this role to a fresher due to the increasing demand for Counsellors in modern times.'

EDU 3 STUDENT MOBILIZER

Job Description

What is mobilization? Every year a large number of children complete class 10 and class 12 and seek admission into vocational courses like ITIs/diplomas, graduation courses like BA and BTech. How does a student get information about a college or a course? She/he finds out through a Student Mobilizer who connects with the parents and students, shares information, and invites the parents to the college. The main objective of a Mobilizer is to ensure that the courses offered are full. She/he sets up and manages a group of agents who work on a commission basis. The profitability of the institute depends upon the success of mobilization and hence this is a critical role.

Typical Responsibilities

- Coordinating and planning end-to-end activities for student mobilization.
- Have a detailed understanding of the courses offered.
- Identify and visit schools, housing colonies to identify prospects.
- Identify new catchment areas for mobilization.
- Set up and manage a battery of mobilization agents.
- Meet parents of prospects.
- Handle student/parent queries and help them understand the courses offered.

- Follow up and collect admission forms/registration forms.
- Take part in education fairs organized by newspapers and TV channels to promote the college and the courses.
- Understand the market demand on courses and update the Centre Coordinator.

Student Mobilizer: A Profile

Likely salary with 1–3 years of experience	Rs 200,000–Rs 250,000 per annum, plus incentives.
Targets	Ensuring more and more students join courses. Convert enquiries into admissions.
Challenges	Acquiring students against intense competition.
Skills	Good networking skills, influencing skills, and an extrovert personality.
Stress	High during the mobilization period.
Travel on the job	A lot of travel is required.
Impact on stakeholders	Students and college management are highly impacted by this role.
Career prospects	After three years you could become a Team Leader and after eight to ten years become the Head of the Mobilization Department.
Future salary with 5–7 years of experience	Rs 300,000–Rs 400,000 per annum, plus incentives.

A Practitioner's View
Student Mobilizer, Rekha, Hyderabad

Ms Rekha worked as a Student Mobilizer for a training institute. When we sought her views about this job as an option for students to start off their career, she said:

'This job involves a lot of communication to be done. We need to constantly call students, answer their queries, take into account their interests, suggest good courses so that they can make a choice, and also give complete details about the course programme. Convincing students and sometimes explaining to their parents can be challenging because views differ from person to person. I loved to interact with people and so enjoyed working in this role. I would also suggest this role to any fresher I know."

EDU 4 SKILL TRAINER

Job Description

When students pass out of colleges, they have to be 'corporate-ready'. Therefore, educational institutions are now hiring Skill Trainers who can help students acquire soft skills such as communication, analytical, logical, and interview skills. In addition to soft skills, Skill Trainers are required to impart technical skills like welding, carpentry, and so on.

What is the primary difference between education and skills? Education is about 'theoretical knowledge on what to do and how to do' and is often assessed by written and oral exams. Skills are about 'doing and demonstrating' and are assessed by practical exams. So Skill Trainers are often practitioners of the skill they teach and hence come with work experience.

Typical Responsibilities

- Taking classes on a daily basis.
- Motivating students to excel in the skill.
- Conduct classes in an atmosphere that promotes positivity.
- Plan, coordinate, and prepare the curriculum.
- Conduct regular assessments.
- Give important practical tips.
- Give one-to-one counselling to students who are struggling in the class.

Skill Trainer: A Profile

Likely salary with 1-3 years of experience	The salary varies depending upon the skill. Skill Trainers can expect from Rs 150,000–Rs 300,000 per annum. Technical skills such as computer, welding, and so on fetch better salaries.
Targets	Most students should pass the external assessments.
Challenges	Staying contemporary in the skill domain and training techniques is essential.
Skills	A lot of patience in dealing with students, good internet research skills. A passion for training.

Stress	Moderate.
Travel on the job	None.
Impact on stakeholders	Students are highly impacted by this role.
Career prospects	In a few years, you can move into a bigger or better-managed institute with higher pay. After eight to ten years, you can become Head of a Skill Training Centre managing a team of Trainers and Student Mobilizers.
Future salary with 5–7 years of experience	Rs 300,000–Rs 400,000 per annum depending on the skill domain.

A Practitioner's View

Skill Trainer, Pallavi (name changed), Hyderabad

Ms Pallavi is working as a Soft Skills Trainer with an institute. When we sought her views about this job as an option for students to start off their career, she said:

'This job involves interacting with students and identifying their positives and negatives. We need to work on areas of concern, as some students are good in group discussions but get nervous during personal interviews while it may be the opposite for some. Some students are extremely shy and take a lot of time to open up. So dealing with such students can be challenging as we first need to strengthen their self-confidence. Sometimes in the process of making students 'corporate-ready', we become more refined individuals. Therefore, I would recommend this role to freshers.'

15

INSURANCE

Some people are the only bread-earners for their families. So if something happens to them, the future of the whole family is at stake. It becomes very difficult for the family to maintain their lifestyle. Therefore, we need to make arrangements for guaranteed financial security while things are going well, and this is where insurance comes in.

SECTION 1
BACKGROUND

Insurance is nothing but a guarantee of compensation provided by a company if there is a loss of life and/or property. It is a form of risk management. Basically, there are two parties involved in insurance: (i) the insurer: the party who undertakes to compensate for losses in exchange for a monthly/quarterly/annual premium paid on time; (ii) the insured: the person or property for which an insurance policy is issued. The insurance policy is the agreement which the insurer gives to the insured. Insurance premium is the amount that the insured agrees to pay the insurer and as long as the premium is paid, on time, the policy is valid. If the unforeseen event happens, the insured/nominee makes a claim and the insurer processes the claim and if found valid, pays the insured amount.

HOW DOES INSURANCE WORK?

An insurance company reaches out and gets many people to take the insurance and each of them pays a premium. This premium is invested by the insurance company. When one of the insured makes a valid claim, the insurance company pays the claim from the invested amount. In effect, all those who are insured and paying regular premiums are pooling their resources so that this may be re-distributed among them in times of calamities such as fire, floods, epidemics, and famine.

TYPES OF INSURANCE

There are many types of insurance policies; we list a few of the more popular ones here.[26]

Life Insurance

This insurance is taken on the life of a person. A person insures him/herself so that in case of death of the policy-holder, the insurance company pays a certain sum to the nominee or the immediate family member. Again, there are various types of life insurance policies and people can choose from the many available options.

Property Insurance

This provides insurance against robbery, loss, or damage of property (for example, fire in a factory). Different policies cover property under different terms and conditions.

Health Insurance

This provides insurance towards any medical expenditure that a person spends on health problems.

Auto Insurance

Any financial loss that occurs to your vehicle due to an accident or theft is covered in this insurance. Third party auto insurance provides compensation to the victim of a road accident.

Travel Insurance

When we travel to different locations, especially to international locations, travel agents always suggest that we get a travel insurance to cover any loss of personal belongings or costs of medical expenses overseas and delays in travel.

Credit Insurance

Sometimes, we purchase assets by taking loans, for example, a housing loan. We need to pay our loans on a regular basis. Sometimes if the policy-holder is not able to pay the loans due to sudden death, then the insurance companies pay off the balance amount of the loan.

HISTORY OF INSURANCE IN INDIA[27]

History of Life Insurance

Prior to 1947, foreign insurance companies dominated the market. An Ordinance was issued on 19 January 1956, nationalizing the Life Insurance Sector and the Life Insurance Corporation (LIC) came into existence in the same year. The LIC had a monopoly till the late 1990s when the Insurance Sector was reopened to the private sector. Since then over 24 private life insurance companies have entered the Indian market. But LIC continues to be the dominant player with a market share (in 2012–13) of around 73 per cent, leaving the balance of 23 players competing for 27 per cent of the market.

History of Non-life (General) Insurance

In 1972 with the passing of the General Insurance Business (Nationalization) Act, the general insurance business was nationalized with effect from 1 January 1973—107 insurers were amalgamated and grouped into four companies, namely, the National Insurance Company Ltd, the New India Assurance Company Ltd, the Oriental Insurance Company Ltd and the United India Insurance Company Ltd. The General Insurance Corporation of India was incorporated as a company in 1971 and it commenced business on 1 January 1973. In 1999, the Insurance Regulatory and Development Authority (IRDA) was constituted as an autonomous body to regulate and develop the insurance industry.

Privatization of the Insurance Industry

The IRDA opened up the market in August 2000 with the invitation for application for registrations. Foreign companies were allowed ownership of up to 26 per cent (now increased to 49 per cent).

INTERESTING FACTS ABOUT THE INSURANCE MARKET IN INDIA[28]

- Today there are 28 general insurance companies including the The Export Credit Guarantee Corporation of India

(ECGC) and Agriculture Insurance Corporation of India and 24 life insurance companies operating in the country.
- Insurance premiums collected by Indian insurers was 3.9 per cent of the GDP in 2013–14.
- After witnessing de-growth since 2010, the life insurance industry rebounded in the first quarter of 2015–16 by recording a growth of 20 per cent in new premium incomes.[29]
- The Indian life insurance industry is the biggest in the world in terms of the number of policies sold (360 million policies).
- LIC is the market leader in life insurance, with 72.7 per cent share in FY 2013, followed by ICICI Prudential, with 4.7 per cent share.
- The non-life or general insurance industry is dominated by motor insurance at 47 per cent share in 2013 followed by health insurance at 22 per cent share in the same year.
- Of India's total population, only 0.2 per cent comes under medical insurance. The Government of India wants every citizen to be covered for health insurance and hence this segment is poised to grow dramatically.

INSURANCE: A GROWING SECTOR[30]

India's growing economy has the potential of developing the Insurance Sector as well as increasing job opportunities. The Life Insurance Sector in particular, is estimated to grow at a compounded average growth rate of 15–20 per cent over the next fifteen to twenty years. The government has targeted life insurance penetration up to 40 per cent, health insurance to 30 per cent, and general insurance to 15 per cent of the total population by 2030.

JOB OPPORTUNITIES IN THE INSURANCE SECTOR

Jobs in Public Sector Insurance Companies

Job opportunities have increased because of the many private players who have entered this industry. Even in a nationalized insurance company like LIC, despite reservation policies and the number of exams one has to clear, it is not very difficult to get a job as a Development Officer.

There are over 1 million people working in this sector and

over 5 million people are associated as Agents, consultants, brokers, sub-brokers, underwriters, and so on. The Associated Chambers of Commerce and Industry of India (ASSOCHAM) estimated manpower requirements in this sector to be 2 million by 2030.[31]

Why should anyone join the insurance industry?

There are four reasons.

Huge demand: There is a huge demand for hardworking graduates who have a flair for selling.

Equal opportunity: Everyone is measured by the same yardstick—meeting targets. This helps people who are winners, to climb the ladder very fast.

Graduate advantage: The industry does not prefer MBAs and graduate qualification is adequate to reach the top.

Living in home town: Insurance is expanding in urban and rural areas. So you can work close to your home.

How Do Insurance Companies Hire?

Public sector companies (PSCs) follow a transparent competitive examination model followed by an interview and medical examination. The private sector prefers to source candidates through advertising, web media, and consultants, and conducts a two-stage interview process.

Before moving on to Section 2, and the entry-level job roles, we would like to highlight a high achiever in the Insurance Sector.

G.V. RAO

Doyen of the Indian general insurance industry, Mr G.V. Rao, was Chairman and Managing Director of the Oriental Insurance Company, India when he retired. A highly experienced and respected professional in the general insurance industry, Mr Rao had a total of over fifty years of insurance experience in domestic and international markets.

He joined the New India Assurance Company Ltd as a Management Trainee and rose to the position of the Chairman and Managing Director of the Oriental Insurance Company. Later, he served as the CEO of Al Ahlia Insurance Company, Oman, for ten years. Apart from India, he had worked in the Middle East and the Caribbean also.

Mr Rao's contribution to the insurance industry was immense

in the post-liberalization era. He was Adviser to several institutions like, HDFC ERGO GI Co., Magma Fin Corp Ltd, State Bank of India, and Midhani Co. Ltd. He was on several important committees of the Insurance Regulatory and Development Authority (IRDA), and was a director on the board of the Institute of Insurance and Risk Management (IIRM). He was Chairman of GVR Risk Management Associates.

Mr Rao was an invited faculty at the National Insurance Academy (NIA), Pune, and participated actively in other insurance forums in India and abroad. A prolific writer, he contributed regularly to several national and international insurance journals. He was regarded in the Indian insurance market as a keen market analyst and many insurance companies and customers sought his professional advice, especially on matters impinging on technical issues of claim settlement, financial analysis, and strategic planning.

SECTION 2
ENTRY-LEVEL JOB ROLES[32]

CODE	ROLE
INS 1	Insurance Agent/Adviser
INS 2	Development Officer/Unit Manager/Agency Manager
INS 3	Underwriting Executive (Trainee)
INS 4	Claims Officer

INS 1 INSURANCE AGENT/ADVISER

Job Description

An Insurance Agent (also called an Insurance Adviser) is someone who is responsible for helping, persuading, and selling an insurance policy to clients. Agents can sell life, health, general, vehicle insurance policies to clients and receive a commission. An Insurance Agent has to pass an exam and is then issued a licence to practise by the Insurance Regulatory and Development Authority of India (IRDAI, commonly referred to as IRDA).

The Role of IRDA

The IRDA is the deciding authority on fixing the maximum commission payable, giving companies the flexibility to offer their agents any rate below that. It reviews the commission structure periodically, and a new commission structure is expected.

How much does an Insurance Agent earn?

This is a very important question because Agents do not get a monthly salary, they get a 'commission'. The commission is a percentage of the insurance premium annually paid by the customer who has bought a policy from the Agent.

The commission varies between Life and Non-life Insurance Policy Agents. It also varies from Agent to Agent and depends upon the commission structure of the company she/he is working for and the number of policies sold.

Life insurance commission structure

Typically, as mentioned above, the commission is a percentage of the annual premium and is paid in instalments—a high premium in the first year, smaller premium in the second and third year, and a small premium from the fourth year onwards. The first year premium percentage, as well as the total premium percentage, rise with the number of years for which the premium is paid. The total commission paid depends upon the insurance product sold.

The first year commission varies from 5 to 25 per cent of the first year premium and goes down to 2 to 5 per cent of the annual premium from the fourth year onwards till the term of the policy.

Non-life insurance commission structure

This also depends on the type of policy—the highest commission is paid for Marine Cargo policies while a lower percentage is paid for Motor Vehicle Insurance. The commission varies from 5 to 15 per cent of the premium paid.

Typical Responsibilities

- Attending training sessions conducted by the company regarding new products/policies.
- Identifying prospective clients.
- Meeting prospective clients and explaining the various policies to them.

- Suggesting the most appropriate policy for clients based on their requirements.
- Collecting details of clients if they agree to buy a policy.
- Ensuring that forms are filled and the required documents are collected.
- Collecting the first premium and delivering it to the company.
- Ensuring that policies are issued on time.
- Ensuring that policies are renewed, on time, in case of non-life insurance.
- Tracking future premiums to ensure that policies do not lapse, in case of life insurance.
- Helping the insured in making claims whenever required.
- Following up with the company to ensure quick disposal of the claim.
- Seeking referrals from existing clients for new clients.
- Complying with the company's policies and procedures.

Insurance Agent/Adviser: A Profile

Likely salary with 1–3 years of experience	Agents are normally not paid a salary, but earn a portion of the insurance premium as a 'commission'. Successful Agents can earn commissions of around Rs 25,000 per month while low-performing Agents may earn as little as Rs 3,000 per month in the first year.
Targets	A minimum number of new policies must be added every year. Value of first year premium from new policies to be above specified level. Default in premium payment by clients should be minimized.
Challenges	Understanding insurance products and identifying the right policy requires financial knowledge and experience. Generating leads on a continuous basis means you have to connect with people you have never met before. Income will be earned only by closing deals. Closing the deal when the competition is willing to do anything is a daily challenge.

Skills	You should be able to write and pass the exam mandated by IRDA and have practical knowledge of the products and competition. Excellent networking and relationship-building skills. Strong tenacity and persuasion skills.
Stress	Moderate.
Travel on the job	You will have to travel locally to meet clients.
Impact on stakeholders	The customers and your Supervisor are highly impacted by this role.
Career prospects	Many successful Agents stay Agents for life because the money they earn is large and they learn the art of getting new leads from existing customers. Some of them grow to become a Chief Life Insurance Agent (CLIA), with a few Agents working under them. Some Agents can join the company as a Development Officer or Agency Manager and move up the management layer. The career prospects for a successful Agent is very high.
Future salary with 5–7 years of experience	Successful Agents earn up to Rs 1 lakh per month in seven years.

A Practitioner's View
Insurance Agent, D. Jayaram, Cochin

Mr Jayaram is working as an Insurance Agent for a reputed company. He has two years of experience in the field. When we asked him to share his views and experiences with us, he said:

'Insurance as a sector is developing very fast. People are now aware of what insurance is and why it is so important to take insurance. I personally like meeting people and talking/explaining to them the advantages of having an insurance policy. Professionally, it helps me gain knowledge about the sector, the company, and about new policies. It is definitely a very good career option as it helps one earn good commissions, based on the number of policies one is able to sell. To convince people is not an easy task so one needs to have high levels of confidence and good knowledge of the variety of policies available in the market. I enjoy doing my job.'

INS 2 DEVELOPMENT OFFICER/UNIT MANAGER/AGENCY MANAGER

Job Description

Insurance Agents are not employees of the insurance company and require continuous supervision, encouragement, and support. The insurance company employee who manages a group of Agents is called a Development Officer (by LIC, India's largest life insurance company), or Unit Manager or Agency Manager (by private insurance companies). We will use the term Development Officer hereafter to refer to all these three designations.

The employee who deals with agents in non-life insurance is also called a Development Officer.

How much does a Development Officer/Unit Manager/Agency Manager earn?

This typically depends on the company you work for as well as your work experience. Your salary is directly proportional to the number of policies your team (you and the Agents under you)—is able to sell and the amount of business it is able to bring. You will be responsible for motivating and training your team of Agents. So the better you motivate and train them, the more business they get and the more you all earn.

Typical Responsibilities

- Discussing targets with superiors and then achieving them.
- Recruiting and training Agents.
- Helping Agents pass the IRDA exam.
- Discussing targets and arriving at action plans with Agents.
- Training Agents on new product launches.
- Monitoring Agents' performance on a daily basis.
- Motivating Agents to achieve sales targets by providing leads, doing joint client calls, and providing them with constructive feedback to boost their confidence.
- Helping Agents get their commissions on time.

Development Officer/Unit Manager/Agency Manager: A Profile

Likely salary with 1–3 years of experience	Rs 300,000–Rs 400,000 per annum plus incentives.
Targets	Meeting targets—new policies acquired, premium earned—assigned by the company. Meeting targets for active Agents.
Challenges	Hiring Agents who get only a commission is the big challenge. Making Agents successful is a bigger challenge.
Skills	Good knowledge of the industry. Strong leadership skills. Good persuasion skills. Networking skills.
Stress	Moderate to high.
Travel on the job	You will have to travel locally in this role to meet clients.
Impact on stakeholders	The customers, your Agents, and the company you work for are highly impacted by this role.
Career prospects	After two to three years as a Development Officer, you can be promoted as an Assistant Branch Manager and later become the Branch Manager. The rate of promotion is faster in the private sector, but in both it depends mainly on performance on the job. Public sector companies like LIC have an extensive training programme for Development Officers who are confirmed at the end of a one-year probation and thereafter, career progression is dependent on performance.
Future salary with 5–7 years of experience	Rs 550,000–Rs 800,000 per annum.

A Practitioner's View

Unit Manager, Omkar Govilkar, Alibaug

Mr Govilkar is working as a Unit Manager for a reputed life insurance company. He has over two years of experience in the field. When we asked him to share his views and experiences with us, he said:

'This job has taught me a lot of things. I have learnt to communicate well and boost my team's spirits to perform well by maintaining good relations. Professionally, it has helped me improve my skills regarding taxation, various banking laws, effective selling techniques, various market funds, and investment opportunities. My day starts with attending calls from my seniors, taking their advice, and preparing an action plan to handle critical situations. Then I guide my Agents regarding different plans and policies, the market status, and daily happenings. I share with them important information. I will recommend this role to freshers because it will help them to improve their position in the society and make them financially independent.'

INS 3 UNDERWRITING EXECUTIVE (TRAINEE)

Job Description

When a proposal (or an application) for insurance is submitted, insurance companies need to check the policy, assess and analyse the risk involved, and then decide how much premium should be paid by the customer based on the documents submitted.

Most Underwriting Executives specialize in any one type of insurance. The main types of insurance are as follows.

- General insurance, which covers household, pets, motor vehicles and travel.
- Life insurance/assurance, which covers illness, injury, and death.
- Reinsurance, where part of the risk is placed with another insurer.

Typical Responsibilities[33]

Daily activities vary according to the type of insurance offered by the company, but may include:

- Studying insurance proposals.
- Gathering and assessing background information in order to effectively assess the risk involved.

- Calculating possible risk and deciding how much individuals or organizations should pay for insurance (the premium).
- Deciding whether the risk should be shared with a reinsurer.
- Computing results for appropriate premiums using actuarial information, other statistics, and own judgement.
- Visiting brokers or potential customers and preparing quotes.
- Liaising with specialists, such as surveyors or doctors, for risk assessment.
- Gathering information and various types of reports (for example, medical records), from specialists.
- Negotiating terms with policy-holders or their brokers.
- Ensuring that premiums are competitive.
- Specifying conditions to be imposed on different types of policies, for example, asking that a property owner install a security alarm.
- Negotiating with brokers and drawing up contracts.
- Writing policies.
- Keeping detailed and accurate records of policies underwritten and decisions made.

Underwriting Executive: A Profile

Likely salary with 1–3 years of experience	Rs 200,000–Rs 400,000 per annum.
Targets	Quantity of proposals processed. Policy turn-around time. Proposal rejection rate.
Challenges	Communicating with customers/Agents to explain and convince them in case the company cannot accept their application.
Skills	Analytical skills. Attention to detail. Verbal and written communication skills.
Stress	Moderate.
Travel on the job	No travel is involved.
Impact on stakeholders	The customers and company you work for are highly impacted by this role.

Career prospects	In the beginning Underwriters usually work as Trainees under Senior Underwriters. Once you gain experience, you can work independently and become a Senior Underwriter.
Future salary with 5–7 years of experience	Rs 500,000–Rs 700,000 per annum.

A Practitioner's View
Underwriting Executive, Ravi, Mumbai

Mr Ravi has worked as an Underwriting Executive with an insurance company. When we asked him about his views, he said:

'The role of an Underwriter is very interesting and crucial. I thoroughly enjoyed doing the role and now I am able to assess situations better. Earlier this role was not very popular and the visibility of an Underwriter was low. Now things have changed. Companies are giving decent importance to Underwriters. The scope and salaries have also improved a lot. Therefore, I would recommend this role to any fresher.'

INS 4 CLAIMS OFFICER

Job Description

The purpose of taking an insurance is to make a claim when an untoward accident happens. Insurance Claims Officers are involved in managing a claim from the beginning through to settlement.

A Claims Officer ensures that insurance claims are handled efficiently. He acts like a broker between the policy-holder and the insurance company. The officer decides on the extent and validity of a claim, checking for any potential fraudulent activity. Apart from communicating with policy-holders, Claims Officers also liaise with external experts such as Loss Adjusters and Lawyers.

Typical Responsibilities[34]

Depending on your experience and level of responsibility, typical activities may include:

- Providing advice on making a claim and the processes involved.
- Processing new insurance claims notifications.
- Collecting accurate information and documents to proceed with a claim.
- Analysing a claim made by a policy-maker.
- Guiding policy-holders on how to proceed with the claim.
- Contacting tradespeople from a network of company-approved professionals, and arranging for them to make repairs on the policy-holder's property.
- Monitoring the progress of a claim.
- Investigating potentially fraudulent claims.
- Identifying reasons why full payment may not be made.
- Ensuring fair settlement of a valid claim.
- Building relationships with Loss Adjusters, Forensic Accountants, and Solicitors, as well as other legal/claims professionals.
- Ensuring the policy-holder is treated fairly and receives excellent service in accordance with industry and company guidelines.
- Handling any complaints associated with a claim.
- Involvement in loss-adjusting activities and in legal discussions relating to settlement.
- Seeking legal recovery of monies paid out.
- Managing a team of Claims Handlers (at managerial level).
- Taking responsibility for productivity and profit.
- Adhering to legal requirements, industry regulations, and customer quality standards set by the company.

Claims Officer: A Profile

Likely salary with 1–3 years of experience	Rs 200,000–Rs 400,000 per annum.
Targets	Quantum of claims handled. Claims ratio which is claims approved as a percentage of claims processed. Cycle time for claim processing.

Challenges	Identifying fake claims. During natural calamities, a large number of claims need to be processed simultaneously.
Skills	Attention to detail. High process orientation. Working under pressure.
Stress	Moderate.
Travel on the job	Very little travel is involved.
Impact on stakeholders	The customers and company you work for are highly impacted by this role.
Career prospects	In the beginning, Claim Officers usually work as Trainees under Claim Managers. Once you gain experience, you can work independently and become a Team Leader and then a Manager.
Future salary with 5–7 years of experience	Rs 500,000–Rs 800,000 per annum.

A Practitioner's View

Insurance Claims Officer, Usha, Hyderabad
(place changed)

Ms Usha was working as a Claims Officer with a reputed insurance company. When we asked her about her views and why would she recommend the role to a fresher, she said:

'The role of a Claims Officer is very crucial in insurance companies. Many people submit wrong claims and try to take the company for a ride, but it is my responsibility to ensure that such situations do not arise. My job involves effective and fair communication with people. It is very interesting as we get to learn about a lot of insurance policies and procedures while doing this role. Considering the learning curve and the knowledge we get, I would certainly recommend this role to a fresher.'

16

CONSTRUCTION, BUILDING, AND INFRASTRUCTURE SECTOR

Everyone who has travelled to the US marvels about the great infrastructure in that country. But very few know the secret of how this was done. Franklin D. Roosevelt, the 32nd President of the US (1933 to 1945) created a publicly funded programme called the 'Works Progress Administration' (WPA) that built infrastructure in 1933. The WPA, between 1933 and 1940 (in just seven years), built, improved, or renovated 39,370 schools, 2,550 hospitals, 1,074 libraries, 2,700 firehouses, 15,100 auditoriums, gymnasiums, and recreational buildings, 1,050 airports, 500 water treatment plants, 12,800 playgrounds, 900 swimming pools, 1,200 skating rinks, plus many other structures. It also dug more than 1,000 tunnels, surfaced 639,000 miles of roads and installed nearly a million miles of sidewalks, curbs, and street lighting, in addition to tens of thousands of viaducts, culverts, and roadside drainage ditches. It provided 8 million jobs in communities large and small. And what those workers put up has never been matched.[35]

Our country, in 2015, is yet to build public infrastructure of the scale that the US built eighty years ago. But the great news is that we are catching up. The Gujarat International Finance Tec-city project, the Delhi–Yamuna Expressway commissioned recently, the Delhi Metro, the Tata Mundra Ultra Mega Power Project, the Yamuna Interceptor sewage system, the Narmada Canal Solar Power Project have all been cited in a list of the world's top 100 innovative projects, compiled by the KPMG in 2014.

Even more impressive is Prime Minister Modi's dream project—the bullet train. According to the final feasibility report prepared by the

Japan International Cooperation Agency (JICA), India's first bullet train corridor between Mumbai and Ahmedabad will cost around Rs 1 lakh crore.[36]

Which is the one sector that will make all this happen and place India among the superpowers of this world? It is the Construction Sector.

SECTION 1
BACKGROUND

DID YOU KNOW THIS?[37]

- The Construction Sector is the second-largest employer in the country. It creates more than 45 million jobs either directly or indirectly. It is highly unorganized (only 20 per cent of the industry is organized), and employs the most labourers, second only to the Agriculture Sector. Labour is highly migratory and largely unskilled.
- The sector is also the largest contributor to the central exchequer, that is, this industry contributes more taxes than any other industry.
- In 2012–13, the market value of the construction industry was estimated at Rs 7,67,400 crore.
- The Real Estate Sector demand is driven by the rapid migration of people to cities. The number of people living in cities will increase from 31 per cent of population to 51 per cent of population by the year 2050 and the Ministry of Urban Development is working on creating 100 Smart Cities by the year 2022. This will drive a huge demand for the construction industry.
- The industry is moving towards mechanization in a big way. The labour force requirement to construct half a million sq. ft fell from 800 in 2002 to 200, due to the use of pre-fabricated structures.

THE MARKET FOR CONSTRUCTION

The Construction Sector is broadly divided into two sub-sectors—infrastructure which contributes 40 per cent and real estate which contributes the balance 60 per cent. The structure of the industry is shown in Figure 16.1.

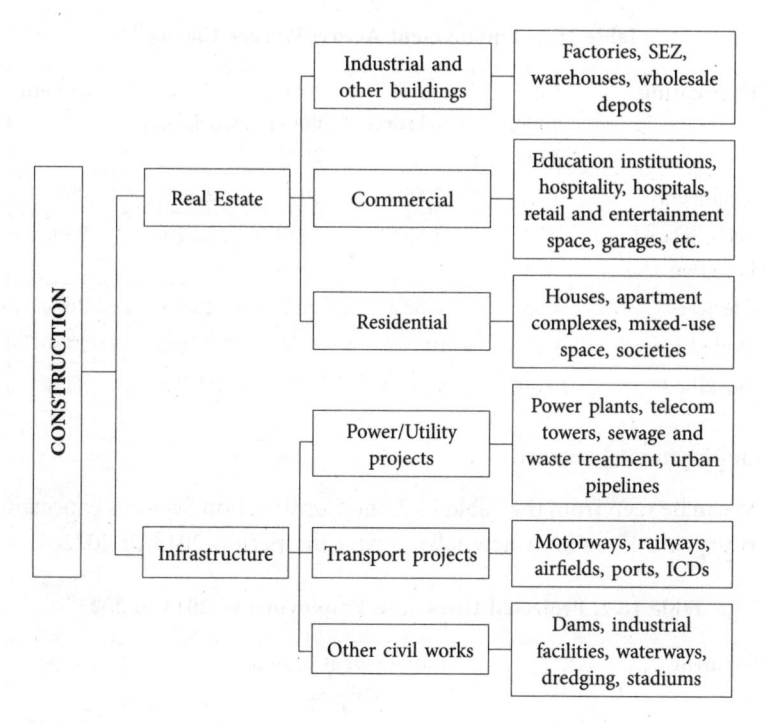

```
CONSTRUCTION
├── Real Estate
│   ├── Industrial and other buildings — Factories, SEZ, warehouses, wholesale depots
│   ├── Commercial — Education institutions, hospitality, hospitals, retail and entertainment space, garages, etc.
│   └── Residential — Houses, apartment complexes, mixed-use space, societies
└── Infrastructure
    ├── Power/Utility projects — Power plants, telecom towers, sewage and waste treatment, urban pipelines
    ├── Transport projects — Motorways, railways, airfields, ports, ICDs
    └── Other civil works — Dams, industrial facilities, waterways, dredging, stadiums
```

Figure 16.1: How Construction Links to Other Sectors[38]

The market will grow to 11,95,400 crore by 2017, making construction one of the most important sectors of the Indian economy.

EMPLOYMENT SCENARIO IN THE CONSTRUCTION SECTOR

As can be seen from Table 16.1, this industry employs a large number of unskilled workers. Graduates are employed as Engineers and Clerks. Diploma-holders and ITI technicians are employed as Technicians and Skilled Workmen. In all 225,000 engineering jobs, 550,000 technician jobs, and 192,000 clerical jobs were added in the period 2005 to 2011. The demand for Engineers, Technicians and non-engineering graduates will continue to grow in this sector.

Table 16.1: Employment Across Worker Classes[39]

Occupation	Nos. (000s) 2005	% of workforce	Nos. (000s) 2011	% of workforce	% growth
Engineers	822	2.65%	1050	2.56%	28%
Technicians/Foremen etc.	573	1.85%	1120	2.74%	95%
Clerical	738	2.38%	930	2.26%	26%
Skilled force	3.267	10.57%	3730	9.10%	14%
Unskilled	25,600	82.45%	34200	83.30%	34%

Employment Forecast

As can be seen from the Table 16.2, the Construction Sector is expected to provide 17 million new jobs during the period 2013 to 2022.

Table 16.2: Projected Growth in Employment—2013 to 2022[40]

Segment	Employment base in million				
	2013	2017	2022	2013–17	2017–22
Building, Construction, and Real Estate	40.14	51.95	66.62	11.81	14.67
Construction of buildings	35.52	45.97	58.96	10.45	12.99
Demolition and site preparation	0.34	0.45	0.57	0.11	0.12
Electrical plumbing and other construction installation activities	1.00	1.29	1.66	0.29	0.37
Building completion and finishing	3.27	4.24	5.44	0.97	1.2
Infrastructure	5.28	7.45	9.93	2.17	2.48
Construction of roads and railways	4.28	6.04	8.05	1.76	2.01
Construction of utility projects	0.79	1.12	1.49	0.33	0.37

Construction of other civil engineering projects	0.18	0.26	0.35	0.08	0.09
Other specialized construction activities	0.02	0.03	0.04	0.01	0.01
Overall Sector	45.42	59.40	76.55	13.98	17.15

Before we go on to discuss the entry-level job roles in this sector, we'd like to draw your attention to a high-achiever in the field—Mr K. Venkataramanan.

K. VENKATARAMANAN

Mr Venkataramanan retired on 30 September 2015 as the CEO and Managing Director of engineering giant Larsen & Toubro (L&T), one of the most admired companies in India.[41] Prior to holding this position he was the whole-time Director and President (Hydrocarbon), L&T. Mr Venkatramanan spearheaded L&T's foray into the world of engineering and construction (E&C) and strengthened every aspect of the engineering-procurement-construction (EPC) value chain, transforming L&T into a respected name in the global EPC fraternity.

Mr Venktaramanan is a chemical engineer from the Indian Institute of Technology (IIT) Delhi, with specialization abroad in design and engineering, and received the Distinguished Alumni Award from IIT Delhi in 2005. He was the first Asian to become the Chairman of the Board of Directors of the Engineering & Construction Risk Institute, Inc., US for a two-year term ending in May 2010. He is an Honorary Fellow of the Institute of Chemical Engineers, UK and the second Indian to receive this recognition from the world's most reputed body in chemical engineering. He is also a fellow of the Indian Institute of Chemical Engineers. He was also the Chairman of the Capital Goods Committee of the Federation of Indian Chambers of Commerce and Industry (FICCI).

SECTION 2
ENTRY-LEVEL JOB ROLES

The Infrastructure Sector provides lot of employment opportunities—both blue collar and white collar. Here we direct the spotlight on three white-collar jobs. Many of the jobs in HR, procurement, and projects have already been covered earlier in the chapters on HR, Finance and Accounts, and Operations and hence are not covered here.

CODE	ROLE
INF 1	Project Civil Engineer
INF 2	Site Supervisor
INF 3	Interior Designer

INF 1 PROJECT CIVIL ENGINEER

Job Description

A Project Civil Engineer manages and oversees construction and maintenance activities of buildings, roads, dams, airports, railroads, bridges, power plants, and so on. A Civil Engineer is responsible for the cost, safety, and timely completion of the project.

Typical Responsibilities

- Visiting project sites and conducting surveys.
- Estimating and managing construction budgets.
- Approving project designs/drawings/reports.
- Preparing blueprints for projects and bids for tenders.
- Liaising with local authorities for various approvals.
- Preparing an estimate of materials, manpower, and machinery required for commencing the construction, and getting the same approved by the management.
- Determining the time that will be taken to complete the project and scheduling work accordingly.
- Constantly inspecting the construction site and materials used.
- Approving contractor bills after verifying the quantum of work.
- Working with the Site Supervisor to ensure the construction is going on as per the actual plan.
- Ensuring that the project is completed within allocated budgets and within timelines.

Project Civil Engineer: A Profile

Likely salary with 1–3 years of experience	Rs 250,000–Rs 350,000 per annum.
Targets	Ensuring timely completion of projects. Ensuring quality of construction. Ensuring safety at the workplace. Ensuring minimum cost over-runs.
Challenges	Working odd hours at the site, because construction can happen round the clock. Meeting project deadlines, despite shortage of manpower and even material. Getting work out of construction teams who are often more experienced than you. Working at project sites which may be far from cities and hence very little social life.
Skills	Solid domain-knowledge in civil engineering. Leadership skills. Problem-solving skills. Planning skills.
Stress	Moderate to high.
Travel on the job	You will be posted to a project site till the end of the project.
Impact on stakeholders	The Project Team and vendors working at the construction site and the customers (users of the civil structures) are directly impacted by this role.
Career prospects	A Civil Engineer can expect a promotion in two years to the post of a Senior Civil Engineer and after three years can become a Site Engineer who manages a whole construction site.
Salary with 5–7 years of experience	Rs 600,000–Rs 800,000 per annum.

A Practitioner's View
Civil Engineer, Aneesh Sule, Mumbai

Mr Sule has nearly three years of experience in this field. When we asked him about his experiences and views about the role and why he would recommend it to a fresher, he said:

"'CIVIL' to me stands for "Construction is Very Important in Life". A man's basic need is food, clothing, and shelter, and a Civil Engineer is responsible for providing an important need that is shelter. Building cities, buildings, and homes requires dedicated, honest, innovative aspiring young professionals like you and me to absorb and implement advanced technology from around the world, making it a better dwelling place. Wide thinking, planning, and action are the three great essentials to prevent a crisis for future generations to struggle through. This job is for people who are self-supporting, hardworking, and strong and who can work with a cooperative spirit.'

INF 2 SITE SUPERVISOR

Job Description

While the Project Civil Engineer is responsible for the engineering aspects of construction, the operational aspects are managed by the Site Supervisor. The individual who ensures the coordination and control of these activities on-site is known as the Site Supervisor.

Typical Responsibilities

- Ensuring the construction site and the facilities there are well maintained.
- Planning and hiring construction equipment materials.
- Planning, procuring, and receiving materials at the site after inspection.
- Constantly inspecting the construction site and materials used, to avoid future problems.
- Hiring of workers and technicians and payments to them.
- Recruiting contractors and sub-contractors.
- Allotting and scheduling work to teams on a daily basis.
- Ensuring safety of workers.
- Dealing with workers' unions.
- Preparing reports on the progress of construction and submitting the same to the management.
- Liaising with the Civil Engineer to see that construction moves ahead as per the actual plan.

◘ Communicating any delays in delivery of materials and equipment to the management.

Site Supervisor: A Profile

Likely salary with 1–3 years of experience	Rs 200,000–Rs 300,000 per annum.
Targets	Ensuring that the construction is carried out as per the plan, without any delays.
Challenges	Meeting deadlines despite unexpected absenteeism and unruly behaviour of workmen. Dealing with trade unions and unhappy workers. Acting promptly during emergencies such as accidents on-site, or any other medical emergency.
Skills	Good understanding about construction practices. Planning and organizing skills. Eye for detail.
Stress	Moderate to high.
Travel on the job	Limited.
Impact on stakeholders	The management, people working at the construction site, and the people who will eventually use the structure that you are constructing, are directly impacted by this role.
Career prospects	The career prospects are also bright as you can grow to become a Project Manager or Site Manager for multiple projects once you gain experience.
Future salary with 5–7 years of experience	Rs 600,000–Rs 800,000 per annum.

A Practitioner's View
Site Engineer, Gangadhar, Hyderabad

Mr Gangadhar is working as a Site Engineer. When we asked him about his experiences and why he would recommend this role to a fresher, he said:

'My role is extremely interesting as you get to learn a lot.

The scope in this field is also increasing in present times and so is the demand. Many Civil Engineers can further opt for this role. I have been working in this field for a very long time now, but even today I get to learn new aspects. That is the beauty of this job. It has helped me learn to manage stress and deal with a variety of people. I would say that the Site Engineer, who has a civil engineering degree, is someone who makes an empty piece of land into a beautiful liveable place/building. Therefore our efforts continue to be seen long after the project is completed. This gives me immense satisfaction.'

INF 3 INTERIOR DESIGNER

Job Description

While the Civil Engineers take care of the structure and the exterior of the building, the Interior Designer is responsible for the interiors. She/he decides on the furniture, furnishings, fixtures, colours, paintings, and lighting of the place and is involved in designing homes and offices or renovating existing places to make them look more attractive and pleasing. An Interior Designer can choose to design the interior of residential as well as commercial buildings.

Typical Responsibilities

The role of an Interior Designer is extremely creative. Typical activities include the following.

- Communicating with clients and understanding their requirements.
- Coming up with a design plan and estimate of expenditure.
- Presenting the design plan to customers.
- Hiring the required personnel to carry out architectural work.
- Suggesting innovative ideas and models to clients on space, layout, furniture, and so on.
- Purchasing all the materials required.
- Supervising the work of contractors, assessing their work, and making payments to them.
- Completing the work within the specified time-frame and budget.

Interior Designer: A Profile

Likely salary with 1–3 years of experience	Rs 200,000–Rs 300,000 per annum for those Interior Designers who work with interior designing firms. Some work on a freelance basis and do not get a salary but receive a commission.
Targets	Timely completion of work at site.
Challenges	Managing client expectations: many customers do not know or do not articulate their expectations clearly, and this leads to a lot of reworking. Estimating the cost when the design is unique is very difficult. Hiring efficient contractors to execute: for example, carpenters are very difficult to control and often delay projects. Collecting payments from clients.
Skills	Excellent domain knowledge of interior designing. Project management skills. Decent communication and convincing skills. Good visualizing ability.
Stress	Moderate to high.
Travel on the job	Travel within the city is extensive.
Impact on stakeholders	The customers and the people working with you are directly impacted by this role.
Career prospects	The career prospects are also bright as you can manage multiple projects once you gain experience and build your clientele to start on your own.
Future salary with 5–7 years of experience	Rs 400,000–Rs 600,000 per annum.

A Practitioner's View
Interior Designer, Deepti (name changed), Delhi

Ms Deepti has been working for the past two years. When we asked her about her role and her experiences, she said:
    'Interior designing is something that is very prominent in

other countries but not very popular in India. But due to the improving economic conditions and opportunities, people get to travel to various international locations. Due to this change in trend, there is a change in the lifestyle as well as people want their homes to look classy and the best. This has shot up the demand for Interior Designers all across the nation. Depending on your clientele, your pay can also be extremely good. It involves a lot of travel, fun, and serious work as well. I love doing this job as I get to travel to various locations to shop for stuff that clients need as well as have the independence of sharing my ideas and turning my imagination into reality.'

17

INFORMATION TECHNOLOGY (IT) SECTOR

India is the world's largest outsourcing destination for Information Technology (IT), accounting for approximately 52 per cent of the US$ 124–130-billion outsourcing market. Indian IT companies, such as Tata Consultancy Services (TCS), have evolved over the years, from being IT body-shopping outfits to integrated MNC-type global operations in just twenty-five years. The industry employs about 12 million Indians (including 3 million direct employees), and contributes significantly to the social and economic transformation in the country. Today the dream of every graduate is to get a job in the IT industry because of the excellent pay and global HR practices.

Before we proceed, let's clarify a few IT terminologies which we are using in this chapter.

- 'Body-shopping': is used when an IT company employs an IT professional who is assigned to work in client premises (called 'on-site') for the client.
- 'Outsourcing': happens when a company decides to get an IT project done by an outside IT company instead of getting it done in-house.
- 'Off-shoring': happens when a company decides to get its IT projects developed outside the country, but will use it back home. For example, many Indian IT professionals are working in India on IT projects that are to be implemented in the US.
- 'Integrated' IT companies: originally Indian IT companies won IT projects to automate business processes. Later, these IT companies started bidding for the business process itself to be outsourced to them. The business process is in the ITeS

domain. 'Integrated' IT companies are thus those which offer both IT and ITeS services.

The evolution of large Indian IT companies is shown in Table 17.1. Many of the large Indian companies have moved from level 1 to level 8 over the last twenty years. Hence the market for IT and ITeS is combined together as a single sector by the National Association of Software and Services Companies (NASSCOM) and the NSDC reports.

Table 17.1: Evolution of Services Offered by Indian IT Companies

Level	IT category	Services offered
1	IT services	Body shopping
2	IT services	IT software maintenance
3	IT services	IT software development
4	IT services	IT testing; IT Implementation
5	IT services	Implementation of business process automation software (like ERP)
6	ITeS	Business Process Outsourcing
7	ITeS	Business Analytics
8	Business Process Management (BPM)	Business Consulting

DO YOU KNOW THIS ABOUT THE INDIAN IT AND ITES SECTORS?[42]

- India's IT industry amounts to 7 per cent of the global IT market, a feat that has been achieved in just twenty-five years.
- Cost of delivering IT services from India is approximately three to four times cheaper than from the US. The story is the same for both IT and ITeS.
- Indian IT companies have helped clients to save US$ 200 billion in the last five years.
- Indian IT companies have become global with delivery centres across the world—approximately 600 offshore development centres for 78 countries.

◘ The sector ranks fourth in India's total FDI share and accounts for approximately 37 per cent of total private equity and venture investments in the country.

MARKET FOR IT AND ITES SECTORS[43]

As can be seen from Figure 17.1, this sector has four sub-sectors.

```
                        IT and ITeS
                             |
     ┌───────────┬───────────┼───────────┐
  IT Services   ITeS      ER & D    Software products
                             |
              Sub-classification of ER & D and software
              products is to understand the pure play
              services and relate to job skills.
```

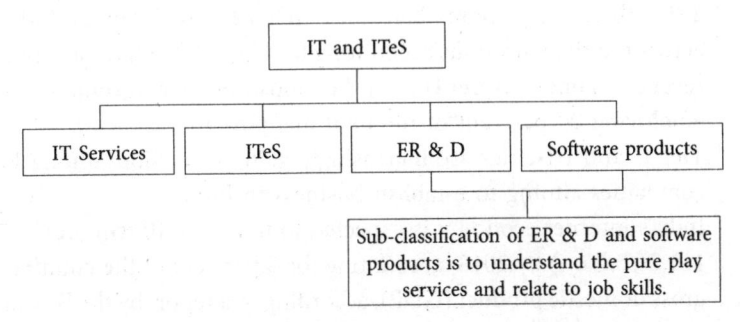

Figure 17.1: Sub-sectors of the IT and ITeS Sectors

IT revenues, domestic and exports, was US$ 118 billion in 2014. Our domestic IT market is also significant at 30 to 33 per cent of the total.

IT services dominate IT exports at 58 per cent, followed by ITeS (also called BPM) at 23 per cent while the balance 19 per cent of the exports are from software products and engineering services.

More Facts

◘ The US has traditionally been the biggest buyer of Indian IT exports; over 60 per cent of Indian IT-BPM exports were absorbed by the US during FY 2013.
◘ Firms in India became multinational companies with delivery centres across the globe—580 centres in 75 countries, as of 2012.
◘ The contribution of the IT Sector to India's GDP rose to approximately 8 per cent in FY 2012–13 from 1.2 per cent in FY 1997–98. This is the reason why every state government is rolling out the red carpet to the IT industry.
◘ TCS is the market leader; accounting for about 10.1 per cent of India's total IT and ITeS Sectors' revenue.
◘ The top six firms contribute around 36 per cent to the total industry revenue, indicating the market is fairly competitive. Of

the total revenue, about 80 per cent is contributed by 200 large and medium players.

- In addition to Indian IT companies, global IT companies like IBM, and Hewlett Packard (HP) have set up Global In-house Centres (GIC), also known as captive centres. They also operate in engineering services and software product development. In 2012, there were more than 760 GICs operating out of India, across multiple locations accounting for US$ 13.9 billion of export revenues, almost 21 per cent of the industry export revenues, and employing 20 per cent of the total manpower.
- Tier II and III cities are increasingly gaining traction among IT companies aiming to establish business in India.
- India's internet economy is expected to touch Rs 10 trillion (US$ 161.26 billion) by 2018, accounting for 5 per cent of the country's gross domestic product (GDP), according to a report by the Boston Consulting Group (BCG) and Internet and Mobile Association of India (IAMAI).

Future Growth Prospects of the IT and ITeS Industry

The IT-BPM Sector in India grew at a Compounded Annual Growth Rate (CAGR) of 25 per cent over 2000–13. Now the growth in this sector is expected to slow down to a CAGR of 9.5 per cent as per IBEF reports. However, as per NSDC reports the industry will see a rising domestic demand and the over-all CAGR will still be at 16 per cent. In either scenario, the growth prospects of this industry are very bright and will be much faster than the growth of other industries in India.

EMPLOYMENT SCENARIO IN IT AND ITES

- India is the world's largest sourcing destination for the IT industry, accounting for approximately 67 per cent of the US$ 124–130-billion market. The industry employs about a 10-million workforce.[44]
- The largest number of people (78 per cent or 2.3 million out of 3 million) are employed in providing IT and ITeS services for the export market.
- The employment in IT and ITeS is spread across large, medium, and small companies as shown in Table 17.2 Many graduates, without

- realizing this, chase jobs only in the large glamorous companies.
- The Indian IT sector primarily operates through six states—Karnataka, Andhra Pradesh, Maharashtra, Tamil Nadu, Haryana, and Uttar Pradesh. Major centres of top IT and ITeS firms such as TCS, Infosys, HCL, Tech Mahindra, Cognizant, and Cap Gemini are based in these states. Also, a majority of these centres are based in Tier I cities of these states, such as Bengaluru, Chennai, Hyderabad, and Noida. As infrastructure facilities in Tier I cities saturate and input costs increase, IT and ITeS companies are shifting their focus towards Tier II and III cities. Some of these cities include Ahmedabad, Pune, Jaipur, Nagpur, Bhubaneshwar, Mangalore, Guwahati, and Chandigarh.
- In the ITeS domain, Gurgaon (part of the National Capital Region) has the largest number of jobs and already many new jobs in this sector are being created in many Tier II cities across India.
- The IT and ITeS Sectors spend 2 per cent of the industry revenue (US$ 1.6 billion) on training employees. In fact IT companies have a huge training infrastructure created in smaller cities like Thiruvananthapuram and Mysore; 40 per cent of total spending on training is spent on training new employees.

Table 17.2[45]

Category	Number of players	Percentage of total export revenue	Percentage of total employees	Work focus
Large	11	47–50%	~35–38%	• Fully integrated players offering complete range of services • Large-scale operations and infrastructure • Presence in over 60 countries
Medium	85–100	32–35%	~28–30%	• Mid-tier Indian and MNC firms offering services in multiple verticals • Dedicated captive centres • Near shore and offshore presence in more than 30–35 countries
Emerging	450–600	9–10%	~15–20%	• Players offering niche IT-BPM services • Dedicated captives offering niche services • Expanding focus towards 500/1,000 firms

| Small | >4,000 | 9–10% | ~15–18% | • Small players focusing on specific niches in either services or verticals
• Includes Indian providers and small niche captives |

- The sector has a relatively large number of women professionals—about 30–35 per cent of the total workforce. This figure is expected to increase to 5 million by the end of 2020. The high number of women in the sector is the result of a working environment conducive to their professional growth and various women-focused initiatives—such as maternity leave, relaxation zones, medico/psycho-counselling sessions, robust grievance redressal mechanisms, committees to handle cases of sexual harassment at work, and effective security and transport mechanisms. This explains why this sector is very popular among women graduates.
- The preference for graduates and postgraduates is almost 100 per cent in this sector. While engineers dominate the IT Sector, non-engineering graduates dominate the ITeS Sector.

Employment forecasts[46]

The huge job growth driven by exports, witnessed in the peak of 2002–09 of 27 to 33 per cent, is over. We will witness a much slower growth as the industry reaches the maturity stage in the immediate future as can be seen from Figure 17.2.

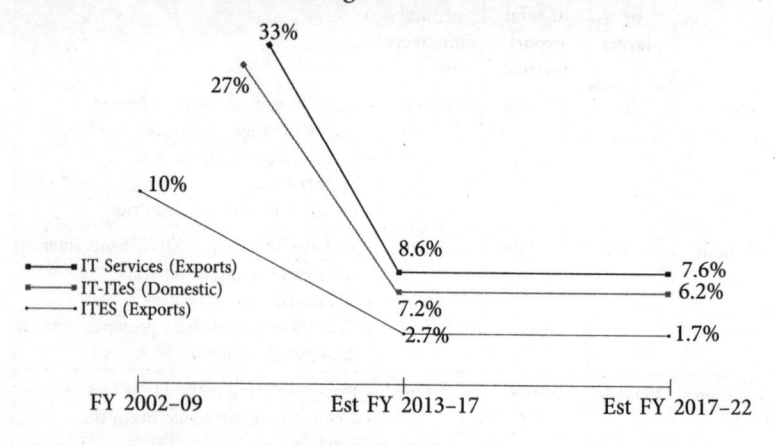

Figure 17.2: IT and ITeS Industry Employment Growth[47]

Despite the employment slowdown, this sector will still be the preferred destination for graduates and will employ over 5.1 million professionals by 2022. Please see Figure 17.3 for details.

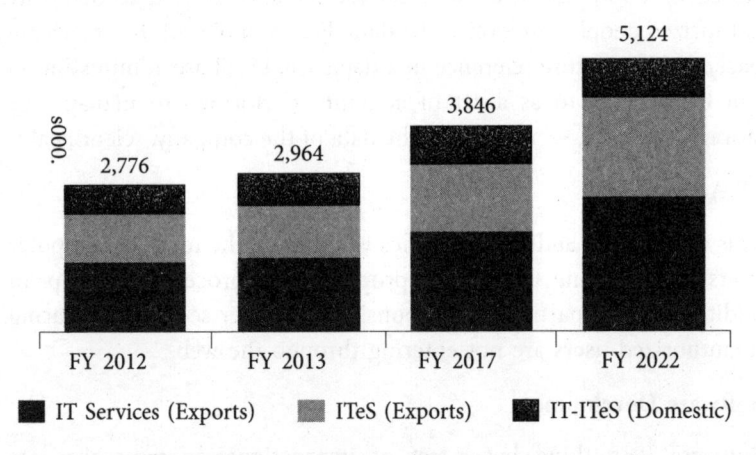

Figure 17.3: IT and ITeS Industry Employment Forecast[48]

WHAT ARE THE ENTRY-LEVEL ROLES IN THE IT INDUSTRY?

The IT industry will create a variety of technical and non-technical jobs like HR, business development, sales, finance and accounting. The non-technical jobs are covered earlier in various departmental jobs, in Chapters 3 to 10. The IT industry also employs a lot of functional specialists who have various industry domains but most of these jobs require work experience and hence not covered in this book. Now lets look at the most popular technical jobs in IT industry (jobs in the ITeS industry are covered separately in Chapter 18).

Systems Integration

There are various software applications which run on multiple hardware—servers, PCs, and laptops—present in an organization, that have to be linked to create a single working system. This process of integrating various sub-systems into one working system is called systems integration.

Database Administration

Ultimately, at the end of every computer program, data has to be stored in a way that it is easily retrievable and secured so that only authorized people can look at the data. For example, all the emails are backed up for future reference in a database. Database administration can be referred to as a set of activities performed to manage the storage, retrieval, security of all the data of the company, scientifically.

IT Audit

This department audits and verifies whether all the internal computer users are following the various processes and procedures set up. In addition, this department is responsible for cyber security—ensuring unauthorized users are not entering through the web.

Software Development

Software is nothing but a set of instructions/programs that are understood by machines. Software development refers to identification of what software is needed, what the specifications are, how the program has to be implemented, how the codes have to be written, how the developed software has to be tested and maintained, and so on. These jobs are performed by Software Developers, Software Testing Engineers, and Systems Designers.

IT Infrastructure Management

The IT infrastructure like PCs, servers, ATM machines need to be managed, often remotely from a central location. The technicians who manage this are Remote Infrastructure Engineers.

Before moving on to the entry-level job roles, let us look at the brief profile of a great achiever in this industry.

NARAYANA MURTHY[49]

In 1981, Narayana Murthy founded Infosys, a global software consulting company headquartered in Bengaluru. He served as the CEO of Infosys during 1981–2002, as the Chairman and Chief Mentor during 1981–2011, and as the Chairman Emeritus during the period from August 2011–May 2013. Under his leadership, Infosys was listed on NASDAQ in 1999. Mr Murthy articulated, designed, and implemented the Global Delivery Model, which has become the foundation for the huge success of the IT services outsourcing industry in India. He has led key corporate governance initiatives in India. He is an IT adviser to several Asian countries. He serves on the boards of Ford Foundation, United Nations Foundation, Rhodes Trust, and the Institute for Advanced Study in Princeton, New Jersey. He has served as a member of the HSBC board and the Unilever board. He has served on the boards of Cornell University, Wharton School, and the Graduate School of Business at Stanford University. He has also served as the Chairman of the Indian Institute of Management, Ahmedabad.

The *Financial Times* ranked Mr Murthy among the top 10 in its list of 'Business Pioneers in Technology', published in March 2015. In 2014, he was ranked 13th among CNBC's 25 global business leaders who have made the maximum impact on society during the last twenty-five years. *The Economist* ranked him among the 10 most admired global business leaders in 2005. He has been awarded the Legion d'honneur by the Government of France, the CBE by the British government, and the Padma Vibhushan by the Government of India. He is the first Indian winner of Ernst and Young's World Entrepreneur of the Year award. He has also received the Max Schmidheiny Liberty prize. He has appeared in the rankings of businessmen and innovators published by *Businessweek*, *Time*, *India Today*, *Financial Times*, *CNN*, *Fortune*, and *Forbes*.

For a person who was born into a middle-class family and who achieved so much through sheer hard work is very commendable. He is truly an inspiration to many.

SECTION 2
ENTRY-LEVEL JOB ROLES

CODE	ROLE
IT IND 1	Systems Integration Trainee
IT IND 2	Database Administrator Trainee
IT IND 3	Software Developer Trainee
IT IND 4	Quality Assurance Testing Engineer
IT IND 5	Remote Infrastructure Engineer
IT IND 6	IT Security Engineer

IT IND 1 SYSTEMS INTEGRATION TRAINEE

Job Description

The Systems Integration Trainee is an individual whose job it is to ensure that both hardware and software (readymade software, customized application software) when combined work well together (or in techie language 'talk to each other') and create a single system that works seamlessly.

Let us understand the systems integration function before understanding this role. Take a railway reservation application as an example. Let us assume that you are booking a railway ticket from a reservation counter. The computer terminal of the Booking Clerk is networked with other terminals as a network with a server in the reservation centre. This server is connected to other servers such as database servers, application servers through another network. There are multiple softwares running—the operating system, the network software, the DB software, the application software, cyber security systems software. Each of these hardware and software components are created by different companies and work differently.

So systems integration is a function that combines all these components to execute the railway reservation system and ensures that it works all the time. It is a very complex job because it must align with individual components so that the overall performance of the application is optimized and hence broad knowledge of both, the individual components and the overall application, is essential. If there is a problem, like if the terminal hangs, then the Systems Integration Team has to figure out what the problem is and fix it quickly.

The systems integration job is to also learn about every new version of the component. For example, if the operating system version changes, then it will impact the other components. So the Systems Integration Specialist has to realign all the components to ensure the overall performance.

One more easy way to understand the systems integration role is to compare it with a general physician (GP, usually an MBBS doctor) whom you visit when you are not well. The GP is a systems integration expert because he knows every part of the body—lungs, liver, kidneys, heart, and so on. He knows how to recommend and analyse diagnostic reports. His job is to find out where the problem is, and then he often recommends you to a specialist.

Similarly a Systems Integration Specialist has a broad knowledge of everything he uses, to figure out where the problem is and tries to fix it with the help of experts. The systems integration role includes integrating and supporting the various systems/components like computers, communication, data, and security.

As a Systems Integration Trainee you will be part of the Systems Integration Team. You will be required to troubleshoot regularly and acquire expertise in your area of work.

Typical Responsibilities

Your role is extremely critical and crucial. As a Systems Integration Trainee, you need to spend a lot of time understanding the various business processes, IT sub-systems, what are the various tools available for integration, and so on. Your daily activities will include the following:

- Working with various departments within an organization to determine their new system needs and problems with their existing systems.
- Analyse current systems for efficiency.
- Decide on modifications to be made to improve the efficiency of current systems.
- Write and submit reports regarding changes to be carried out.
- Design, develop and test new cost-effective systems.
- Conducting research on new technologies and new products.
- Develop and design automated testing tools.

Systems Integration Trainee: A Profile

Likely salary with 1–3 years of experience	Rs 300,000–Rs 500,000 per annum.
Targets	Ensuring the systems perform as per consumer/user/client requirements without any maintenance issues. Plan and implement new software/hardware without unplanned downtime.

Challenges	Working on tight deadlines that can cause stress. Developing new skills and learning continuously to keep abreast with fast-changing technologies. Collaborating with Technology Team members, end-users, and other stakeholders who pull in different directions.
Skills	Good analytical, problem-solving skills. Continuous learning skills as you may encounter a new problem every day, which will require a new approach to solve the problem. Ability to work under pressure. Excellent communication skills.
Stress	Moderate to high.
Travel on the job	Systems Integration Specialists normally may have to work at client sites and try to solve problems remotely from there. You will have to travel to different locations to understand and solve problems.
Impact on stakeholders	Employees and clients who depend on the system managed by the Systems Integration Specialists are impacted by this role.
Career prospects	The career prospects are very bright as there is a heavy demand for this role.
Future salary with 5–7 years of experience	Rs 500,000–Rs 900,000 per annum.

A Practitioner's View

Systems Integration Trainee, Ruchi Bansal, Delhi

Ms Bansal has three years of experience working as a Systems Integration Trainee. When we asked her about her experiences, she said:

'I have three-plus years of experience in the field of systems integration in a large organization and for me there is lots of learning with new IT products in the market. In this field we have to coordinate with the customer directly, which improves my confidence and knowledge as well. I have learnt one more thing in my job "Always work hard and help others also" and this is the key to success.'

IT IND 2 DATABASE ADMINISTRATOR TRAINEE

Job Description

To understand this role, you first need to understand what an IT database is and why it is needed.

You must have booked your railway ticket through a computerized railway reservation system. Every day, lakhs of tickets are either booked or cancelled through a computer system. Where are all the bookings retained in the computer? In a centralized IT database. So whenever a new customer wants to book a berth, the computer needs to know the current status (like are there berths on a specific train?) and hence connects and checks with the IT database. Now you can visualize it—thousands of computers across various booking centres are seeking information from the IT database simultaneously. The answers must come correctly and quickly or else there will be chaos. That is not the end. Imagine that after you book your ticket, someone enters the database, deletes your booking and inserts his booking for the same berth. Imagine the chaos when both of you enter the compartment and start fighting for the berth. The data, once entered, must be protected from unauthorized modifications.

IT databases are storehouses of all master data and transactions in a computer. The way this data is organized, the way database tables are designed, the way databases are accessed will determine the speed and accuracy of the database. In addition, many cyber criminals will try to seek unauthorized access to the database which is protected through firewalls (software that provide secure access) that must be installed and managed. All this is done by a Database Administrator (DBA).

Typical Responsibilities

- Designing, developing, and keeping databases up-to-date.
- Managing and monitoring database access.
- Designing database maintenance procedures.
- Ensuring databases meet user requirements.
- Liaising with Programmers, Applications/Operational Staff, IT Project Managers, and other technical staff.
- Implementing database security measures.
- Writing reports, documentation, and operating manuals.

- Testing and modifying databases accordingly.
- Providing user training, support, and feedback.

Database Administrator Trainee: A Profile

Likely salary with 1–3 years of experience	Rs 200,000–Rs 500,000 per annum.
Targets	The DBA is measured by the uptime (how long is the database working without breakdown) and response time (how fast does the database respond to software requests).
Challenges	Keeping your skills and qualification up-to-date with fast changing database software.
Skills	Good problem-solving and logical skills. Ability to work under pressure. Good knowledge of the database software—Oracle, IBM, Microsoft are some of the big database companies and hence your software expertise is linked to the database company.
Stress	Moderate to high.
Travel on the job	There is no travel involved in this role.
Impact on stakeholders	The customers and users of the software are impacted by this role.
Career prospects	If you are keen on specializing and staying in the database administration area, then you can become a Senior Administrator or head the Database Administration Team. Alternatively, you could move into software projects.
Future salary with 5–7 years of experience	Rs 400,000–Rs 1,000,000 per annum.

A Practitioner's View
Database Administrator, Anita Jadhav, Pune

Ms Jadhav is currently working as a Database Administrator. She has one and a half years of experience in this field. When we spoke to her regarding her experiences, she said:

'My job is extremely creative and at the same time complex. I get to monitor how a database is performing and also develop new systems to improve performance. Being a girl, I first felt this is not a job for me because many organizations expect Database Administrators to work 24/7. But as I started learning and gained some experience, I started liking my job and would definitely recommend this role to a fresher because the prospects and learning is very high.'

IT IND 3 SOFTWARE DEVELOPER TRAINEE

Job Description

Before understanding what software development is, let us understand what software is. Software is nothing but a set of instructions called software codes that a computer can read and execute. Computers need instructions in a language that a computer can understand. The language is called programming language.

The purpose of the software is to automate a repetitive task. A good example is a railway ticketing software. Today you can book a railway ticket by going online from your computer or cell phone or going to the nearest railway booking centre. Railway reservation is a repetitive task (called a software application, that is being automated through software called Railway Reservation System).

Software development is nothing but the process of designing, developing software codes in programming languages. Whose job is it to develop these software codes? It is the job of a Software Developer. A Software Developer is someone who designs, writes the codes and tests them. It is a very critical role and requires a lot of expert knowledge.

As a Software Developer, you will be responsible for writing software codes that work all the time without bugs and to modify the software as and when required. You will mostly work on modifying and integrating new software to the existing software application. Attaining efficiency in the shortest possible time is not as easy as it sounds because many things can go wrong. The hardware (machine) may not work properly or software logic may be wrong or parts of the software, like databases where all the data is stored, may not work properly. But the user will blame the software on the whole and the

Developer who writes the software codes, for any issues. That's why your work is generally very technical and complex in nature.

As a Software Developer Trainee, you will be part of a team of Developers, Testers, and a Project Manager.

Typical Responsibilities

- Analysing and understanding user requirements and specifications.
- Researching and identifying existing software components that can be integrated.
- Writing software codes.
- Writing operational documentation with technical authors.
- Liaising with Programmers, Designers, Developers, IT Project Managers, and other technical staff.
- Correcting software defects (called 'bugs').

Software Developer Trainee: A Profile

Likely salary with 1–3 years of experience	Rs 200,000–Rs 400,000 per annum.
Targets	To deliver software applications as per specifications, within a specified time-frame, as per the best coding practices, which will work without bugs when integrated with the other components.
Challenges	Meeting daily deadlines and working late nights, as required. Working in teams with high dependencies on the output of other team members. Being flexible to make up for the slippages of other members in your team. Being agile and open to receiving changes in specifications, even in the last minute. Upgrading skills on a timely basis, because the software industry keeps coming up with new software and updates. Threat of the 'bench'—the term used for those not on any project. For many people it is frustrating to watch others work. Salary may also be lower.

Skills	Good programming skills. Good analytical and problem-solving skills. Ability to work under pressure. Excellent communication (both oral and written skills). Good team-playing skills.
Stress	Moderate to high.
Travel on the job	Most of the time, Trainees will be working out of the development centre in India.
Impact on stakeholders	The software users, co-workers, and clients are impacted by this role.
Career prospects	Typically, the Software Programmer gets promoted to a Senior Programmer or a Team Lead in about three years. If you manage your team well, you can get promoted to the next level of an Associate Manager in the next two to three years.
Future salary with 5–7 years of experience	Rs 400,000–Rs 1,000,000 per annum.

A Practitioner's View
Software Developer, Anil Vallala, Hyderabad

Mr Vallala has five-plus years of experience in this field. When we spoke to him and asked him his views on this job role and why he would recommend it to freshers, he said:

'My job involves interacting with clients, taking their business requirements and specifications, showing them various samples of the software called prototypes that I have developed, suggesting the best option according to their requirements. Programming and implementing various new concepts is what interests me the most. The scope in this role is extremely high as there is a high demand for Software Developers. If a fresher spends one to two years working in this role, she/he gets to learn various aspects of software development. It is a very interesting and exciting role.'

IT IND 4: QUALITY ASSURANCE TESTING ENGINEER

Job Description

A Quality Assurance Testing Engineer is responsible for effective testing of software systems to identify any issues and bugs that need to be rectified. Your work will involve mostly testing for functionality. 'Functionality testing' in the software industry, means testing the behaviour of a software feature under various situations (called 'use cases'). You will need to help the programmer debug software by sharing your test results. It is a highly technical and important role.

Typical Responsibilities

- Analyse the 'use case' scenarios.
- Design and develop test scenarios, using automated testing tools that address areas such as database impacts, software scenarios, negative testing, error or bug retests, or usability.
- Document software defects, using a bug tracking system, and report defects to software developers.
- Document test procedures to ensure compliance with standards.
- Develop or specify standards, methods, or procedures to determine product quality or release readiness.
- Recommend new testing methods, including new testing tools.

Quality Assurance Testing Engineer: A Profile

Likely salary with 1–3 years of experience	Rs 200,000–Rs 400,000 per annum.
Targets	Your target will be making sure that the software performs, when deployed in a live environment, without any maintenance issues.
Challenges	Investigating and solving problems under strict timelines. Continuous learning of new testing tools. Visualizing and aligning testing to the 'live' environment when the software is deployed.

Skills	Expertise in test methods and testing tools. Analytical and problem-solving skills. Understanding of the software development process. Documentation skills.
Stress	Moderate.
Travel on the job	This role involves occasional travel.
Impact on stakeholders	The employees (programmers) and users are impacted by this role.
Career prospects	Good, because once you gain experience you can become a Senior Testing Engineer and go on to manage a team.
Future salary with 5–7 years of experience	Rs 400,000–Rs 800,000 per annum.

A Practitioner's View
Software Quality Assurance Testing Engineer, Sanjay Singh, Pune

Mr Singh has been working as a Software Quality Assurance Engineer for the last three years. When we asked him about his experiences regarding this job and why he would recommend this role to a fresher, he said:

'As a Quality Assurance Engineer, ideally you are expected to provide a system with zero per cent defects that could be passed on to the customer. The whole reputation of the company depends on it, as the customer would choose a company which develops and delivers the best bug-free software in the market. Now when being a Quality Assurance Engineer, the first thing that you should learn is getting to know the end-to-end functionality of the software that only you can test. In my experience, I have learned that it is not a very complex task to perform the testing of the software when you have a deep knowledge of it. Also, one should never restrict oneself to any domain, any technology. The market keeps changing with new emerging technologies hence we should also be ready to learn. Technically speaking, one should have knowledge of various operating systems, databases, application servers, and so on, so that one can test the software on any platform.

'To freshers I would say that the more you enjoy your role, the better you will perform it. That is the point you keep in mind while working. I always try to enjoy my work and it helps me keep off the frustration of the workload or any other problems. While testing, think that you are the customer who uses that software so that you would think of all the possible scenarios of testing. A career as a Quality Engineer is very interesting and challenging where you can learn many new things. All you have to do is improve on your grasping power.'

IT IND 5 REMOTE INFRASTRUCTURE ENGINEER

Job Description

The Remote Infrastructure Engineer/Executive is responsible for efficient handling of all remote access systems of a particular company, as well as planning and designing remote access infrastructure. A good example is the bank ATM which is monitored remotely.

Typical Responsibilities

- Support remote networks.
- Maintenance of security and WiFi systems.
- Solving operational issues faced by the team.
- Liaising with third-party vendors and the clients' support channels, reporting and managing faults.
- Provide change management services.
- Work closely with engineers on timely resolution of 'incidents' and routine service requests.
- Reporting of security events.
- Implementing appropriate policies and procedures.

Remote Infrastructure Engineer: A Profile

Likely salary with 1–3 years of experience	Rs 200,000–Rs 400,000 per annum.

Targets	Your target will be avoiding network security lapses and ensuring uptime of the infrastructure as per the norm.
Challenges	Keeping oneself updated with emerging technologies.
Skills	Sound domain knowledge including Wide Area Networks (WAN). Good communication skills. Good organizational skills.
Stress	Moderate.
Travel on the job	This role involves occasional travel.
Impact on stakeholders	The company, employees, and users are impacted by this role.
Career prospects	Your career prospects will also be good because once you gain experience you can move into senior roles.
Future salary with 5–7 years of experience	Rs 400,000–Rs 700,000 per annum.

A Practitioner's View
Remote Infrastructure Engineer, Vamshi
(name changed), Hyderabad

Mr Vamshi was working as a Remote Infrastructure Engineer. When we asked him about his experiences regarding this job and why he would recommend this role to a fresher, he said:

'Managing networks and ensuring that they are run without any issues is very challenging. There are many tough situations that we may come across but that is when we get to learn and figure out solutions for issues. I would recommend the role to any fresher who wants to start a career in IT due to the high level of learning.'

IT IND 6 IT SECURITY ENGINEER

Job Description

The role of an IT Security Engineer (or Cyber Security Engineer) is very crucial in any company. An IT Security Engineer is responsible for protecting important and confidential data like client records and financial records from cyber theft by computer hackers and cyber criminals.

Typical Responsibilities

- Support manager in installing and managing IT security software and fire walls.
- Maintain systems and controls to protect information asset integrity.
- Design procedures to prevent unauthorized access, disclosure, modification, and deletion of confidential information.
- Interact with network specialists to enhance authentication, authorization, and encryption solutions.
- Anticipate information security leak events and develop solutions to prevent them.
- Regularly test existing security solutions for vulnerabilities as per industry standards and submit formal reports on test findings.
- Review and revise purchase specifications for security software, hardware, or services.
- Respond to information security issues quickly.

IT Security Engineer: A Profile

Likely salary with 1–3 years of experience	Rs 250,000–Rs 400,000 per annum.
Targets	Ensuring all confidential information is secure.
Challenges	Keeping oneself updated on new cyber security threats and defensive mechanisms.
Skills	Sound technical knowledge in security systems, including firewalls, intrusion detection systems, anti-virus software, authentication systems, log management, content filtering. Experience with network technologies and with system, security, and network monitoring tools. Thorough understanding of the latest security principles, techniques, and protocols.

	Familiarity with web-related technologies (Web Applications, Web Services, Service-oriented Architectures) and of network/web-related protocols. Problem-solving skills and ability to work under pressure.
Stress	Moderate to high.
Travel on the job	This role involves occasional travel.
Impact on stakeholders	The company, employees, and users are impacted by this role.
Career prospects	This role is in demand with excellent prospects for growth as Team Lead and Cyber Security Manager. You can also become an entrepreneur after five years of experience.
Future salary with 5-7 years of experience	Rs 400,000–Rs 900,000 per annum.

A Practitioner's View
IT Security Engineer, Naveen, Hyderabad

Mr Naveen has been working as a IT Security Engineer for the last three years. When we asked him about his experiences regarding this job and why he would recommend this role to a fresher, he said:

'My job is very challenging as one has to be alert always and keep oneself updated with various cyber threats/thefts. This job comes with a lot of responsibility. It teaches you to become a problem-solver, managing time, activities, and people in a better way.'

18

IT-ENABLED SERVICES (ITES)

Information Technology-enabled Services (ITeS) are provided when companies use IT to deliver business processes (for example, customer support) services to customers. In turn, when these companies seek ITeS services, they are opting for Business Process Outsourcing (BPO).

SECTION 1
BACKGROUND

WHAT IS A PROCESS?

When a set of activities are executed together to achieve an objective, it is called a process. A good example is the cooking of rice. Typically cooking rice is a seven-step activity—(i) clean and wash raw rice; (ii) add adequate water and rice to a rice/pressure cooker; (iii) place the cooker on the gas stove, close the lid; (iv) put the pressure cooker weight on top; (v) allow the rice to cook and wait for the steam to whistle; (vi) shut down the flame; (vii) let the rice simmer in the cooker for 10 minutes—and the rice is ready to serve. This seven-step activity is called a process.

WHAT IS A BUSINESS PROCESS?

Every company has to do many things—called business processes—to serve its customers. These business processes include manufacturing, distribution, marketing, sales, procurement, accounting, HR management, legal and knowledge management, technology management.

Traditionally, every company carried these processes out in-house. Then some companies decided that they could cut costs and improve their efficiency by shutting down, or downsizing the internal teams and 'outsourcing' or asking an external company to take over this process. For example, Coca-Cola has several franchisees that actually buy the Cola concentrate and manufacture and bottle the Coca-Cola that we drink, as per a contract signed with the Coca-Cola Company. This is called outsourcing of the manufacturing/operations process.

WHAT IS BUSINESS PROCESS OUTSOURCING (BPO)?

It refers to a business process contracted out to a third-party service provider. According to Wikipedia, 'BPO is typically categorized into "back-office outsourcing", which includes internal business functions such as human resources or finance and accounting, and "front-office outsourcing", which includes customer-related services such as contact centre services. A BPO that is contracted outside a company's country is called "offshore outsourcing". A BPO that is contracted to a company's neighbouring (or nearby) country is called "near-shore outsourcing". Knowledge Process Outsourcing (KPO) and Legal Process Outsourcing (LPO) are some of the sub-segments of the BPO industry.'

In 2010, the Philippines surpassed India as the largest BPO industry in the world.

THE BPO INDUSTRY IN INDIA

When this industry started its operations in India, it created ripples. People often referred to BPO jobs as 'call centres' because the first wave of outsourcing was focused on Customer Support, wherein an US customer could call his Customer Support telephone number in the US and the call would be automatically diverted to India, answered by an Indian Call Centre Executive. Today, outsourcing to India has expanded to cover many more areas such as HR management, accounting, payroll processing, data entry, back-office support, transcription, knowledge and data management, legal services, and tax services.

Since its inception, it has created numerous job opportunities and provided employment to many young graduates. The sector currently employs more than a million people. According to an article in a leading Indian news website:[50] "'Exports from the BPO sector in India have grown despite the global economic crisis," Minister of State for Communications and IT Milind Deora said in a written reply to the Lok Sabha in 2013. He stated that "The market share of the Indian BPO sector in the global BPO industry has increased from 34 per cent in 2009 to an expected 37 per cent in 2012. The global BPO sourcing market has grown from $ 36–38 billion in 2009 to $ 48–50 billion in 2012," Deora said. He added that "The total size of the Indian BPO sector has grown from $ 14.7 billion in 2009–10 to an expected $ 20.9 billion in 2012–13 and has provided an estimated employment to 917,000 people in 2012–13."'

Table 18.1: Comparative Growth of the BPO Sector

BPO industry	2009–10	2012–13	Annual growth rate
India's market share in global BPO	34%	37%	
Size of global market	36–38 US billion dollars	48–50 US billion dollars	9%
Size of India's BPO Sector	14.7 US billion dollars	20.9 US billion dollars	12.5%

BPO companies are betting big on sectors like Banking, Financial Services and Accounting, Supply Chain, and Healthcare to drive the next phase of growth which will increase employment opportunities in the sector.

EMPLOYMENT IN THE BPO INDUSTRY

Broadly there are two types of BPOs—Global and Indian—based on the location of the customers they serve. Global BPOs service customers outside India (in the US, UK, and other countries), whereas Indian BPOs serve customers in India. Global BPOs operate during the late evening/night (when it is daytime in the customer country), and require high-quality English-speaking skills. Indian BPOs operate normal working hours and require excellent vernacular language skills (such as in Hindi, Telugu, Tamil).

Before we look at the entry-level job roles available in the ITeS/BPO sector, we would like to briefly profile a high achiever in the ITeS/BPO sector.

RAMAN ROY

Mr Roy is one of the pioneers of the BPO industry in India. A Chartered Accountant based in the NCR-Delhi region, he is currently the CEO of his venture capitalist-funded BPO company Quatrro. Raman started his BPO work with American Express in 1984, when the company started its Japan and Asia Pacific (JAPAC) support operations based out of New Delhi in India. The work was largely accounting and back-office based.

After American Express, Raman moved to GE International Capital Service (GECIS). GECIS was GE's captive BPO arm started in Gurgaon before Gurgaon built its reputation as an MNC hub. In 2000, with funding from a venture capitalist firm, Chrysalis Capital, Raman started the company Spectramind in New Delhi. Spectramind was a pioneer BPO in India, as it was among the first few companies incorporated in India to get into the third-party business.

By 2002, Spectramind had expanded to 9000 employees spread across New Delhi, Mumbai, and Pune. At this time Wipro bought out Spectramind for US$ 175 million. Raman served in Wipro as the CEO of the BPO entity till 2006, when he left along with a large number of senior Spectramind resources to start a new venture called Quatrro.

Thus Raman Roy, Chairman and Managing Director of Quatrro Global Services, has the distinction of starting the Indian BPO revolution. Roy is also one of the founders of Indian Angel Network.

Considering his contributions, he can be called the Father of the BPO Sector in India.

SECTION 2
ENTRY-LEVEL JOBS IN BPO/ITES SECTOR

There are numerous job roles in the BPO/ITeS Sector but we are covering only a few entry-level roles based on their popularity among graduates.

CODE	ROLE
ITeS 1	Inbound Call Centre Executive
ITeS 2	Outbound Call Centre Executive
ITeS 3	Process Analyst

ITeS 4	IT Tech Support Executive
ITeS 5	Geographical Information Systems Trainee

ITES 1 INBOUND CALL CENTRE EXECUTIVE

Job Description

When products are shown on television, customers are given numbers to call and place their orders. Let us assume you are shopping from one of these channels and you call up on the numbers flashed on your TV screen. Your call is received by an Inbound Sales Call Centre Executive who takes your order. She/he asks you for your complete address, phone number, and other details, and informs you by when your order will be processed. The Inbound Sales Call Centre Executive then records your information in a computer which shares the order with various other departments to process your order.

Typical Responsibilities

- Receiving calls from customers.
- Patiently handling customer enquiries with regard to different products, pricing, offers, discounts.
- Taking down customer details correctly.
- Meeting sales targets by converting prospective enquiries into sales.
- Providing reports to superiors on calls attended and sales generated.
- Cross-sell other company products.
- Answering quality complaints on the calls that you handle.
- Constantly upgrading one's telephone etiquette.

Inbound Call Centre Executive: A Profile

Likely salary with 1–3 years of experience	Rs 150,000–Rs 250,000 per annum.
Targets	Handling and closing the stipulated number of calls (daily, weekly, or monthly). Minimizing call escalations. Meeting sales targets (daily, weekly, or monthly).

Challenges	Talking non-stop for hours and staying fresh and energetic every minute of the shift. Night shifts and donning a pseudo personality at international call centres. Handling difficult and cranky customers. Dealing with fake customers who call up only to pass time and are not serious about buying the product.
Skills	Good command over English or local language. Problem-solving skills. Good influencing skills. Time management skills.
Stress	Moderate to high. Stress reduces once you start enjoying the job.
Travel on the job	There is no travel involved in this role. It is a desk job.
Impact on stakeholders	The customers who call to place their orders and the company are impacted by this role.
Career prospects	Initially you will join as an Executive but with an experience of two or more years, you will become a Team Lead and thereafter, an Assistant Manager at the BPO. In seven years you can lead a process.
Future salary with 5–7 years of experience	Rs 250,000–Rs 500,000 per annum.

A Practitioner's View

Inbound Call Centre Executive, Thomas, Hyderabad

Mr Thomas is an Inbound Sales Call Centre Executive with a local cab company that provides pick-up and drop services to customers. When we asked him about his role and how he likes his job, he said:

'My job involves taking calls from customers who call up to avail our taxi services. I take down customer details and based on their pick-up and drop location, I check with our cab database and see if any cab is available in that particular area to service the customer. I then assign the cab for that customer pick-up. The job is hectic as we continuously receive calls. We also need to be prepared for nasty responses from customers in case there is a delay or for some reason the cab does not reach the location. But it certainly is a learning experience and anyone who likes communicating with people, organizing data, and working on the system will love the job.'

ITES 2 OUTBOUND CALL CENTRE EXECUTIVE

Job Description

Many of us often receive phone calls asking us if we are interested in taking a personal loan, insurance policy, home loan, and so on. Companies hire Tele-representatives to call customers and generate sales/leads. These representatives are called Outbound Sales Representatives. An Outbound Sales Call Centre Executive is someone who makes calls to prospective and existing customers and persuades them to buy more or buy another item.

Typical Responsibilities

- Generating a prospective list of customers you need to call. They can be individuals or a business entity.
- Connecting and talking to customers as per the planned script.
- Providing correct information regarding the product or service to customers.
- Responding patiently to customer enquiries.
- Explaining the process of sales (if any) to the customer.
- Taking down customer details correctly.
- Maintaining customer databases.
- Meeting sales targets.
- Providing reports to superiors on calls made and sales generated.

Outbound Call Centre Executive: A Profile

Likely salary with 1–3 years of experience	Rs 150,000–Rs 300,000 per annum plus incentives.
Targets	Meeting daily, weekly, or monthly targets on sales, calls made, calls converted. Minimize customer complaints.

Challenges	Handling unruly customers: some customers speak very rudely as they may be sleeping, travelling, or in the middle of doing some work, and may not like it if someone calls them up at the wrong time. So dealing with such situations is a challenge. Meeting sales targets, especially when there is no apparent demand for the product\service.
Skills	Selling and influencing skills. Good command over English or local language. Influencing skills. Time management skills.
Stress	High.
Travel on the job	None.
Impact on stakeholders	The customers you call and the company you work for are impacted by this role.
Career prospects	There is a shortage of people in this role. Initially, you will join as an Executive but with two years' experience or more, you can become a Team Leader/Assistant Manager/Manager, depending on your performance.
Future salary with 5–7 years of experience	Rs 400,000–Rs 700,000 per annum.

A Practitioner's View

Outbound Call Centre Executive, Madhu, Hyderabad

Mr Madhu works as an Outbound Sales Call Centre Executive for an insurance company and shares his views with us:

'The job is exciting especially for those who are interested in selling and marketing. I found it challenging initially to meet targets because some customers speak rudely and are not interested in listening to what you say. But after being in this field for four years now, I understand the trick of attracting customers' attention. I would certainly recommend this job for any fresher who wants to pursue a career in marketing/selling, as it is a good starting point.'

ITES 3 PROCESS ANALYST

Job Description

Let us assume that you plan to shift your residence and need packers and movers to move your luggage. When you call the packing and moving company, your call is received by a Call Centre Executive who takes down your details like address, phone number, location, whether it is a local or domestic or international transfer. Then you are informed that an assessor from the company will come for a personal visit and finalize things. The assessor comes on the promised date and makes an assessment of how much it will cost you, based on the items that have to be shifted. Once the assessment is done and you both agree upon a certain amount, the same is communicated to the company. On the day of shifting, a team of packers and movers are sent to your residence to shift the items. After packing, the goods are shipped to the destination. This is an example of a streamlined process and the people who design these processes are called Process Associates/Analysts.

A Process Analyst is someone who identifies, analyses, plans, designs, and manages business processes and streamlines the flow of work.

Typical Responsibilities

- Understanding the end objective of the process and the workflow.
- Designing a process to achieve the objective. If there is already an existing process, review the same and modify as required.
- Checking if the designed process is executable.
- Designing process flow-charts.
- Interacting with users of the process as well as the management to identify loopholes.
- Documenting and storing process flow data.
- Training users of the process.
- Taking feedback from parties involved regarding any improvements that need to be made to the designed process.
- Continuously improving the process.

Process Analyst: A Profile

Likely salary with 1–3 years of experience	Rs 200,000–Rs 400,000 per annum.
Targets	Designing new processes, or modifying existing processes that work efficiently.
Challenges	Convincing stakeholders (employees, management, and clients) to implement any process or process change. Taking feedback constructively to make further enhancements and improvements. Planning for process failures.
Skills	Good networking skills. Problem-solving skills. Good communication skills. Good knowledge of flow-charts, Excel, and other process-designing tools.
Stress	Moderate.
Travel on the job	There is no travel involved in this role.
Impact on stakeholders	The process users and their supervisors are directly impacted by this role.
Career prospects	Initially, you will join as an Analyst but with an experience of two or more years, you can become a Senior Analyst and thereafter, an Assistant Manager in your division.
Future salary with 5–7 years of experience	Rs 450,000–Rs 700,000 per annum.

A Practitioner's View
Process Manager, Pramila N., Hyderabad

Ms Pramila is working as a Process Manager with a mutual fund investment company. She has around five years of work experience in this field. When we asked her about her experiences, she said:

'I joined as a Process Trainee initially when I was a fresher, and realized that process is extremely important in all that we do. After two years I became a Senior Process Analyst. Can you imagine a world if things are not organized or there is no process in place? I cannot. Therefore, this job has taught me to be more organized and professional. There is lot of learning as you get to deal with the intricacies of how a business should function and how you should streamline things. I would recommend this role to freshers because the learning is high and the pay and prospects are very good.'

ITES 4 IT TECH SUPPORT EXECUTIVE

Job Description

Let us assume that you are working on your system in office and sending some important files and documents to your seniors and clients. You notice that the mail is taking its own sweet time to get sent and suddenly your mailbox crashes. What do you do? Whom do you approach? You rush to the IT Department to raise a request for solving your problem. You will then be contacted by an internal IT Tech Support Executive, who will help you resolve the issue. Similarly, you have bought the latest Apple MAC computer and take it home. While installing the software like MS Office, you encounter difficulties. You will call an IT Tech Support Call Centre set up by Microsoft. A Tech Support Executive will guide you step-by-step to install the software. This is the second type of Tech Support Centre—the External IT Tech Support Centre.

Tech support is also offered for devices with built-in software such as mobile phones or iPads or laptops. Tech support is delivered by different methods—telephone, SMS, online chat, email, support forums. There are four tiers or levels in tech support.

Level 1, also called first line support, is offered to customers to solve basic issues such as software installation, or hardware connections. Level 2 to level 4 are higher levels of support, mostly offered by advanced specialists to technical people at one or two levels below them. For example when the level 1 Tech Support Executive is not able to solve the customer problem, she/he will escalate the problem to a level 2 expert who will assist her/him, but if the level 2 expert is unable to solve it, she/he may approach a level 3 expert.

This job role is about level 1 external IT tech support. The purpose of this role is to understand the customer's problem, seek basic information by asking a sequence of questions, identify the root cause by analysing the symptoms, and finally trying to guide the customer to a solution. Since the problems are technical in nature, the people who do this role are technically qualified and are trained before they start taking customer calls.

Typical Responsibilities

- Receive customer calls or emails.
- Understand the customer's complaint—which is often the symptom and not the root cause—for example the 'error code' shown on the screen.
- Ask structured questions to gather as much information as possible from the customer.
- Analyse the data.
- Identify probable causes.
- Ask more questions to arrive at the root cause.
- Once the root cause is arrived at, guide the customer to implement corrective action.
- Verify if the problem is solved.
- If not, recheck the data and arrive at a new cause, and take new corrective action till the customer's problem is solved.
- If the solution is not arrived at after all the above steps have been taken, refer the matter to a Tech Support Level 2 Executive, seek answers, call the customer and implement corrective action.
- Respond to calls/mails from users professionally.
- Educate the customer on the resolved problem, informing them on how to handle it themselves, if the problem occurs again.
- Maintain a record of all calls attended and issues resolved.
- Set up new users' accounts and profiles and deal with password issues.
- Prioritize and manage many open cases at one time.
- Build and maintain good relations with customers and level 2 professionals.
- Escalate to management if a technical complaint occurs repeatedly.

IT Tech Support Executive: A Profile

Likely salary with 1–3 years of experience	Rs 200,000–Rs 300,000 per annum. The salary varies according to the complexity of the technology supported.
Targets	Quantum of cases resolved. Quality of complaint resolution: customer ratings, escalations post-resolution, and so on.
Challenges	Customers come with a variety of problems and expect instant solutions. Customers are not trained to articulate their problems accurately, and often get irritated with detailed questions. You need a lot of tact and telephone etiquette to get answers. Continuous work pressure.
Skills	Excellent knowledge of the technology on which support is delivered. Telephone skills. Probing skills. Problem-solving skills.
Stress	Low to moderate.
Travel on the job	None.
Impact on stakeholders	Customers are directly impacted.
Career prospects	You can become a Team Lead in two to three years, and the Head of a Tech Support Process Group at a managerial level in three to four years.
Future salary with 5–7 years of experience	Rs 350,000–Rs 550,000 per annum.

A Practitioner's View

IT Tech Support Executive, Jai Chandran, Chennai

Mr Jai Chandran has seven years of experience in the field of IT. When we asked him about the role he says:

'There are lots of opportunities in the field of IT. I get to explore a lot of things and I feel very important as a lot is dependent on IT. If there is any issue regarding systems or software, customers look to us. Therefore, I have to constantly keep upgrading myself regarding any new developments or upgradations. I have to keep a cool head when customers get angry and frustrated when the system does not work. In many cases, the users are at fault but tend to blame the system. I believe a lot of customer training is required to make my role easier!'

ITES 5 GEOGRAPHICAL INFORMATION SYSTEMS TRAINEE

Digitization is a method by which a map printed on paper or a survey plan, is transferred into a digital medium through the use of a CAD (Computer Aided Design) program, and geo-referencing capabilities.

A Geographic Information System or GIS is a computer system that allows you to map, model, query, and analyse large quantities of data within a single database according to location. A GIS allows you to record a base map with a geospatial referencing system (longitude and latitude), and then to add additional layers of other information. Dozens of map layers can be arrayed to display information about transportation networks, hydrography, population characteristics, economic activity, and political jurisdictions. GIS is a tool used by individuals and organizations, schools, governments, and businesses to make better decisions.

Job Description

As a GIS Trainee Analyst your responsibilities include preparing customized GIS maps and manipulating data to serve a variety of purposes. You will read and interpret maps. You may also need to manipulate and understand digital land data and manage data entered into a GIS database.

Typical Responsibilities

- Collecting information about assets using GIS tools.
- Converting paper data or images to GIS maps.
- Creating and maintaining GIS databases.
- Presenting geographical information by creating programs.
- Managing the flow of all cartographic information.

- Maintain records and files of all the data worked on.
- Train and get expertise in the customized GIS tools.
- Mapping of features from various sources by working on various GIS platforms.

Geographical Information Systems Trainee: A Profile

Likely salary with 1–3 years of experience	Rs 150,000–Rs 250,000 per annum.
Targets	Daily output. Extent of error and rework.
Challenges	Working on tight deadlines can cause stress. Daily productivity norms must be met.
Skills	Attention to detail and ability to concentrate for long periods of time. Good command over the customized GIS tools.
Stress	Moderate.
Travel on the job	None.
Impact on stakeholders	GIS data users are highly impacted by this role.
Career prospects	You can become a Senior GIS Engineer and then a Manager, once you gain experience.
Future salary with 5–7 years of experience	Rs 300,000–Rs 400,000 per annum.

A Practitioner's View
GIS Trainee Analyst, Preethi, Hyderabad

Ms Preethi is working as a GIS Trainee with one of the big GIS companies in India. She has around one and a half years of experience in this field and when we asked her about the role and her experiences, she said:

'It is a very interesting role and I like doing my job because I get to work on so many interesting applications and tools. Earlier, this role was not so popular but now it has gained popularity and so many people want to explore this opportunity. It is highly technical in nature and many people rely on your work. Therefore, you must make sure that whatever data you provide is accurate. There is no scope for error. I would recommend this role to a fresher because of the high amount of learning.'

19
LOGISTICS

The courier industry is about movement of documents, small parcels, messages, and mail. It is different from other similar forms such as postal services, in terms of its features like speed, security, tracking, customization of delivery terms and lastly, a commitment to deliver as per agreed timelines and consequently, it is more expensive.

Logistics is the management of movement of goods, including documents and also people. It involves many things—transportation, warehousing, and shipment through multiple modes like air, road, and sea, and rail, inventory management, tracking management, material handling, packaging, delivery tracking, delivery documentation, and even collection of payment.

SECTION 1
BACKGROUND

LOGISTICS SECTOR IN INDIA

The Logistics Sector plays a very key role in any economy—by transporting people, goods, documents. Since goods have to be stored or warehoused before and after transportation, warehousing is considered part of the Logistics Sector. India's spending on logistics activities (13 per cent of its GDP), is higher than that of the developed nations due to the relatively higher level of inefficiencies in the system, with lower average trucking speeds, higher turnaround time at ports, and high cost of administrative delays.

The NSDC Human Resource and Skill Requirements reports divide the Logistics Sector into seven sub-sectors. As stated in Table 19.1, the bulk of the jobs in this sector are either for graduates, or lie in the government sector and hence the coverage in this book is limited.

Table 19.1: The Seven Sub-sectors in the Logistics Sector

Sub-sector	Purpose	Remarks	Coverage in this book
Passenger railways	Transport people	Indian Railways is a monopoly player.	Limited. Railways hire through entrance tests.
Freight railways	Transport cargo	Indian Railways is a monopoly player.	Limited. Railways hire through entrance tests.
Passenger roadways	Transport people	Intra-city transport: dominated by government transport corporations. Inter-city transport: dominated by the private sector.	Bulk of the jobs are for non-graduates. Graduate jobs are limited.
Freight roadways	Transport cargo	Dominated by the private sector.	Bulk of the jobs are for non-graduates. Graduate jobs are limited.
Packaging	Package cargo	Dominated by the private sector.	Bulk of the jobs are for non-graduates. Graduate jobs are limited.
Warehousing	Store cargo	Dominated by the government till recently. Private sector expanding rapidly.	Bulk of the jobs are for non-graduates. Graduate jobs are limited.
Courier	Transport documents	Dominated by the private sector. Postal department is the government player.	Bulk of the jobs are for non-graduates. Graduate jobs are limited.

Anything that is larger than a parcel is called 'cargo'. Cargo cannot be transported as easily as documents and parcels, and forms part of the Logistics Sector. Cargo needs to be transported to different locations via air, rail, sea, and road. Depending on the location and urgency, the mode of transport is decided. Some cargo requires special arrangements for storage and transport. A good example is the transport of milk, which is transported by special refrigerated trucks.

A very easy example to understand logistics

You go to an online site like www.BigBasket.com and order groceries. The company takes your order and promises delivery within 24 hours to your home. Many things must happen to keep this promise. The company should have the goods you have ordered, at the warehouse nearest to your home, the items must be packed, the likely delivery time must be intimated by SMS, a delivery boy must be assigned, he must reach your house, show you that the items that you ordered have been delivered in good packed condition, and complete the documentation. If there is a refund involved, you collect the money and he ensures that confirmation of the delivery reaches the company and lastly, makes you happy enough to order online again. A separate set of people are involved in replenishing the stocks in the warehouse. This entire delivery system is called Supply Chain Logistics.

FUTURE GROWTH OF THE INDUSTRY

The logistics industry is expected to witness high growth over the next ten years due to the following reasons.

1. Increased outsourcing: more companies are willing to outsource their logistics operations to focus on their core activities.
2. The emergence of global 3PL (third-party logistics) companies is expected to drive outsourcing of transport and logistics activities.
3. Global 3PL companies will drive professionalization and improve the employment scenario, both in terms of salaries and better working conditions.
4. Emergence of specialized value-added services, such as Liquid Logistics and Cold Chain will increase the demand for skilled professionals.
5. IT penetration will increase productivity, leading to better salaries and demand for higher skills.
6. Explosion of e-commerce operators will significantly increase logistics' business opportunities.

COURIER SERVICES

A courier service is a specialized service involving either an individual or a company, which transports, dispatches, and delivers important messages, documents, and goods, at your doorstep within a stipulated time period, with a little more cost to you than the regular postal service. Couriers can be sent via rail, road, sea, and air. In courier services in all cases, the delivery is point-to-point.

Parcel Couriers

These are used to transfer small parcels/goods from one location to another, where delivery is guaranteed between 48–72 hours.

Domestic Couriers

These are used to transfer documents and parcels to different locations in the same country.

International Couriers

These are used to transfer documents and parcels to international locations, using air as the mode of transfer.

India presently has 2300 courier companies and the courier industry on the whole is worth Rs 7000 crore and is growing at the rate of 25 per cent every year.

EMPLOYMENT OPPORTUNITIES IN THE LOGISTICS INDUSTRY[51]

Poor working conditions, low pay-scales relative to alternate careers, poor or non-existent manpower policies, and prevalence of unscrupulous practices have added to the segment's woes, creating an image of the segment that holds few attractions for those seeking employment. However, this scenario will significantly change in the years to come.

Demand for People in this Industry

Employment in this industry is expected to grow from 16.74 million in 2013 to 28.40 million by 2022 as given in Table 19.2.[52]

Table 19.2: Heading, centre align: Incremental Human Resource Requirement (2013–17, 2017–22) and Skill Gaps
Workforce is expected to reach 28.40 million by 2022

	Employment (in million)			Employment growth 2013–17	Employment growth 2017–22
	2013	2017	2022	(in million)	(in million)
Courier services	0.23	0.30	0.36	0.07	0.06
Packaging	0.22	0.26	0.30	0.04	0.04
Passenger railways	0.83	1.11	1.35	0.28	0.24
Passenger transport roadways	9.10	12.59	15.60	3.49	3.01
Rail freight	0.13	0.18	0.22	0.05	0.04
Road freight	5.79	7.99	9.88	2.20	1.90
Warehousing	0.43	0.57	0.69	0.14	0.12
Total	**16.74**	**23.00**	**28.40**	**6.26**	**5.41**

- The sector currently employs over 16.74 million employees and is slated to employ more than 28.4 million employees by 2022. This implies additional creation of 11.7 million jobs in the nine-year period.
- The period 2013–17 will see a marginally higher growth in employment vis-à-vis 2017–22 due to an expected increase in the level of automation in logistics and warehousing operations, leading higher productivity levels of the workforce.

Before moving on to Section 2 we would like to briefly profile a high-achiever in this sector.

SUBHASISH CHAKRABORTY

DTDC Courier and Cargo Ltd was founded in the year 1990, with Mr Chakraborty as the Founder, Chairman, and Managing Director. He has been instrumental in building DTDC's 240+ networks and also taking DTDC global. The company is doing extremely well under his leadership.

Mr Chakraborty is a Gold Medallist in Chemistry from the University of Calcutta and has an Advanced Management Programme Diploma from the Indian School of Business (ISB) to his credit.

He has won various accolades and awards for his outstanding work. Through his unique vision of a franchise-based business model, he has taken DTDC to newer heights and provided employment to 5500 people who are his direct employees and to 5800-plus Channel Partners. He is commonly looked up to as the 'Guru' in his company. He truly is a living inspiration to many.

SECTION 2
ENTRY-LEVEL JOB ROLES

CODE	ROLE
LOG 1	Courier Executive
LOG 2	Transport Logistics Executive
LOG 3	Warehousing Executive

LOG 1 COURIER EXECUTIVE

Job Description

Courier Executives are generally employed by courier companies to pick-up and deliver messages, parcels, and so on at the customer's doorstep within stipulated timelines. They follow a route plan to deliver or pick-up the packages, figure out the correct address, reach the place, pick-up/deliver and complete the required documentation. Though this job is done by non-graduates too, many graduates start their career in this industry in this role but quickly move up the ladder to supervisory levels. The courier industry believes in the dignity of labour and so many top industry professionals started their career in this role.

Typical Responsibilities

The role of a Courier Executive involves a lot of travel within the city and in the case of Air-Travel Couriers, a lot of outstation travel. You will first need to reach the main office and collect the parcels/couriers to be delivered and start going to places as per the schedule and location allotted to you.

Your activities include the following.
- Collecting packages that need to be delivered from the office.
- Taking from a roster, the customer addresses and contact details.

- Seeing that the packages are placed properly in the delivery vehicles.
- Keeping packages safely so that they don't get damaged.
- Calling customers in case there is any confusion regarding addresses.
- Delivering the package.
- Completing the delivery documentation.
- Submitting the sheet at the office by the end of the day.

In case of a pick-up, the process is the reverse. The packages are picked up, weighed, packed as per the company procedures, the required documentation completed, and the package is finally delivered to the designated office for onward transportation.

Courier Executive: A Profile

Likely salary with 1–3 years of experience	Rs 80,000–Rs 110,000 per annum plus reimbursements of conveyance and travel expenses.
Targets	Quantum of pick-up. Error-free documentation. Ensuring correct billing in case of a pick-up.
Challenges	This job is repetitive and very transactional and there are daily and hourly deadlines to be met, which is the biggest challenge. Dealing with thefts or damages en route.
Skills	Apart from basic communication and documentation skills, you must have a good idea about the local geography in which you operate and must also know how to drive a two-wheeler.
Stress	Low to moderate.
Travel on the job	Extensive travel is required.
Impact on stakeholders	The customers and the courier company are highly impacted by this role.
Career prospects	Your career prospects will depend upon your hard work and commitment to the company. Since the industry is growing very fast, graduates can quickly move into an office role in logistics, and in five to eight years become the Manager of a local office or become a Franchisee of the courier company.

Future salary with 5–7 years of experience	Rs 250,000–Rs 350,000 per annum.

A Practitioner's View
Courier Executive, Pratap, Hyderabad

Mr Pratap from Hyderabad has been working as a Courier Executive for the past four years. When we asked him about his experiences, he said:

'I work to earn a living. Initially, when I joined this profession, I did not know anything about the job but as I started working I gained some experience. I had to travel to offices, collect couriers from there and send them to different cities. I now have knowledge about how the company works. It has helped me become more confident and has also helped me improve my communication. I now have respect in society as, even though I do not hold a very big official position, I am employed and independent.'

We also talked to an experienced Courier Executive who works with a company that delivers packages overseas. He said:

'I like doing this job because I like to travel. I have learnt to organize my time so that I can deliver couriers on time. I have also developed good relations with my co-workers. I am the kind of person who loves to travel all day in a vehicle, and have been doing this role for the last fifteen years!'

LOG 2 TRANSPORT LOGISTICS EXECUTIVE

Job Description

Imagine a courier company which picks up parcels from one place (in one city) and delivers them to another place (in another city). Typically, there may be hundreds of pick-up sites and drop sites. All these pick-ups must be completed within a specified time-frame, brought to a common place and sorted based on the destination cities, and then shipped to those destinations. Again, at those destinations, all parcels are received at a common place. They are sorted based on drop destinations and then dispatched. Many vehicles are involved in the process. Inter-city shipments may happen through air, road, or rail.

Irrespective of which mode you use, the parcel must reach the right destination on time, without damage, at the lowest cost.

The Transport Logistics Executive has the required skills to manage, coordinate, and direct transportation activities within the organization. She/he is responsible for managing schedules and routes, managing budgets, the workforce of drivers, and also providing training to them. Transport Logistics Executives are employed mostly by courier/parcel companies, transportation companies, manufacturing companies, and e-commerce companies.

Typical Responsibilities

- Ensuring the billing is done as per company policies.
- Supervising the team to ensure proper distribution of work to ensure that all deadlines are met.
- Understanding the company's transport policies and adhering to them.
- Communicating work schedules to drivers.
- Managing budgets and costs.
- Planning and scheduling routes.
- Monitoring vehicle movement and solving the Delivery Team's problems.
- Scheduling vehicle maintenance.
- Maintaining necessary records about employees, vehicles, drivers, routes, and so on.
- Coordinating and communicating with other internal departments to prioritize tasks.
- Managing the safety of employees, parcels, and other items.
- Handling customer complaints on non-delivery or damaged delivery.

Transport Logistics Executive: A Profile

Likely salary with 1–3 years of experience	Rs 180,000–Rs 250,000 per annum.
Targets	Ensure on-time delivery percentage. Minimize customer complaints. Minimize revenue-loss due to wrong billing. Optimize cost of operations.

Challenges	This job is very transactional and there are daily and hourly deadlines to be met, which is the biggest challenge. Defective documentation is one of the biggest reasons for delayed delivery and the challenge is ensuring that the team gives priority to documentation. Ensuring that the safety norms are met by drivers and other employees who tend to take shortcuts.
Skills	An eye for detail. Good planning skills. Good organizing skills. Problem-solving skills.
Stress	Moderate.
Travel on the job	You may need to travel occasionally.
Impact on stakeholders	The customers are impacted by this role.
Career prospects	Transport Logistics Executives can be promoted to Senior Executives in two years, become Branch Managers in five to seven years, and Regional Managers in ten years.
Future salary with 5–7 years of experience	Rs 350,000–Rs 500,000 per annum.

A Practitioner's View

Logistics Team Leader, Usha D., Bengaluru

Ms Usha has around three years experience in the area of logistics management. When we asked her to share her experiences with us, she said:

'The job involves a lot of co-ordination activities. You need to maintain strong relations with the workforce of the company. When I was a Logistics Executive, I had to assign a particular location to a particular vehicle, arrange for all the parcels and documents pertaining to that area to be loaded into the allotted vehicle, provide the drivers with the addresses of people to whom the courier had to be delivered, note the driver's details, track the vehicle, and ensure that parcels were being delivered as per schedule.

'It requires lot of patience to handle and coordinate so many activities, but the experience is one of its kind. As you gain experience, you will move into the management and supervision mode. It is definitely a good career option for freshers who wish to have an exposure in this particular area.'

LOG 3 WAREHOUSING EXECUTIVE

Job Description

To understand this role, you need to understand how a consumer goods company ensures that the supermarket closest to your house always stocks the brand of toothpaste that you regularly buy. The supermarket (called the dealer) orders and receives the toothpaste not from the company's factory, but from the nearest stocking point or warehouse. The Warehouse Executive's job is to ensure that his warehouse never runs out of the popular toothpaste brand that your dealer orders. He does this by placing orders and receiving stocks from the company's manufacturing plant or stock point, in time.

A Warehouse Executive is someone who is responsible for assisting the Warehousing Manager in a wide range of warehousing duties/activities.

Typical Responsibilities

- Placing orders for supplies.
- Ensuring that the warehouse is stocked with required goods/material in a scientific and safe manner.
- Examining and inspecting the items for any defects or breakages and update the Manager regarding the same.
- Keeping the warehouse clean and organized.
- Maintaining a record of all activities taking place in the warehouse at all times.
- Keeping a record of inventory.
- Conducting a quality check of products before dispatch.
- Preparing despatch documentation.

Warehousing Executive: A Profile

Likely salary with 1–3 years of experience	Rs 100,000–Rs 200,000 per annum.
Targets	Minimize inventory levels in the warehouse, but do not create a 'stock-out'. Perfect documentation.
Challenges	To keep the warehouse operational at all times. Controlling pilferage and breakages. Periodic stock-checking and reconciliation.
Skills	An eye for detail. Excellent documentation skill.
Stress	Low.
Travel on the job	No travel, since you will be working from the warehouse itself.
Impact on stakeholders	Your dealers and customers are influenced by this role.
Career prospects	You can become Warehouse In-charge in five years. Career progression thereafter, depends upon picking up additional skills.
Future salary with 5–7 years of experience	Rs 250,000–Rs 350,000 per annum.

A Practitioner's View
Warehouse Manager, Rahul Jadhav, Ahmedabad

Mr Jadhav has been working in Ahmedabad as a Warehouse Manager for the last two years. When we spoke to him and asked him about his views regarding the job, he said:

'My job involves dispatching against sales orders, raising and maintaining tax invoices, maintaining stocks in the depot, and so on. I am very comfortable working in this role as I like dealing with my customers (dealers who sell the stock to consumers are my customers), maintain strong relations with them, and understand what exactly their needs are. If someone wishes to pursue a career in the Supply Chain Sector, then it is a very good starting point to understand the process flow.'

20

MEDIA AND ENTERTAINMENT SECTOR

According to a National Council of Applied Economic Research (NCAER) 2010 report, 'a literate youth spends on an average five hours a day consuming one form of media or another', which seems rather a lot.

Some youth are addicted to news and information, but most are addicted to music, TV serials, and films. So media and entertainment are closely linked. Media delivers the entertainment that we need every day to make our life more interesting. Be it a corporate professional, a daily wage earner, or a housewife, entertainment is essential for all.

SECTION 1
BACKGROUND

ENTERTAINMENT

Entertainment has three main sub-sectors: films and TV content, music, and animation/special effects/gaming.

Films

Do you know that India is the largest producer of films in the world, even bigger than Hollywood? That over 23 million people watch a movie every single day?[53] Three billion tickets are sold every year.

As many as 1,600 films in various languages of India were produced annually in 2012.

Media

The media has five sub-sectors: print, radio, TV, outdoor media, and the internet.

That India is the second-largest newspaper market in the world after China even though the average newspaper penetration in India is low at around 15 per cent? That the penetration exceeds 70 per cent in cities and suburban areas, but in villages it is as low as 5 per cent?

That over 98 per cent of all Indian newspapers are home-delivered and the scale of operations is really big—over 300,000 vendors and beat boys deliver approximately 45 million copies of newspapers every morning in over 5,000 cities and towns? That 67 per cent of newspaper revenue comes from advertising; subscription revenue (the money you pay when you buy the newspaper) contributes only 33 per cent of total newspaper revenue? That, of the top 10 circulated newspapers, only one is English (*Times of India*) and growth is also mainly in the Hindi and vernacular mediums.

Television

Television first came to India in the form of Doordarshan (DD)—the national television network of India—on 15 September 1959. Today there are 15 private TV companies.

As per Wikipedia, as of June 2014, seven direct to home (DTH) operators served 68 million subscribers of whom 38 million were active. India is poised to overtake the US, to be the world's largest DTH market soon.

Radio

All India Radio (AIR) was established in 1936 and today is one of the largest radio networks in the world, including AIR FM.[54] With over 36 FM Operators, the FM channels are likely to go up to 839 from the current number of 245. Interestingly, many media houses like the Times Group, Star TV, and Malayala Manorama today own radio stations.

MEDIA AND ENTERTAINMENT (M&E) INDUSTRY SIZE

With the massive reach of TV, the advent of web technology, digitization, increase in regional media, in the numbers of movie-goers and several other factors, the Indian M&E industry is growing rapidly. With over 1000 movies produced each year, 600 TV channels, 70,000 newspapers, and over 20 radio FM stations, the industry's future looks very bright.

The M&E industry is expected to double to Rs 178,000 crore between 2013 to 2018. TV, print, and films contribute 86 per cent of the revenues.

EMPLOYMENT OPPORTUNITIES IN THE M&E INDUSTRY

The total current employment in the M&E Sector is estimated at ~0.46 million, and is projected to grow at a compound annual growth rate (CAGR) of 13 per cent to reach 0.75 million by 2017.

The Film and Television Sectors employ a 56 per cent of the workforce in the M&E industry. The bulk of job roles in the M&E industry, are depicted sub-sector wise in Table 20.1. However, many of these jobs require experience. Jobs for fresh graduates are limited.

M&E jobs are spread over five hubs, namely, Delhi/NCR/Haryana, Maharashtra, West Bengal, Telangana, and Karnataka.

This industry will add 0.9 million jobs during the period 2013 to 2022 (please see Table below for details).

Table 20.1: Employment in M&E Sub-sectors[55]

Sub-sector	Employment (in million)		
	2013	2017	2022
Television	0.14	0.28	0.64
Print	0.06	0.07	0.13
Radio	0.02	0.03	0.04
Animation, VFX, and gaming	0.02	0.03	0.04
Films	0.16	0.24	0.44
Overall Sector	**0.4**	**0.65**	**1.3**

Employment challenges in the M&E industry

Lack of regular employment in the film industry

Across India, approximately 25 per cent of the total people employed in the M&E Sector work in the film industry. A majority of them are contract workers/freelancers as opposed to full-time employees. On the contrary, in 2010 in the UK, only 5 per cent of the total media and entertainment workforce was employed in the film sector with only 25 per cent freelancers. A large number of people are self-employed as freelancers even in TV content production.

The job growth in print media is poor

Internet and TV are severely impacting the job growth in the print media industry especially in the English media.

Wages in print media

A government-appointed wage board governs journalists' wages and journalists also have strong unions. These two practices have resulted in 'non-professional' wage and employment practices like contract staffing and low wages for vernacular journalists.

Before moving on to entry-level job roles, we'd like to briefly profile a high-achiever in the media world.

PRANNOY LAL ROY[56]

Prannoy Roy is a well-known award-winning Indian journalist and media personality. He along with his journalist wife Radhika Roy founded NDTV (New Delhi Television), of which he remains the Executive Co-chairperson. He is also a qualified Chartered Accountant, a fellow of the Institute of Chartered Accountants (England & Wales), and has a PhD in Economics from the Delhi School of Economics.

He has been an Economic Adviser in the Indian government's Ministry of Finance and an Associate Professor at the Delhi School of Economics and has, in his avatar as a media person, interviewed many political leaders during his career. In addition to winning international and national awards for his programmes, Roy has been adjudged 'Television Personality of the Millennium' by an *Indian Express* poll.

Roy's network has focused on a number of social issues through campaigns like the annual 'Greenathon', '7 Wonders of India', and the 'Save Our Tigers' campaign, which won the Best Public Service Campaign for a Brand by a News Channel in 2011. Other campaigns include 'Support My School' and 'Marks for Sports' in 2010 and 2011. The *'Jeene ki Aasha'* campaign, which focuses on maternal and childcare issues around the country was launched in 2011 with the Gates Foundation. NDTV also honours deserving people from all walks of life with its 'Indian of the Year' Awards. Prannoy Roy truly is an example of excellence to many.

SECTION 2
ENTRY-LEVEL JOB ROLES FOR GRADUATES

CODE	ROLE
M&E 1	Print Content Editor
M&E 2	Radio Jockey
M&E 3	News Reporter (Print/TV)
M&E 4	TV Anchor/Presenter
M&E 5	Public Relations Officer (PRO)

M&E 1 PRINT CONTENT EDITOR

Job Description

Every morning when you read the newspaper do you ever wonder how the readability is maintained every day? Many reporters write their reports in different styles, but when published, all these reports have something in common—they are easy to read and comprehend. Who does this job? It is the Print Content Editor.

A Print Content Editor's main job is to edit and rewrite any content from the readers' point of view. Most writers, in the excitement of writing, may not focus on the point that the audience must understand what they are writing. So the Print Content Editor is someone who makes an article readable by simplifying complicated sentences, breaking up the copy into paragraphs, adding headlines, and so on.

They work on the copy (the written matter that has to be edited is called 'copy'), check it for any factual mistakes, logical/grammatical errors, and make sure that the content is properly formatted. They also edit or remove any negative or controversial content that can affect the reputation of the publication.

One of the key responsibilities of a Print Content Editor is to ensure that editorial guidelines are met. They also edit English or vernacular content. Vernacular content editing is a new emerging field.

Typical Responsibilities

- Comprehending and interpreting editorial guidelines.
- Editing articles, online advertisements, books, newspapers, websites, and so on.

- Correcting errors in spelling and grammar.
- Suggesting catchy headlines to attract reader attention.
- Rewriting the entire copy if necessary, without changing the meaning.
- Cross-checking the data that goes into an article and validating the same before it is published.
- Working closely with content writers, individual writers, and reporters.
- Overseeing the activities of Trainee Editors, supervising and training them.
- Attending editorial meetings and providing ideas for new stories.

Print Content Editor: A Profile

Likely salary with 1–3 years of experience	Rs 200,000–Rs 400,000 per annum.
Targets	You will be measured by the quality (nil errors, high readability) and speed of editing (number of words per hour). The challenge is achieving both speed and quality. Strict adherence to editorial policies.
Challenges	Adapting to various styles of writing of different writers. Cross-checking data for validation. Working under enormous deadline pressure.
Skills	Good communication and writing skills. An eye for detail. An excellent grip over the language you are editing in. Good general knowledge. Very advanced computer and internet research skills.
Stress	Moderate.
Travel on the job	None.
Impact on stakeholders	Readers are impacted by this role.
Career prospects	Print Content Editors are traditionally hired by newspapers and book publishers. With the arrival of the internet, they are also used for editing e-learning and web content. Career progression would mean promotion to Senior Editor and Desk Head, managing a team of Editors.

| Future salary with 5–7 years of experience | Rs 400,000–Rs 600,000 per annum. |

A Practitioner's View
Print Content Editor, Fernandes, Kerala

Mr Fernandes is working with an online content company. When we asked him about his experiences and the job role, he said:

'Editing is a mission for me, personally. It may surprise you to learn that many who seem to have a good command over the language, don't write as well they speak. Editing thus enhances the quality of written material and makes reading it enjoyable. There are writers who tend to make silly mistakes and sometimes we do come across articles that we read with a sense of irritation. One of the aspects of good writing is not making silly mistakes.

'I like doing this job because I can improve what people write, and educate them towards better and more effective writing. Personally, I have learnt to understand my own limitations as an Editor. In addition, I have learnt to appreciate other people's points of view on any subject. Professionally too, I have learnt various technical skills required for the job. I am indebted to my colleagues for their feedback on my work. Yes, on the whole this role provides satisfaction that you are doing something worthwhile.

'Before I recommend this job to a fresher, I would look to see whether they are well read, have excellent language skills, and have an eye for detail. I encourage people to opt for this job because it provides challenges and great job satisfaction. Despite the pressures of deadlines and quality, I have found that this job is as gratifying as teaching, which I did for many years.'

M&E 2 RADIO JOCKEY

Job Description

Radio channels are coming up with many new and interesting programmes for listeners. The people who host these talk shows and make them exciting for the listener are called Radio Jockeys. People can communicate with Radio Jockeys through live calls and emails. They play songs as per the request of the listeners; interact with audiences over a particular topic or provide general knowledge on a topic to the public.

Typical Responsibilities

- Selecting and shortlisting music to be played during your programme.
- Providing traffic and weather updates to listeners on a regular basis.
- Preparation and presentation of content and sound bytes from people for your show.
- Giving voiceovers for promos, teasers, advertisements.
- Connecting with PR agencies for contacts with celebrities.
- Updating programme details on the website on a daily basis.
- Taking sound bytes of celebrities during festivals, programmes, events, and so on.
- Interacting with audiences during live broadcasts.

Radio Jockey: A Profile

Likely salary with 1–3 years of experience	Rs 200,000–Rs 350,000 per annum.
Targets	Increase the number of listeners by implementing innovative ideas. Keep listeners engaged and maximize audience participation.
Challenges	Audiences are very demanding and the programme must keep evolving to keep them engaged. Competition is very intense and advertisers tend to opt for only the top programmes. Reaching the top is difficult and staying there is even more difficult.

Skills	Excellent command over the language and voice modulation. Ability to connect with young audiences is a must. A fertile and imaginative mind.
Stress	Moderate.
Travel on the job	This job does involve limited travel to cover events.
Impact on stakeholders	The listeners and the radio channel you work for are impacted by this role.
Career prospects	Your career prospects are excellent because every channel wants to grab the best.
Future salary with 5–7 years of experience	Rs 400,000–Rs 600,000 per annum.

A Practitioner's View
Radio Jockey, Aabir Lahiry, Jabalpur

Mr Aabir has been working as a Radio Jockey with Radio Mirchi for over a year. He hosts a morning breakfast show 'Hello Jabalpur', which is mainly based on current issues. When we asked him about his experiences, he said:

'It feels very good when you start creating an impact on a lot of people's lives through a programme. From being a totally unknown person to becoming a little master, this experience has been very hi-energy. The experience is incomparable, as at the end of the day what you get is ultimate satisfaction, and of course, money. I have learnt a lot of things.

'Trust me, if you are here in this job and you are working with your soul, this will turn out to be the best job in the world for you. Every time you just enjoy, laugh, giggle, and innovate. This job has taught me how to handle tough situations. This job is more about dealing with tough times. It is also about time management. This job has given me joy and happiness which I think is needed by almost everyone these days. Those who don't know, Radio Mirchi is a part of the Times of India Group. So being a part of India's biggest media house has obviously given me a lot of professional acclaim.'

M&E 3 NEWS REPORTER (PRINT/TV)

Job Description

A Reporter is someone who keeps the general public informed about happenings, news, and events. Reporters are responsible for visiting the event site, interviewing people, collecting data, writing the report and in case of TV, presenting the news stories. Their main target is to present factual and relevant news to the general public. They cover various fields such as news and politics, sports, entertainment, arts and science, finance and equity markets.

Typical Responsibilities

- Scanning the web, talking to people, regularly visiting important places like the State Assembly or the High Court, for current happenings.
- Identifying news which will be of interest to the audience and getting prior approval for the story.
- Connecting with key people involved to get evidence and validate the news.
- Covering breaking news (in the case of TV) by reporting from the event site. Writing the story as per the editorial policy and submitting it to the Sub-editor (in the case of a Print Reporter).
- Interviewing newsmakers, celebrities, film stars, sports stars, bureaucrats, politicians, entrepreneurs, social workers, and information experts like lawyers/doctors.
- Re-writing scripts and stories as per the Editor's feedback.
- Working closely with seniors, Editors, Sub-editors, Cameramen, other Reporters.

News Reporter (Print/TV): A Profile

Likely salary with 1–3 years of experience	Rs 200,000–Rs 350,000 per annum.
Targets	Maximize the number of original stories submitted. Minimize the number of important stories missed. Quality of the story as measured by reader/viewer feedback, and the story picked up by the competition.

Challenges	Reporting first at the place of action, before competitors arrive (in the case of TV). Being up and running all the time to cover current happenings, even during odd hours. You have to be the first to spot the story and cover it. News events are happening all the time. You are known by the stories you break first. In the face of intense competition, identifying the breaking story ahead of seasoned reporters requires an extensive contact network which has to be built over time. Cross-checking data/facts for validations. Error in reporting can be costly, including litigations, loss of credibility, and so on. Ensuring that you present facts to people and not your opinion. You will get various versions of the event/incident, but you have to analyse and present a balanced and true version. Due to negative reporting, celebrities are not accessible and tend to avoid the media, but you are expected to reach them and get a quote, within strict deadlines.
Skills	An eye for detail and an ability to convert mundane news into an engaging story. Enormous patience and listening skills. Networking skills (for building news sources and getting access to celebrities). Researching skills, writing skills (for print), and presentation skills (for TV). Wide knowledge about various subjects like history, economics, politics, and the ability to spot the news value.
Stress	Moderate to high.
Travel on the job	Yes. This job involves travel both in the city of posting and to nearby coverage areas. Much of the travel will be unplanned.
Impact on stakeholders	The viewers/public at large and the employer are impacted by this role.
Career prospects	In three to five years, you can become a Senior Reporter and in ten-plus years you can join the Editorial Desk (in case of Print), or become the News Chief for the publication/channel for your area of work. You will be invited to speak on TV or

	radio shows after acquiring experience and knowledge. Many Reporters stay in reporting for life, because it is intoxicating and the contact network of politicians and celebrities is very useful.
Future salary with 5–7 years of experience	Rs 400,000–Rs 600,000 per annum. Reporters' salaries are generally low except for the top few.

A Practitioner's View

Chief Correspondent, Radhika Mohan Iyer, Bengaluru

Ms Iyer is NDTV's Chief Correspondent, South India, and has around ten years of work experience in this field. When we asked her about her experience as a Reporter and why she would recommend it to a fresher, she said:

'I am ten years old in the Indian news media industry. I began my reporting stint in Doordarshan in 2003. I was presenting a news bulletin called "States Scan" and then moved to the India Today group. I have begun my ninth year at NDTV now.

'Journalism is more than a just a "job". It is empowerment. It has made me a sensitive being. Covering terror attacks, bomb blasts, air crashes, tsunami, floods, and earthquakes not only requires courage but a great deal of sensitivity. The job is very challenging, physically, emotionally, and mentally. It has made me a better person apart from a better writer and presenter. It is a job which teaches you the significance of truth no matter how tough it may be to believe.

'I recommend journalism only to those who have grit and courage to stand by accuracy and transparency at all times. It demands a lot of your time. Give it all the time, because you must be born for it. If you do not have the passion, you will not be able to sustain the pressure. Many think presenting news requires glamour. If it were only about glamour, I wouldn't have been here.'

A Practitioner's View
Senior Reporter, V. Swathi, Hyderabad

Ms Swathi is a Senior Reporter with *The Hindu*. When we asked her about her experiences working as a Print Journalist/Reporter and why she would recommend it to a fresher, she said:

'I love my job because no day is the same in this field. I get to meet newer challenges every day. The job carries a positive power with which I can bring a change in people's lives. Being a journalist has brought a great change in my persona. It has made me a better thinker, broadminded, and less selfish with less inhibitions and obviously, more social skills. At a professional level, it gave me an identity and a purpose.

'The job offers a very good exposure to life to begin with. It constantly opens up newer horizons and fresh perspectives for any curious youngster ready to explore life and the world. Once a journalist, you don't want to be anything else, but at the same time, you get the attitude to be anything if need be.'

M&E 4 TV ANCHOR/PRESENTER

Job Description

It is a fact that all the news channels have the news programme at the same time, so how do you select the channel to watch? You select it based on who is the News Presenter and how the news is presented.

To build a viewership for news, two things are very important—credibility and viewer engagement. Credibility comes from accuracy of the news and the News Presenter is partly responsible (along with the News Editor) for selecting the news that will go on air. The viewer engagement comes from the way the news is presented. Hence the role of the News Presenter is crucial to the success of any programme.

Many of the viewers also want to hear an analysis of the news from many experts and this news debate often determines the popularity of the news programme. Someone has to decide the experts to call, prepare the questions in advance, and moderate the discussions. A Programme Anchor does this.

The Programme Anchor hosts a variety of programmes in addition to the news, such as reality shows, sports events, movie and entertainment shows, one-on-one celebrity interviews on TV.

Typical Responsibilities

- Conducting detailed research on various topics that need to be featured in the news programme.
- Identifying experts to be invited for panel discussions and TV shows.
- Moderating panel discussions.
- Preparing, reading from auto cues, memorizing scripts.
- Coordinating with various other members of the Production Team like Field Reporters, Cameramen, and interviewees.
- During the news programme:
  - speak to various people on the field;
  - interview politicians, spokespersons, sports personalities, celebrities, and others;
  - take calls from the general public and interact with them; and
  - provide viewers with the right information.

TV Anchor/Presenter: A Profile

Likely salary with 1-3 years of experience	Rs 300,000–Rs 550,000 per annum.
Targets	Rating of the programme which determines the advertising revenue from the programme.
Challenges	Reading the news correctly and confidently without making any mistakes. Conducting a balanced and unbiased discussion, despite provocation from panellists. Holding engaging conversations with a variety of experts, despite having superficial knowledge yourself. Responding well to unplanned events that may suddenly arise while you are presenting the news.

Skills	Excellent communication skills and command over the language.
	Sound researching and interviewing skills.
	Comfortable in front of the camera—camera presence.
	An analytical and incisive mind.
	Strong memory for facts.
Stress	Moderate.
Travel on the job	Minimal.
Impact on stakeholders	The audiences/viewers of the programme and the broadcasting agency you work for are impacted by this role.
Career prospects	You join as a Junior Presenter and can then grow up to the level of a Senior Presenter after three to five years. After seven to ten years, you can run your own show.
Future salary with 5–7 years of experience	Rs 400,000–Rs 750,000 per annum.

A Practitioner's View
News Presenter, Nagaraju, Hyderabad

Mr Nagaraju is a journalist who has been working as a News Presenter since 2009. When we asked him why he likes the job and why would he recommend this role to a fresher, he said:

'It was my passion to be a journalist and a news reader. It gave me a platform to learn and share on a daily basis. I get to share any recent developments, news, events with the society. If feels good to furnish people with right information. It is an extremely satisfying and challenging job at the same time. For someone who wishes to pursue a career in journalism/broadcasting journalism, this is a very good option.'

M&E 5 PUBLIC RELATIONS OFFICER (PRO)

Job Description

Let us take the example of an airline company that was functioning very well but had to suddenly shut down its operations due to huge debts.

During this crisis situation the management could not directly interact with the public. Therefore, they relied on their Public Relations Officer to handle the situation.

The Public Relations Officer (PRO) is thus an employee who advises the management on 'What to say' and 'Whom to talk to.' PROs can be hired by public bodies (like the government, railways), as well as private bodies.

So, basically, Public Relations is nothing but managing the reputation of the company. Thus, PROs use various forms of communication and media to maintain and enhance the image/ reputation of the organization they work for.

While large organizations have PROs on their rolls, many medium-sized companies hire PR firms which employ PR professionals, to do this job.

Typical Responsibilities

- Planning, preparing, presenting, and implementing PR strategies and promotional campaigns.
- Preparing an effective PR media plan and communications budget.
- Responding to calls and queries raised by the public, media, and competitors and answering the same via emails and phones.
- Drafting and releasing press releases as and when required, with the involvement of the management.
- Measuring media coverage/reach of the organization.
- Writing case studies and articles, and preparing speeches for the top management.
- Keeping a track of all promotional material like leaflets, brochures, and videos.
- Organizing, representing, and conducting press conferences during special events, making announcements.
- Training the senior management of the organization on how to deal with the media.

Public Relations Officer: A Profile

Likely salary with 1–3 years of experience	Rs 175,000–Rs 300,000 per annum.

Targets	Maximize positive coverage that enhances the reputation of the company. Minimize adverse publicity.
Challenges	Handling crisis situations. Managing media journalists with an agenda and a large ego.
Skills	Good communication skills. Good knowledge about various social media tools. Inter-personal and networking skills. Influencing skills. Organizing skills.
Stress	Moderate.
Travel on the job	You may have to travel occasionally to organize/conduct fairs, exhibitions, and conferences on behalf of the company.
Impact on stakeholders	The public at large, the customers, the management, and the investors of the company are impacted by this role.
Career prospects	There are two career paths for a PRO. The first option is to work with the PR Department of a large print/public sector/government body. The second option is to work for a PR agency which provides PR services to many customers.
Future salary with 5–7 years of experience	Rs 400,000–Rs 500,000 per annum.

A Practitioner's View
Public Relations Officer, Sanjeev Dixit
(name changed), Mumbai

Mr Dixit, has been working as a PRO for the past three years. When we asked him about the job, he said:

'Public Relations is a tough job. You need to be very careful with whatever you say or do, because it will affect the company's reputation. You need to have complete knowledge about the latest happenings and developments taking place so that you can be prepared to take on any questions from the media/public. Confidence is the key to doing your job well. Good networking skills can take you a long way.'

21

RETAIL SECTOR

SECTION 1
BACKGROUND

Our Retail Sector accounts to 23 per cent of the gross domestic product (GDP) and 8 per cent of employment, making India the fifth largest global retail investment destination. The Indian Retail Sector has undergone tremendous transformation over the last few years—from traditional (your neighbourhood *kirana* store) to organized retail (supermarkets, malls). Several new players—global and Indian—have entered into organized retail, making the competition stiffer.

CURRENT STATUS OF THE RETAIL INDUSTRY[57]

- The industry is moving towards a modern concept of retailing. The size of India's retail market was estimated at US$ 435 billion in 2010. Of this, US$ 414 billion (95 per cent of the market) was traditional retail and US$ 21 billion (5 per cent of the market) was organized retail. Hence organized retail is still very small in India but is expected to grow much faster than traditional retail.
- India's retail market is expected to grow to US$ 850 billion by 2020. Traditional retail is expected to grow to US$ 650 billion (76 per cent), while organized retail is expected to grow to US$ 200 billion by 2020.
- Organized retail is no more an urban phenomenon. It is estimated that Tier II and smaller cities will evolve fast to constitute the majority share of the Organized Retail Sector in the coming years.

The Retail Sector is divided into the following eight sub-sectors. Of the eight, food and grocery is by far the biggest with 69 per cent of the market, while apparel stores are the second biggest at 8 per cent of the market, followed by jewellery and consumer durables, IT at 6 per cent each. The remaining 11 per cent is shared between pharmacy, furniture/furnishing, footwear, and others.

WHERE IS THE INDIAN RETAIL MARKET HEADING?

According to *Retail 2020: Retrospect, Reinvent, Rewrite* (published in February 2015),[58] the Indian retail market is expected to grow to US$ 1 trillion by 2020. (While earlier researchers had put the estimate at US$ 880 billion).

Online Retail vs. Organized Retail

The online retail market is also seeing tremendous growth, as many people are welcoming online shopping due to the convenience and competitive prices. The online retail market is expected to grow from US$ 3.1 billion in FY 2013 to US$ 22 billion (from 10 per cent to more than 15 per cent of the organized retail market) by FY 2018.

The Government of India allows Foreign Direct Investment (FDI) up to 100 per cent in single brand retail and 51 per cent in multi-brand retail. This is likely to attract several global retailers in India and will give the organized retail a big push and professionalize this industry.

Job Opportunities

India has over 12 million retail outlets, employing 33 million-plus people. The Organized Retail Sector is the new hub of job opportunities, with many new malls and stores coming up.

ORGANIZED RETAIL OPERATES IN MANY FORMATS

- Convenience stores are street-corner or petrol pump stores with limited items for sale—for example, the Twenty-four-seven Stores of the Modi group.
- Neighbourhood general stores/kirana stores stock a variety of items for household needs.
- Supermarkets such as Food World, are self-service department stores with separate areas for different items.

- Hypermarkets such as Shoppers Stop/SPAR, are very large multiple-floor stores.
- Cash N Carry stores are stores where you have to buy in bulk or large quantities—for example, the Metro Cash N Carry stores.
- Discount stores such as Brand Factory, offer items at a discount because the stock is old or has some minor defect.
- Variety stores stock inexpensive household items that are not normally stocked in supermarkets.

Only 7 per cent of employment is in the Organized Retail Sector and the balance 93 per cent is in the Unorganized Retail Sector. Big Indian retail employers include Pantaloon Retail (Aditya Birla Nuvo Ltd), Shoppers Stop Ltd, Spencer's Retail (RPG Enterprises), Lifestyle Retail (Landmark Group). Other major domestic players in India are Bharti Retail, Tata Trent, Globus, Aditya Birla 'More', and Reliance Retail.

Some of the major foreign players who have entered the segment in India are Germany-based Metro Cash & Carry, Walmart USA, British retail chain Tesco in partnership with Tata Trent, Marks & Spencers in partnership with Reliance Retail.

The total employment in the retail industry is expected to reach 56 million (from the current 38.6 million) by 2022. For details see Table 21.1.

Table 21.1: Retail Sub-sector-wise Employment Growth Estimates[59]

Sub-sector	Employment (in million)			Employment growth 2013–17	Employment growth 2017–22	Employment growth 2013–22
	2013	2017	2022	(in million)	(in million)	(in million)
Food and grocery	19.6	21.36	24.44	1.76	3.08	4.81
Health and personal care	1.7	1.86	2.28	0.16	0.42	0.58
Home improvements	4.4	5.11	6.63	0.71	1.52	2.23
Leisure	0.8	0.84	0.92	0.04	0.08	0.12
Lifestyle	4.5	5.17	6.10	0.67	0.93	1.60
Auto sales	1.5	1.68	1.95	0.18	0.27	0.45

Jewellery retail	1.5	2.04	3.14	0.54	1.10	1.64
Food services	4.6	7.05	10.49	2.45	3.44	5.89
Total	**38.6**	**45.11**	**55.95**	**6.51**	**10.84**	**17.35**

Interestingly, it is one of the rare sectors where 77 per cent of the workforce is at entry-level.

WHAT ARE THE ENTRY-LEVEL JOBS IN RETAIL FOR GRADUATES?

At the core of retail lies store operations, which command anywhere between 70–95 per cent of total employment in organized retail. Buying and merchandising, as well as supply chain management and logistics (often outsourced) constitute about 5 to 10 per cent each. The other functions form about 2 to 5 per cent.

Jobs for graduates in store operations are limited to the roles of Customer Service Associate and Cashier since the bulk of the other entry-level jobs like delivery boys, pickers, and packers require only class 10 and class 12 qualifications. Other roles such as Assistant Store Manager requires work experience of two years or more. Hence only these two roles are covered here.

KISHORE BIYANI[60]

Mr Kishore Biyani is the Managing Director of Future Retail Ltd and the Group Chief Executive Officer of Future Group. Considered a pioneer of modern retail in India, Kishore's leadership has led Future Retail's emergence as India's leading retailer, operating multiple retail formats that cater to the entire basket of Indian consumers.

Kishore Biyani led the company's foray into organized retail with the opening of the Pantaloons family store in 1997. This was followed in 2001 with the launch of Big Bazaar, a uniquely Indian hypermarket format that democratized shopping in India. It blends the look and feel of the Indian bazaar with aspects of modern retail like choice, convenience, and quality. This was followed by a number of other formats including Food Bazaar, Central, and Home Town.

The year 2006 marked the evolution of Future Group that brought together the multiple initiatives taken by group companies in the areas of retail, brands, space, capital, logistics, and media. Kishore Biyani advocates 'Indianness' as the core value driving the group and the corporate credo 'Rewrite Rules, Retain Values.' Regularly ranked among India's most admired CEOs, he is the author of the book, *It Happened in India*. He has won numerous awards from government bodies and the private sector in India and abroad and is on the board of a number of bodies, including the National Innovation Foundation in India and the New York Fashion Board.

SECTION 2
ENTRY-LEVEL ROLES

CODE	ROLE
RTL 1	Billing Executive/Cashier
RTL 2	Customer Service Associate

RTL 1 BILLING EXECUTIVE/CASHIER

Job Description

When we visit Lifestyle, Shoppers Stop, Hypercity, and other big retail stores, we select products and head to the billing counter where a Billing Executive/Cashier takes charge. She/he collects the products, makes a bill and hands it over to us. She/he also informs us about offers available and also the benefits of becoming a member of the retail group.

Typical Responsibilities

- Receiving payment by cash, cheque, credit/debit cards.
- Issuing receipts, refunds, credits, or change due to customers.
- Resolving billing issues by directing them to the Customer Service Executive.
- Maintaining billing records and also records of all bills issued to customers.
- Training juniors by providing them practical experience.
- Receiving and processing all payments according to standard operating procedures (SOPs).

▫ Counting money in cash drawers at the beginning of your shift to ensure that amounts tally correctly with the sum left behind at the closure of the shop the previous day, and that there is adequate change.

Retail Billing Executive: A Profile

Likely salary with 1–3 years of experience	Rs 250,000–Rs 350,000 per annum for organized retail companies only.
Targets	Speed of billing services. Minimize customer quality complaints. Minimum billing errors.
Challenges	A very repetitive job. Managing rude customers.
Skills	Cash-handling skills. Communication skills.
Stress	Moderate.
Travel on the job	None.
Impact on stakeholders	The company you work for and the customers are impacted by your work.
Career prospects	You join as a Billing Executive/Cashier and can thereafter, move into a supervisory role managing many Executives.
Future salary with 5–7 years of experience	Rs 200,000–Rs 400,000 per annum, for organized retail companies only.

A Practioner's View
Retail Billing Executive, Jaya Lakshmi, Hyderabad

Mrs Jaya Lakshmi has been working as a Billing Executive with one of India's biggest supermarkets. She has around four years of experience in this field. When we spoke to her and asked her why she would recommend this role to a fresher, she said:

'This job has given me an opportunity to work with people with different personalities. My superiors, my co-workers, and customers who walk into the store to buy products, all have different ways of thinking and so the learning is high. Sometimes due to a customer's request we may have to cancel a product from the bill once the billing is done. This may cause a problem to us as superiors think we did not check with the customer before billing the product, and customers say, "Call your superiors", if we refuse to cancel or ask them to go to the Customer Service counter. Some are very impatient and do not like standing in the line for billing and so they try to break the line. If we refuse to bill their products, they get annoyed. So actually it is very challenging. Through these experiences only we learn how to deal with tough situations. Remaining positive is very important and also having a smile on your face can work wonders, making it easy for customers as well as us. There are a lot of new malls, outlets, showrooms coming up and so the opportunities are also immense. Therefore, I would certainly recommend this role to a fresher.'

RTL 2 CUSTOMER SERVICE ASSOCIATE

Job Description

Let us assume that you visit an outlet and shop for clothing. Once you come home and try it on, you realize that you picked a smaller size and you decide to exchange the shirt. When you go back to the store, you are asked to meet the Customer Service Executive.

Alternately, when we purchase something and find discrepancies in the bill, it is the Customer Service Associate who helps settle disputes.

Typical Responsibilities

- Responsible for handling complaints and solving disputes.
- Passing on positive feedback given by customers to the management.
- Accepting goods that have to be returned or exchanged.

- Ensuring that proper refunds are given to customers when required.
- Activating gift cards, membership cards, and vouchers.
- Constantly interacting with customers and taking their feedback.

Customer Service Associate: A Profile

Likely salary with 1–3 years of experience	Rs 150,000–Rs 250,000 per annum for organized retail companies only.
Targets	Ensuring customer satisfaction. Providing good service to walk-in customers.
Challenges	Convincing customers in case of any discrepancies, and also explaining the issue to the management.
Skills	Good interaction and communication skills. Presentable personality. Attention to detail.
Stress	Moderate.
Travel on the job	None.
Impact on stakeholders	The retail group you work for and the customers are impacted by your work.
Career prospects	You join as a Customer Service Executive and thereafter, opt for a supervisory role in the Administrative Department of the company.
Future salary with 5–7 years of experience	Rs 300,000–Rs 400,000 for organized retail companies only.

A Practitioner's View
Customer Service Associate, Ram Prasad (name changed), Hyderabad

Mr Prasad has been working in Hyderabad as a Customer Service Associate for a big retail group for the last three years. When we spoke to him and asked him about his views regarding the job, he said:

'My job is very interesting, as we get to deal with a variety of issues. Sometimes it gets challenging as customers do not cooperate and do not give us sufficient time to attend to the issue. But when we are able to solve customer issues it gives immense happiness because that is what our job demands. The prospects are very bright and so I would recommend a career in this field for freshers as the exposure is high and so is the learning.'

22
TELECOM SECTOR

SECTION 1
BACKGROUND

Human messengers, pigeons, beacons of light, drum beats, telegraphs, telephone, tele printers, radio, wireless telephones, email, satellite phones, SMS, chats, smartphones, video conferencing, Voice over IP (Skype)—we have come a long way in telecommunications technology. Telecom today, is the lifeline of any business. Healthcare, agriculture, defence, manufacturing, education, media, and almost every other sector depend on telecom. Finally, telecom has made the world a global village—a grandmother in a village in India can speak to her grandson in New York in an instant. The internet, which all of us take for granted, exists because of the telecom network.

Phones were a luxury item as recently as the 1980s. Today India has over 900 million subscribers, the world's second-largest telecommunications market with a market size of Rs 57,400 crore (as of September 2013), and has registered exceptional growth over the years.

The Telecom Sector has the following sub-sectors: Telecom Service Providers, Telecom Infrastructure Providers, Telecom Equipment Manufacturing, Telecom Network and IT Management, and Telecom Retail.

DID YOU KNOW THIS?

- India is No. 1 in the world in terms of telecom affordability, in a survey of 144 nations. Call rates in India are the cheapest in the world, with the average realization per minute (ARPM) of Rs 0.48.

- India's telecommunication network is the second largest, after China, in the world.
- According to the TRAI report dated 23 November 2015, mobile phone subscriber base in India recorded 6.71 per cent year-on-year growth to 980.81 million users in quarter-2 of 2015.
- Teledensity or the number of telephones per 100 individuals, was 136 in urban India (1.3 phones per person) and 42 in rural India. Most of the new connections will have to come from rural India.
- Mobile phone penetration is expected to grow to 72 per cent by 2016.
- India is the second largest mobile-handset market in the world with revenues of Rs 36,000 crore in 2012–13.
- Telecom requires a lot of specialized software (it's called telecom software), which connects telecom devices and computers.
- India is expected to be one of the top 10 broadband markets in the world.
- 90 per cent of the Rs 50,000-crore telecom equipment market is imported, and one of the big priorities of the central government is to make companies manufacture/assemble telecom equipment in India.
- According to a Microsoft report, India will emerge as the leading player in the virtual world by having 700 million internet users (of the 4.7 billion global users) by 2025, growing from 165 million users in March 2013 and holding the third position in 2012.
- With the advent of 4G mobile technology, in five years, most of us will be using video telephony with the smart handset.

THE TELECOM MARKET

Telecom Service-providers Market

Among the two technologies in this space—wired line and wireless—clearly the wireless is growing in leaps and bounds while the wire line market, where BSNL holds a 65 per cent market share, is declining. Airtel leads the market (22 per cent share), Reliance (13 per cent), Vodafone (18 per cent), Idea (15 per cent), BSNL (11 per cent), Tata (7 per cent), and Aircel (7 per cent), with the remaining share being held by other small operators.

Telecom Infrastructure

Many of the Telecom Service Providers have hived off their telecom tower infrastructure to specialist infra companies like Indus, or GTL. But this sub-sector is unlikely to witness major growth in the immediate future.

Network and IT

This sub-sector is dominated by Tech Mahindra, Tata Consultancy Services (TCS), Wipro, Infosys, HCL Technologies, and Sasken Communication Technologies. These are traditional IT companies with specialized divisions for the telecom industry.

Telecom Equipment

This sub-sector is dominated by foreign companies like Ericsson, Nokia Siemens Networks (NSN), ZTE Corp., Huawei, Alcatel, and Samsung. This sub-sector is struggling for profits.

Handset and Retail

The top three players—Samsung, Micromax, and Microsoft (Nokia)— together had a market share of only 43 per cent in the year 2014 and the remaining 57 per cent market was shared by many smaller brands.

While many retail stores opened in 2014 and 2015 for selling mobile phones, the 'e-tailers' like Flipkart and Amazon are quickly gaining the market share at the cost of the 'brick and mortar' retailers.

WHAT ARE THE EMPLOYMENT OPPORTUNITIES?[61]

The Indian Telecom Sector is expected to create 4 million direct and indirect jobs over the next five years on the back of the government's efforts to increase penetration in rural areas, along with growth in the smartphone numbers and internet usage, according to estimates by Randstad India.

In the next few years, the telecommunications industry is expected to generate a significant number of new jobs. Key segments include the following:

- Retail and distribution.
- Service-providers.
- Network and IT vendors (managed services).

Workforce requirement[62]

The total employment in the Telecom Sector will double from 2.08 in 2013 to 4.16 by 2022 as can be seen from Table 22.1. The growth till 2017 will be slow but thereafter growth will pick-up.

The employment in sub-sectors in Telecom in 2013 and in 2022 is shown in Table 22.2 below. As can be seen the major employment growth will be in retail of handsets, followed by Telecom Service Providers.

Table 22.1: Telecom Sector Employment in 2013 and 2022[63]

Sector	Employment (2013)	Employment (2022)	Employment growth between 2013 and 2022
	All figures are in million		
Telecom service-providers	0.60	1.20	0.60
Infrastructure providers	0.10	0.13	0.03
Telecom equipment manufacturing	0.45	0.64	0.19
Network and IT	0.45	0.77	0.32
Handsets and telecom retail	0.46	1.44	0.98
Total	**2.06**	**4.18**	**2.12**

WHERE ARE THE LARGEST NUMBERS OF ENTRY-LEVEL ROLES?

The Telecom Service-providers Sector, like the Pharma Sector, has a strong preference for graduates and postgraduates where 70 per cent of the new jobs will be for graduates and above.

Some of the jobs are for technical specialists like Telecom and Electronic Engineers, and some of them require prior relevant experience. Jobs for freshers are limited, and even they require specific training. The Telecom Sector Skill Council is doing great service by listing job roles and training and certification requirements. So fresh graduates can enrol into one of these courses and get certification from the Telecom Sector Skill Council, which will greatly enhance their employability.

General skills that telecom companies look for while recruiting candidates[64]

- Product companies largely seek engineering graduates (who have a background in computers, electronics, or telecommunications) since the nature of the job is technical.
- Application development and maintenance provides opportunities to Application Developers with strong programming skills in database and graphical user interface (GUI) development.
- Engineers with a background in IT, computers, and electronics have an edge over the others, due to their knowledge of computer architecture and systems design.
- Skills like coding and software testing are essential in the network and IT domain of the Telecommunications Sector.
- Entry-level roles in telecommunications can vary from a Management Trainee to an Executive of any vertical stage in the present-day Telecommunications Sector.

Before we discuss the entry-level roles for graduates, let's discuss the profile of a great achiever in the Telecom Sector.

SUNIL BHARTI MITTAL

Sunil Bharti Mittal is the Founder and Chairman of Bharti Enterprises which has interests in telecom, retail, realty, financial services and agri products. Bharti Airtel, the group's flagship company, is a global telecommunications company with operations across South Asia and Africa. Bharti has joint ventures with several global leaders: SingTel, Softbank, AXA, and Del Monte.

Mr Mittal is currently Vice Chairman of the International Chamber of Commerce (ICC). He also serves on the Prime Minister of India's Council on Trade and Industry, the World Economic Forum's

International Business Council, the Telecom Board of International Telecommunication Union (ITU), Commissioner of the Broadband Commission, and the Singapore Prime Minister's Research, Innovation and Enterprise Council. He has been appointed by the Prime Minister of India as Co-chair of the India–Africa Business Council and India–Sri Lanka CEO Forum as well as a member of the India–US, India–UK, and India–Japan CEO Forums. Earlier, he served as the President of the Confederation of Indian Industry (CII, 2007–08), the premier industry body in India. He is a recipient of the Padma Bhushan, one of India's highest civilian awards.

Mr Mittal believes that a responsible corporate has a duty to give back to the community in which it operates. This belief has resulted in the Bharti Foundation, which operates 254 schools as well as remedial centres and renders quality support to government schools, providing holistic education to over 50,000 under-privileged children in rural India. He was ranked among the Top 25 Philanthropists in the World in 2009 by *Barron's* magazine. He is also a Member of the Board of Trustees of Qatar's 'Education Above All' Foundation, an initiative of Her Highness Sheikha Moza Bint Nasser al Missned.

SECTION 2
ENTRY-LEVEL JOB ROLES

Even though there are various roles a fresher can opt for, we are covering only the most popular roles mentioned by industry experts.

CODE	ROLE
TEL 1	Fault Management/Support Engineer
TEL 2	Optical Fibre Splicer
TEL 3	In-shop Promoter
TEL 4	Service/Repair Executive (Handset)

TEL 1 FAULT MANAGEMENT/SUPPORT ENGINEER

Job Description

A Fault Management/Support Engineer is responsible for monitoring the network from the main location and ensure that faults are resolved within a stipulated time-frame to avoid big issues. The Engineer gives directions to the team who carry out the directions to correct faults.

Typical Responsibilities[65]

- Constantly monitoring the network.
- Guiding the team in case any fault arises, by providing them with an appropriate solution.
- Monitoring alarms, localizing, correcting faults and verification resolution from a Remote Delivery Centre.
- Liaising with customer care organizations regarding network outages.
- Coordinating with internal/external customers, and Operation Teams for resolution/restoration.
- Providing support and coordination with sub-contractors and third parties to resolve faults.
- Supporting end-to-end support, coordination, and control of assigned trouble tickets and work-order.
- Providing Incident Reports and RCA (Root Cause Analyses) for the outages in the network.
- Supporting major service outage investigations and follow-up.
- Ensuring planned outages are carried out/rolled back in the maintenance window.
- Ensuring Operator Customer Care is fully updated for service affecting outages.
- Carrying out proactive preventive measures to improve network availability.
- Following NOC (Network Operations Centre) procedure/process and being ready to work in 24×7 environments.

Fault Management/Support Engineer: A Profile

Likely salary with 1–3 years of experience	Rs 200,000–Rs 400,000 per annum.
Targets	Ensuring the network is maintained well and faults are resolved as early as possible.

Challenges	Sometimes it becomes challenging to communicate with field staff due to issues in the network. So coordinating with them and arriving at a solution may become challenging.
Skills	Good interpersonal and communication skills. Analytical and technical skills. Attention to detail. Problem-solving skills.
Stress	Moderate to high.
Travel on the job	Travelling to fault locations may be required at times.
Impact on stakeholders	The company you work for, the team, and customers/subscribers are impacted by your work.
Career prospects	You can opt for a network managerial role in the company.
Future salary with 5–7 years of experience	Rs 500,000–Rs 700,000 per annum, depending on the company you work for.

A Practitioner's View

Fault Management/Support Engineer, Venkatesh, Hyderabad (Rural)

Mr Venkatesh has been working in the Telecom Department for a long time. He also served as a Fault Management Engineer during his tenure. When we spoke to him about the job, he said:

'The job is very challenging. We need to be technically sound and have a good grip of various subjects dealing with network management as a lot of things are interconnected. So if a fault occurs, thousands of connections get affected and this puts high pressure on us to resolve the issue as fast as possible. Sometimes we face complex situations where it may take days for the issue to get resolved. So by dealing with tough situations, we get to learn a lot of new things and solutions. It can be a good platform to hone skills that one has learnt from college and therefore, I would recommend this role to a fresher.'

TEL 2 OPTICAL FIBRE SPLICER

Job Description[66]

Optical Fibre Splicing Technicians are also known as Telecommunications Line Installers and Repairers. They specialize in fibre optic cables, which are used in phone, television, and data networks. They splice and terminate fibre optic cables while maintaining fibre optic networks and are required to have a technical diploma or degree and complete formal classroom and on-the-job training before deployment.

Typical Responsibilities[67]

- Preparing cables for splicing operations.
- Ensuring availability of tools and spares.
- Performing splicing operations as per standard procedure, including stripping the protective coating of cables, at areas where splicing has to be performed, precision cleaving of fibre ends, aligning fibres using fusion machine or mechanical sleeves, verify and protect the slice with heat-shrink sleeves.
- Testing effectiveness and performing joint closures by testing the fibre joint with an optical time-domain reflectometer (OTDR), a special equipment to confirm conformance to design requirements, ensuring that the optical losses are within limits, sealing the joints with heat shrink\mechanical sleeves, strengthening the joints as specified, testing for cross-fibre instances, placing the joint in the chamber, placing spare cable in the chamber, filling up the chamber with sand, and covering the chamber.
- Ensuring health and safety at site by following all the approved safety procedures.
- Reporting and recording the activities including appropriate cable marking and installation of chambers and route-markers for direction and route identification, preparation of jointing record for future reference, and completion of the OTDR register showing complete record of jointing tests.

Optical Fibre Splicer: A Profile

Likely salary with 1-3 years of experience	Rs 120,000-Rs 240,000 per annum.
Targets	Speed: quantum of joints completed per day. Quality: number of errors in jointing/splicing.
Challenges	The optical fibres are very expensive and hence errors are costly. Intense concentration is required since this is a precision job.
Skills	Mechanical skills, including good hand-eye coordination. An eye for detail.
Stress	Moderate.
Travel on the job	Travelling to project sites for installing fibre optic systems is required.
Impact on stakeholders	The customers/subscribers who will use the cable network installed by you will be impacted by your work.
Career prospects	Vertical progression into Team Lead and Project Lead is possible.
Future salary with 5-7 years of experience	Rs 300,000-Rs 400,000 per annum, depending on the company you work for.

A Practitioner's View
Optical Fibre Splicer, Reddy, Hyderabad

Mr Reddy worked as an Optical Fibre Splicer for nearly five years. When we spoke to him about the job and asked his views, he said:

'I got into this job after taking training in Fibre Optics. There is lot of travelling involved in my job. Sometimes during breakdowns, we need to travel to the site to check the issue and resolve it. The job involves maintenance and repair work and also examining lines and use electrical equipment to test for damage. We troubleshoot a line to locate a fault and splice in new line to replace damaged cable. I find the role very interesting as we get to know a lot of new things about fibre optics by practically working on them.'

TEL 3 IN-SHOP PROMOTER

Job Description

An In-shop Promoter is someone who explains about the look and feel and features of the product (a mobile phone, a land phone, cordless phone, other accessories) to walk-in customers. She/he helps customers finalize on what product to buy, by comparing various products and explaining why the chosen product is the best.

Typical Responsibilities[68]

- Demonstrating and explaining products, methods, or services in order to persuade customers to purchase products or utilize services.
- Identifying interested and qualified customers in order to provide them with additional information.
- Keeping areas neat while working, and returning items to correct locations following demonstrations.
- Practising demonstrations to ensure that they run smoothly.
- Preparing and altering presentation contents to target-specific audiences.
- Providing product information using lectures, films, charts, and/or slide shows.
- Providing product samples, coupons, informational brochures, and other incentives to persuade people to buy products.
- Recording and reporting demonstration-related information, such as the number of questions asked by the audience and the number of coupons distributed.
- Researching and investigating products to be presented to prepare for demonstrations.

In-shop Promoter: A Profile

Likely salary with 1–3 years of experience	Rs 200,000–Rs 300,000 on an average, per annum depending on the company you work for.

Targets	Influencing a customer in such a way that she/he purchases the product. Converting a product enquiry into a sale.
Challenges	Taking customers into confidence so that they purchase the product is a huge challenge, as every customer is different and has his/her set of questions which the Promoter should be able to answer.
Skills	Good interpersonal and communication skills. Networking skills. Influencing skills. Good product knowledge.
Stress	Moderate to high.
Travel on the job	Very little.
Impact on stakeholders	The company you work for, the superiors, and customers are impacted by your work.
Career prospects	You can opt for a Sales Supervisor role in the company.
Future salary with 5–7 years of experience	Rs 400,000–Rs 500,000 per annum, depending on the company you work for.

A Practitioner's View
In-shop Promoter, Sampath K., Hyderabad

Mr Sampath is working as an In-shop Promoter in one of the big mobile showroom outlets. When we spoke to him about the job and asked his views, he said:

'My job involves explaining to customers about a particular phone, its features and why it is better from many other phones of the same category, for example, smartphones. Generally, customers do an online review of the product and walk into the showroom with a fixed mind-set. To be able to change their thinking and to be able to explain to them that online reviews are not always reliable is a challenge we Promoters face on a regular basis. The exposure is high as we get to meet different people. The role is good and so I would recommend it to a fresher.'

TEL 4 SERVICE AND REPAIR EXECUTIVE (HANDSET)

Job Description

We use landline phones almost on a daily basis. Sometimes these phones have problems such as numbers not getting pressed on the keypad, or noise while talking, or some keys not working, and so on. When we complain to the Service-provider and register a complaint, they send a Service and Repair Executive, who initially sees if it is the issue with the line or if the handset itself is faulty.

The same is the case with mobile phones. Here, we take mobiles to the Service Centre where the Service Executive checks for any hardware or software issues. She/he would also let us know if any part needs to be replaced.

Typical Responsibilities

- Checking line connections for the landline phone and replacing the set if it is faulty.
- Do a complete check-up by calling the telephone exchange from the landline phone once the repairs are done.
- Taking the Complaint Register from the Customer Care Executive about complaints received.
- Working on the handset to see if there is any virus that has caused any issue.
- Updating the software.

Service and Repair Executive (Handset): A Profile

Likely salary with 1–3 years of experience	Rs 150,000–Rs 250,000 on an average, per annum depending on the company you work for.
Targets	Ensuring that all repairs are carried out properly and no customer complains about the service rendered.
Challenges	To identify the exact cause and resolve issues.
Skills	Good technical knowledge. Decent communication skills. Analytical skills.
Stress	Moderate to high.

Travel on the job	Travelling to customer locations is required at times.
Impact on stakeholders	The company you work for, the superiors, and customers are impacted by your work.
Career prospects	You can opt for a supervisory role in the company.
Future salary with 5–7 years of experience	Rs 300,000–Rs 400,000 per annum, depending on the company you work for.

A Practitioner's View

Service and Repair Executive, Krishna, Hyderabad

Mr Krishna worked as a Service Executive in the Telecom Department. When we spoke to him about the job and asked him why he would recommend it to a fresher, he said:

'My job involves attending to customer complaints and solving their issues. We have to explain to them how to use certain features on the land phone. We are given a set of complaints on a daily basis that need to be solved and the status has to be reported at the end of the day. It is sometimes challenging to finish all the assigned tasks, as some repairs take a longer time to be resolved. It can be a good starting point to learn how handsets and land phones work before moving into higher roles. So, for learning and gaining experience, I will recommend this job.'

23

TRAVEL, TOURISM, AND HOSPITALITY

SECTION 1
BACKGROUND

DO YOU KNOW THAT TOURISM IS ONE OF THE WORLD'S BIGGEST BUSINESSES?[69]

Today, tourism is a major source of income for many countries, and affects the economy of both the source and host countries, in some cases being of vital importance.

Tourism is an important, even vital, source of income for many countries. Tourism brings in large amounts of income into a local economy in the form of payment for goods and services needed by tourists, accounting for 30 per cent of the world's trade of services, and 6 per cent of overall exports of goods and services. It also creates opportunities for employment in the Service Sector of the economy associated with tourism.

The service industries which benefit from tourism include transportation services, such as airlines, cruise ships, and taxicabs; hospitality services, such as accommodations, including hotels, restaurants, resorts, and vacation homes; and entertainment venues, such as amusement parks, casinos, shopping malls, music venues, and theatres. This is in addition to goods bought by tourists, including souvenirs, clothing, and other supplies through retailers and shopping arcades.

TOURISM IN INDIA

International Tourism[70]

We received over 7 million tourists in 2014 and this is expected to grow at the rate of 6 per cent per annum. But the unfortunate reality is that India gets only 0.6 per cent of the global tourists.

Domestic Tourism

Did you know that the inter-state travel of domestic tourists crossed 1 billion in 2012 and is expected to grow at the rate of 14.5 per cent per annum?

Hotel companies in India are betting big on India's growing middle class with 350–500 million people having the money to spare on travel.[71] Around 300 branded hotels are expected to come up over the next three years across India, constituting about 17 per cent of Asia's hotel contribution pipeline.[72]

EMPLOYMENT IN TRAVEL, TOURISM, AND THE HOSPITALITY SECTOR

Where are the jobs in this sector?

To answer this question, we need to understand the industry value chain as shown in Figure 23.1.

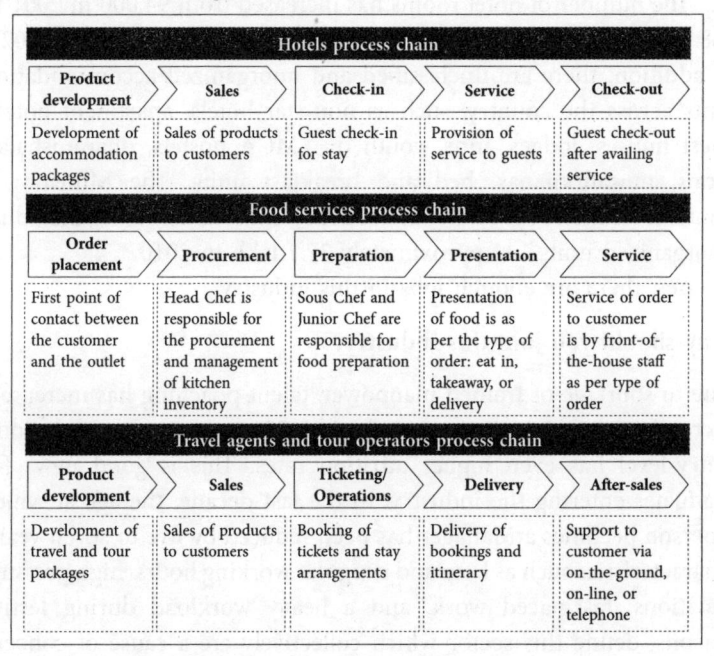

Hotels process chain				
Product development	Sales	Check-in	Service	Check-out
Development of accommodation packages	Sales of products to customers	Guest check-in for stay	Provision of service to guests	Guest check-out after availing service
Food services process chain				
Order placement	Procurement	Preparation	Presentation	Service
First point of contact between the customer and the outlet	Head Chef is responsible for the procurement and management of kitchen inventory	Sous Chef and Junior Chef are responsible for food preparation	Presentation of food is as per the type of order: eat in, takeaway, or delivery	Service of order to customer is by front-of-the-house staff as per type of order
Travel agents and tour operators process chain				
Product development	Sales	Ticketing/ Operations	Delivery	After-sales
Development of travel and tour packages	Sales of products to customers	Booking of tickets and stay arrangements	Delivery of bookings and itinerary	Support to customer via on-the-ground, on-line, or telephone

Figure 23.1: The Industry Value Chain[73]

In each segment of the value chain, there are employment opportunities. For example, for a food services outlet to run, we need stewards to take the order, Head Chefs to procure and stock the raw materials ready for cooking, cooks to prepare the food, delivery boys or waiters to deliver the food, and the Manager of the outlet to ensure that the customers are happy and come back.

EMPLOYMENT IN THE HOTEL INDUSTRY[74]

Are there enough jobs in this industry?

The hospitality industry employs over 50 million people in India and, on an average, has added 55,000 jobs per month since the beginning of 2013, compared to 30,000 jobs per month in 2012.[75]

According to the World Travel and Tourism Council (WRRC), the industry will grow exponentially to create 8 million additional jobs in India over the next ten years.

The number of hotel rooms has increased from 94,000 in 2001 to 168,000 rooms in 2013 which will increase to 238,000 rooms in 2022. In addition, there are unclassified and unorganized accommodation units across the country, such as non-star hotels, apartment hotels, guest houses, lodges, inns, youth or YMCA hostels, dharamshalas, sarais, musafirkhanas, bed and breakfast units. The Ministry of Tourism estimates the total number of accommodation units, including unorganized units, at approximately 27.1 lakh in 2010.

Yes, there are enough jobs in this industry.

Why should you join this industry?

Due to shortage of trained manpower, talent poaching has increased. Increase in the attrition rate is as high as 50 per cent across functions. Entry-level has even higher attrition rates. This is good news for graduates entering the industry. In the last decade, the age at which a person becomes a Manager has been reduced by five to seven years. Characteristics such as long and irregular working hours, high pressure situations, fast-paced work, and a heavy workload during festive seasons, define this sector which collectively are a cause of concern for current and prospective employees. So if you want a peaceful nine to five job, this is not suitable for you. This is an ideal place for all those who are willing to work hard and learn quickly.

Due to saturation in big cities, new properties will come up in smaller towns. Graduates from big cities are unwilling to move to smaller towns. This is good news for graduates in smaller towns, for two reasons—less competition and starts your career closer to home. The hotel industry today employs youth in significant numbers and hence you can expect a young peer group. In addition, this employee mix is cosmopolitan. Both these are great for young graduates.

Before we move on to any entry-level job roles, let us look at the career of an exceptional hotelier who has become a legend in his own lifetime and is often termed the Father of the Indian Hotel Industry. We are talking of none other than the Founder of the Oberoi Group, Mr M.S. Oberoi.

MOHAN SINGH OBEROI[76]

Founder of Oberoi Group of Hotels, Mr M.S. Oberoi was born in 1900 and was among the first few individuals to recognize the potential of the tourism industry and its ability to contribute to economic growth and generate direct and indirect employment.

His first job was that of Front Desk Clerk at the Cecil Hotel, Shimla, at a salary of Rs 50 per month. He took up many additional responsibilities there and caught the eye of Mr Clarke, who was the manager. Soon Mr Clarke hired him as manager for his own hotel. Mr Oberoi did an excellent job and in 1934, when Mr and Mrs Clarke were returning to England, he sold his wife's jewellery, acquired additional funds, and bought Clarke's Hotel from his mentor. Later, he bought the Cecil as well, now known as the Oberoi Cecil, and eventually went on to own hotels across the world.

However, more than just ownership, it was his personal attention to detail and quality that he refused to compromise on, that won the Oberoi Group its unmatched reputation and the trust of thousands of customers globally.

Mr Oberoi received many awards and honours during his lifetime, and was also awarded the Padma Bhushan in 2001. He passed away in 2002, at the age of 102. A man of this stature is truly an inspiration!

SECTION 2
ENTRY-LEVEL JOB ROLES

There are various jobs available in this industry.

CODE	ROLE
HOS 1	Front Office Executive
HOS 2	Housekeeping Executive
HOS 3	Banquet Executive
HOS 4	Chef

HOS 1 FRONT OFFICE EXECUTIVE

Job Description

The Front Office Executive is the first person whom guests meet when they visit a hotel.

Typical Responsibilities

- Managing customer arrivals to maximize relationship-building opportunities.
- Making reservations over the phone or checking-in walk-ins.
- Documenting details of guests who visit the hotel.
- Preparing bills and accepting payments.
- Handling check-ins and check-outs.
- Taking messages over the phone on behalf of guests if they are not available.
- Responding quickly to any queries raised by guests regarding the hotel facilities, sightseeing tours, and so on.
- Dealing and assisting customers in case of any issues.
- Following a proper dress code and telephone etiquette.

Front Office Executive: A Profile

Likely salary with 1–3 years of experience	Rs 200,000–Rs 300,000 per annum plus benefits such as free or subsidized meals while on shift.
Targets	Minimize check-in and check-out time of guests. Ensuring delightful customer experience—minimum complaints and maximum compliments.

Challenges	Dealing with unruly guests.
Skills	Multi-tasking skills. Excellent communication skills. Very sharp memory for faces and names.
Stress	Moderate.
Travel on the job	None.
Impact on stakeholders	The customers who visit the hotel are highly impacted by this role, because Front Office Executives act as the face of the organization.
Career prospects	You can get promoted to Front Office Manager or any other suitable managerial roles in the hotel within three years and thereafter move on to Banquet Sales, Guest Relations, or Public Relations roles.
Future salary with 5–7 years of experience	Rs 400,000–Rs 600,000 per annum.

A Practitioner's View
Front Office Executive, Harsh Ratwal, Delhi

Mr Ratwal has been working as a Front Office Executive for a little over two years. When we spoke to him and asked him to share his experiences about his job with us, he said:

'A front office job is for young and dynamic personalities, because as a Front Office Executive, you are the FACE of the hotel. You make the first and last impression on the guest.

'I love this job because I get to meet a lot of new guests, answer their questions, and assist them in making their stay a memorable one. My positive attitude towards work has helped me progress well and also improved my personality. I feel that in the front office, being a fresher or a candidate with experience doesn't make any difference, because it is the attitude that makes a difference!'

HOS 2 HOUSEKEEPING EXECUTIVE

Job Description

When we visit a hotel, the first thing we observe is how neat it is, how well it has been maintained. Inside a hotel room, we expect the bed to be made, the toilets to be clean, the towels fresh, toiletries in place, and so on. All of this is managed by the Housekeeping Department.

Basically, the Housekeeping Executive manages the look and feel of the place. Housekeeping Executives are appointed in hotels, hospitals, corporate offices, and at public places like airports. They are responsible for ensuring that the facility is maintained hygienically.

Typical Responsibilities

As a Housekeeping Executive, your day will involve guiding and managing the housekeeping staff whose job is to clean the place. Your typical activities on a daily basis will be:

- Supervising the daily routine of the housekeeping staff.
- Inspecting to ensure that offices, reception, washrooms, seating areas, public places are all cleaned and well-maintained—and doing so without inconveniencing employees and guests.
- Guiding and motivating the housekeeping staff.
- Hiring and training new staff.
- Keeping a track of the housekeeping inventory.
- Making necessary purchases of supplies and inventories.

Housekeeping Executive: A Profile

Likely salary with 1–3 years of experience	Rs 120,000–Rs 250,000 per annum.
Targets	On-time completion of daily tasks. Minimize complaints.
Challenges	Managing housekeeping staff who are not disciplined. Meeting the expectations of demanding customers. Attending to customer requests at odd hours.

Skills	Good organizing skills. An eye for detail. Excellent listening skills so that you can understand and effectively respond to guest requirements.
Stress	Low to moderate.
Travel on the job	There is no travel involved in this role.
Impact on stakeholders	The hotel guests and the management are highly impacted by this role.
Career prospects	In three years you can expect to become a Senior Executive and in five to seven years, become the Head of the Housekeeping Department.
Future salary with 5–7 years of experience	Rs 300,000–Rs 400,000 per annum.

A Practitioner's View
Housekeeping Executive, Rashmi, Mumbai

Ms Rashmi has been working as a Housekeeping Executive for the last two years. When we asked her about her experience she said:

'Working in this role has taught me patience. I like to keep things spic and span and so my job complements my nature. Many people feel that it is an inferior role but I believe in the dignity of labour. We get to learn a lot of things that help us become organized individuals.'

HOS 3 BANQUET EXECUTIVE

Job Description

When you decide to conduct family functions like a birthday celebration, a wedding reception, naming ceremony, at a hotel, you meet a Banquet Executive. She/he is responsible for understanding your requirements and then showing you the hotel's banqueting facilities, so that you can choose the one that fits your needs and your budget. She/he will negotiate with you to provide you the best quote, explain the terms and conditions of using the banqueting facility, and will also note down your menu requirements. During events/functions, she/he must ensure that guests are not having any problem and also monitor the food and beverages that are being served. After the function, she/he needs to conduct a thorough check of the banquet hall to detect for damages/theft so that the loss of hotel property can be billed to the customer.

Typical Responsibilities

As a Banquet Executive, your day will be busy as you will have to manage activities related to banquet sales, maintenance of banquet facilities, manage functions, and guest relations. Your typical activities will be:

- Making sales calls to sell the use of the facilities for events to corporate houses as well as receiving walk-ins who want to discuss holding a family event such as a party/wedding reception at the hotel.
- Ensuring that the infrastructure present in the banquet hall is intact and properly maintained.
- Maintaining records of inventory, food cost, and labour cost.
- Handling bookings and suggesting the best menu and decorations.
- Ensuring that customers receive the best service during functions.
- Checking the availability of food and beverages during functions.
- Dealing with any issues/complaints that customers are having.
- Billing the customer and collections.

Banquet Executive: A Profile

Likely salary with 1–3 years of experience	Rs 240,000–Rs 400,000 per annum.
Targets	Revenue target from banquets. Managing costs to achieve profitability targets. Customer satisfaction measured by referrals.
Challenges	Managing demanding customers and negotiating costs. Coordinating activities among the Housekeeping and Food and Beverage (F&B) Departments to see that services are delivered as per customer requirements.

	Accommodate any last-minute changes such as last-minute requests for music/DJ facilities.
Skills	Good communication skills. Excellent negotiation skills. Organizing skills.
Stress	Moderate.
Travel on the job	This role does not involve travel outside the city, but you will be required to travel within the city.
Impact on stakeholders	The customers and the hotel's management are highly impacted by this role.
Career prospects	In three years you can move to other senior roles in the hotel such as corporate sales. In seven years you can lead a small team as Banquet Manager.
Future salary with 5–7 years of experience	Rs 400,000–Rs 600,000 per annum.

A Practitioner's View
Banquet Manager, Ravi, Hyderabad

Mr Ravi works with one of the best hotels as a Banquet Manager. When we asked him about his experiences he said:
'I love my job. We get to interact and communicate with customers and negotiate with them regarding their requirements. We need to have excellent organizing and management skills to be able to perform well in this role. The trick lies in striking a balance between what the customer demands and what the management expects out of you. It is a good career option for anyone who wants to make a career in the Hospitality Sector.'

HOS 4 CHEF

Job Description

A Chef is trained in culinary skills. She/he ensures that whatever is prepared in the kitchen is made to the best hygienic standards and is presented exceptionally well. She/he also helps in maintaining accounts, meets customers on a regular basis to ensure that they like what is being served, and in case of any feedback she/he uses it in a constructive way to help the team improve.

Specific Education and Training

Culinary education is available from many institutions offering diploma, associate, and bachelor degree programmes in culinary arts. Depending on the level of education, this can take one to four years. An internship is often part of the curriculum. Regardless of the education received, most professional kitchens follow the apprenticeship system, and most new Chefs will start at a lower-level first or second cook position and work their way up. The usual formal training period for a Chef is two to four years in catering college. They often spend the summer in work placements.

Typical Responsibilities

As a Chef, your day will be busy as you will have to manage the whole kitchen and guide a team of Junior Chefs to carry out activities. There is immense planning involved in this role. As a Chef you will need to tackle the following tasks.

- Plan the menu.
- Decide on how the items need to be prepared and presented.
- Plan staff requirements.
- Prepare a budget for supplies and take necessary approvals from the management.
- Manage the inventory of ingredients.
- Monitor/inspect the quality of ingredients, utensils, equipment that will be used to prepare food.
- Decide on the quantity of food that needs to be cooked on a daily basis.
- Constantly guide juniors during preparation of food and beverages and share valuable tips with them.
- Taste the food and check the presentation before serving customers.
- Constantly interact with customers to take their views.
- Dispose of the excess food hygienically.
- Change the menu according to the season to bring in variety.

Chef: A Profile

Likely salary with 1–3 years of experience	Rs 300,000–Rs 400,000 per annum. Salaries in the initial years are low because experience is essential to be a great Chef.
Targets	The main target is to ensure the quality of dishes served. On-time delivery of food on the table. Innovate on the menu to attract customers not staying in the hotel.
Challenges	Determining the exact quantity of food that needs to be prepared on a daily basis, to avoid wastage. Cooking large quantities for big events without losing the taste. Odd working hours, especially late hours.
Stress	Moderate to high.
Skills	Excellent culinary skills. Good communication skills. Good leadership skills. Multi-tasking and organizing skills.
Travel on the job	Low.
Impact on stakeholders	Customers and the hotel's management are highly impacted by this role.
Career prospects	You will join as a Trainee Chef and slowly move towards becoming a Sous Chef and once you gain considerable amount of experience, you will become a Chef/Master Chef/Executive Chef over a period of ten to fifteen years.
Future salary with 5–7 years of experience	Rs 700,000–Rs 1,400,000 per annum.

A Practitioner's View

General Manager (started career as a Chef),
Abhay Desai, Mumbai

Mr Desai is working as a General Manager with Grand Cuisines Banquets. He has eleven years of experience in the hospitality industry. When we asked him to share his views with us, he said:

'After graduating from the Institute of Hotel Management, Mumbai, I started off as a Trainee Chef at Thackers Hospitality Services. I underwent on-the-job training to sharpen my culinary skills. The training process also involved people management skills. As I moved on to the Orchid Hotel, Mumbai, as a Management Trainee, I was imparted culinary skills along with introduction to a new repertoire, as well as management skills. Management classroom sessions combined with on-the-job training, helped in understanding the hospitality business.

'After two years of training, we were inducted into the system as a Sous Chef, which is a supervisory position in the kitchen production department. My third job, with Grand Cuisines, helped me to rise from Sous Chef to Corporate Chef and eventually, to General Manager. Speciality skills supported with management skills helped in understanding the hospitality business in a unique way.

'It has changed my outlook towards life. It has taught me to access various situations in a logical way. Every person working in a particular sector has a sense about their product as to how is it performing in the market. Professionally, the Hospitality Sector, even with the world economies slowing down, has not been affected as food is not just about eating food and filling your stomach. Today, eating food that carries a certain panache and edge, and makes a statement in society, is what foodies and connoisseurs alike want to explore.'

24

PHARMA AND HEALTHCARE SECTOR

Healthcare is about hospitals, clinics, and diagnostic centres. Pharma is about drugs/medicine manufacturing and marketing. According to National Family Health Survey-3,[77] the private medical sector remains the primary source of healthcare for 70 per cent of households in urban areas and 63 per cent of households in rural areas. The Indian healthcare system, funded by the government, is very poorly funded and administered. Having said that, healthcare is one of the key priority areas for the Indian government, and a key area for investment for private and MNC investors.

On the other hand, the pharma industry is a big success story, is globally competitive, and the ideal sector for the 'Make in India' campaign. It is also one of the most attractive sectors for employment for knowledge workers including graduates, pharmacists, doctors, engineers, postgraduates, and PhD scholars

SECTION 1
BACKGROUND

These interesting statistics tell the story of the Indian Healthcare Sector.[78]

ABOUT OUR HEALTHCARE SYSTEM

- The World Health Organization's 2000 World Health Report ranks India's healthcare system at 112 out of 190 countries.
- In 2013, India spent only around 4.1 per cent of its national GDP towards healthcare goods and services (compared to 18 per cent by the US).
- A staggering 70 per cent of the population still lives in rural areas and has no or limited access to hospitals and clinics.

- Almost 70 per cent of Indian patients pay for their hospital visits and doctors' appointments with cash, without payment arrangements. According to the World Bank and National Commission's report on Macroeconomics, only 5 per cent of Indians are covered by health insurance policies.

Healthcare Industry is Poised for Excellent Growth

- The Healthcare Sector which stood at Rs 4.8 lakh crore in 2012 is expected to double by 2017 to Rs 9.64 lakh crores. Although the expenditure on health has been on the rise, the per capita expenditure on health in India (INR 3,844) in 2012 is significantly less than that in other developing countries—for example, it is INR 16,988 in China. With the rising income and growing size of the middle class, the per capita expenditure is expected to grow.
- The healthcare industry is also receiving a lot of foreign direct investment or FDI (US$ 1.2 billion during 2011–13).

Components of the Healthcare Sector

- The Indian healthcare industry which serves Indian and foreign patients consists of sub-sectors like hospitals, pharma companies, medical equipment companies, medical insurers, and other service-providers, and medical diagnostic companies. Hospitals, at 71 per cent of the industry sales are the biggest. The pharma industry which manufactures and markets the drugs that these patients use is the next biggest at 13 per cent of the industry sales.

ABOUT OUR PHARMA INDUSTRY

- The following terms must be understood before we talk of the pharma industry:
  - Formulations are the drugs that the doctors prescribe and we consume. Drugs can be in many forms but the most popular forms are capsules, tablets, injectables, ointments, inhalers.
  - These formulations contain one or many APIs (short form for Active Pharmaceutical Ingredients), which is the drug we need. The APIs are mixed with other inert substances to make the drug delivery effective. For example, when your doctor

prescribes Asprin 650 mg for pain or fever, your chemist will give you a tablet (formulation type) containing 650 milligrams of aspirin (the API). Bulk drugs are another term for APIs.
- Branded drugs are the drugs discovered and marketed by a pharmaceutical company under their brand name. Since any pharma company has to invest thousands of crores of rupees to discover and test the drug, the company gets a patent protection for a period of time to recover the investment. Once the patent period ends, other pharma companies can copy and make drugs which have the same efficacy and these drugs are called generic drugs.

- The Indian pharmaceutical industry currently tops the chart amongst India's science-based industries with wide-ranging capabilities in the complex field of drug manufacture and technology.
- Currently, the Indian Pharmaceuticals Sector ranks third globally in terms of volume sales and tenth, in terms of value.
- India accounts for about 10 per cent of the global pharmaceutical production.
- India is the third-largest exporter of pharmaceutical products in terms of volume.[79] Around 80 per cent of the market is composed of generic low-cost drugs which seem to be the major driver of this industry.
- Indian drugs are exported to more than 200 countries in the world, particularly to the US.
- India accounts for over 60,000 generic brands across 60 therapeutic categories and manufactures more than 500 different APIs.
- India has 119 manufacturing sites approved by the USFDA (US Food and Drug Administration), the highest in any country outside the US.
- Manufacturing costs in India of the USFDA-approved plants is only 35 to 40 per cent of the manufacturing costs in developed countries such as the US.
- Approximately 80 per cent of the formulations produced are consumed indigenously, while a majority of the bulk drugs/APIs manufactured are exported.

- Our pharma industry serves almost 95 per cent of India's pharma needs. The vast range of medicines that are manufactured include simple headache pills to sophisticated antibiotics and complex cardiac compounds.
- MNC pharma players have only around 25 per cent market share of the Indian market (in March 2013). The big Indian players dominate the formulations market.
- The government regulates the formulations' pricing in the domestic market of essential and key drugs.
- Pharma is a highly organized but fragmented industry. There are 300 to 400 organized big players in the industry. The rest are over 8,000 SMEs.
- The Indian Pharma and Life Sciences Sector is a big success story (like our IT industry) and had a steady and strong growth in the last five years—even when other manufacturing sectors struggled—from US$ 19 billion in 2010 to US$ 34.5 billion in 2015 at an annual growth rate of 12.6 per cent. Interestingly, Indian companies dominate the industry while the MNCs have only 25 per cent market share.
- The top ten pharma players in India based on net sales value are— Sun Pharma, Lupin Labs, Dr Reddy's Labs, CIPLA labs, Aurobindo Pharma, Cadila Pharma, Glaxo Smith Kline, and IPCA labs.[80]

EMPLOYMENT IN THE HEALTHCARE INDUSTRY (EXCLUDING THE PHARMA INDUSTRY)

- With a diverse range of medical services, there are over 11 lakh allied health professionals in the country in the categories of nursing associates, sanitarians, medical assistants, medical equipment operators, optometrists, traditional and faith healers, physiotherapists, dieticians, and dental assistants which is still short of the current demand.
- Permanent staff form less than 50 per cent of all employees (the rest are on contract) in the healthcare industry.
- Allied healthcare professionals (professionals other than doctors, nurses, and pharmacists) constitute 56 per cent of the head count and most of them are on a contract basis.
- Total employees in healthcare will grow from around 3.6 million

in 2013 to around 7.4 million in 2022. Nurses and midwives will see the maximum growth—see Table 24.1.[81]

Table 24.1: Manpower Requirements in the Healthcare Sector[82]

Sub-category	Employment in thousand		
	2013	2017	2022
Doctors (allopathic)	434	494	621
Specialists	218	248	311
Dentists	78	88	111
Nurses and midwives	973	1753	3645
Pharmacists	264	300	377
Allied and other healthcare professionals	1425	1622	2039
Total	3595	4739	7398

Problems of high attrition is observed in general profiles like nursing which see as much as 50 per cent attrition levels, due to low job satisfaction and uncertainty of tenure due to most of the employees being contractual.

Table 24.2: Manpower Requirement of Allied Health Professionals

Sub-category	Employment in thousand		
	2013	2017	2022
Technicians	567	645	811
Health workers (Male)	464	528	664
Rural healthcare workers	327	372	468
Doctor (AYUSH)	67	76	96
Managerial categories	205	233	293
Total	1630	1855	2332

Technician jobs will increase by over 0.35 million between 2013 and 2022.

EMPLOYMENT IN THE PHARMACEUTICAL INDUSTRY[83]

- There are about 24,000 manufacturing units in India.
- Due to the rapid growth of the industry, there will be a shortage of Managers which means faster promotions and career progression for youth joining the industry.
- The pharma industry is the preferred employer for management graduates and Accountants for commercial roles while the production and research roles are popular with science and pharmacy graduates.
- In 2012–13, 1145 pharmacy colleges in India had an intake of 121,652 students for diplomas, undergraduate, and postgraduate degrees in pharmaceutical sciences.
- Maximum number of employees (about 70 per cent) in the pharma sector are engaged in the production and quality control division.
- PhD/MTech/MSc account for 5–8 per cent of the workforce in the chemicals and pharmaceuticals segment, while 75 per cent of the people employed in the sector have an educational background of class 12 or above. Up to 45 per cent of the workforce comprise graduates (engineers and non-engineers).
- Overall employment in the industry is expected to double in nine years to reach over 3.5 million by 2022. Please see Table below.

Table 24.3: Employment in the Pharma Industry[84]

Segment	Employment (in million)			Employment growth 2013–17	Employment growth 2017–22	Employment growth 2013–22
	2013	2017	2022	(in million)	(in million)	(in million)
Manufacturing	0.69	0.89	1.15	0.20	0.25	0.45
R&D	0.07	0.09	0.11	0.02	0.02	0.04
Wholesale	0.20	0.29	0.42	0.09	0.13	0.22
Pharma retail	0.90	1.32	1.90	0.43	0.58	1.00
Total	1.86	2.60	3.58	0.74	0.98	1.72

Before moving on to entry-level job roles in the health and pharma industry, we would like to briefly profile an outstanding achiever of this industry.

DR K. ANJI REDDY[85]

All of us know about Dr Reddy's Laboratories Ltd, popularly known as DRL or Reddy Labs. The company was founded by Dr K. Anji Reddy, in the year 1984. He was born in Tadepalli in Guntur district of Andhra Pradesh. After graduating from Bombay University in BSc (Tech) with specialization in pharmaceutical science and fine chemicals, Dr Reddy obtained his PhD in chemical engineering from the National Chemical Laboratory (NCL), Pune. Then came a stint at the state-owned Indian Drugs and Pharmaceuticals Ltd (IDPL), following which he became an entrepreneur and founded DRL in 1984. Under Dr Reddy's leadership the company has evolved into a pioneer in the Indian pharmaceutical space.

Dr Reddy's passion for research had led DRL to take up basic drug discovery research in 1993, thereby becoming the first pharmaceutical company in India to do so. Dr Reddy's mission was to provide innovative new medicines for healthier lives, at a price the common man can afford. Dr Reddy was also the Founder of the Hyderabad-based Institute of life sciences, a public–private partnership with the government of Andhra Pradesh focused on cutting-edge research in life sciences. A humanitarian, Dr Reddy's work in the field of outcome-based institutionalized philanthropy is legendary. His sustained efforts in this area have had a tremendous impact on improving the lives of nearly 5 million underprivileged people in India, especially youth and children.

Dr Reddy served as a Member of the Prime Minister's Council on Trade and Industry, Government of India. He was a Fellow of the Indian National Academy of Engineering and the Chairman of the Andhra Pradesh Industrial Development Corporation (APIDC). He was also the President of the Indian Pharmaceutical Alliance and had served as a Board Member of GAIN, Switzerland (Global Alliance for Improved Nutrition) and a Board of Directors for TB Alliance, New York (Global Alliance for TB Drug Development).

Dr Reddy was a recipient of several national and international recognitions and Lifetime Achievement Awards. In April 2011 the Government of India honoured him with the Padma Bhushan (the third highest civilian award in the country) for his contribution to the Indian pharmaceutical industry.

SECTION 2
ENTRY-LEVEL JOB ROLES

There are multiple job roles that exist in these industries of which we are covering only the most popular entry-level roles.

CODE	ROLE
P&H 1	Junior Doctor
P&H 2	General Nurse
P&H 3	Emergency Medical Technician
P&H 4	Laboratory Assistant/Technician
P&H 5	Quality Control Chemist (Factory)
P&H 6	Hospital Billing Executive
P&H 7	Medical Transcriptionist
P&H 8	Pharmacy Assistant
P&H 9	Medical Representative

P&H 1 JUNIOR DOCTOR

Job Description

When you visit a hospital to see a specialist, you are initially screened by the Junior Doctor who asks you a few questions to understand what exactly is the issue and then conveys it to the Senior Consultant. The Junior Doctor also provides primary and continual medical care for patients, after the course of treatment is decided. Junior Doctors go on to specialize in a specific area like anaesthetics, general medicine, gynaecology, paediatrics, among others, over a period of time.

Typical Responsibilities

- Advising and counselling patients under the guidance of Senior Doctors.
- Supervising nursing and para-medical staff to ensure medications and tests are done as per instructions of the Senior Doctor.
- Assisting Senior Doctors during all medical procedures and operations.
- Responding in times of emergencies and providing necessary treatment before the Senior Doctor arrives.
- Participating in medical camps organized by the hospital.

- Explaining the implications and complications of a surgical procedure and providing moral support to the patient as well as his/her family.
- Constantly learning and upgrading medical knowledge.

Junior Doctor: A Profile

Likely salary with 1–3 years of experience	Rs 300,000–Rs 600,000 per annum.
Targets	Provide right and timely medical care in a professional manner to patients. Many hospitals attach billing targets to doctors and Consultants that must be achieved.
Challenges	Responding to emergency situations. Ensuring that the inexperienced nursing staff perform their role. Almost 24×7 work timings.
Skills	Sound domain knowledge. Good inter-personal skills; specially handling nursing staff and patients' relatives' queries. Attention to detail.
Stress	High.
Travel on the job	Generally, no. But you may have to travel for conferences and medical camps organized by the hospital.
Impact on stakeholders	The hospital you work for, the Senior Doctors/Consultants and the patients are impacted by your work.
Career prospects	You join as a Junior Doctor. After a few years you could become Shift In-charge. Most doctors then appear for PG (postgraduate) admissions. After PG, you can then grow to the level of a Senior Doctor and become a Specialist or a Super-specialist and a Consultant, based on your area of specialization.
Future salary with 5–7 years of experience	Rs 800,000–Rs 1,500,000 per annum subject to PG qualification.

A Practitioner's View
Junior Doctor, Dr Arunima, Hyderabad

Dr Arunima is working as a Junior Doctor. When we asked her about her experiences and why she would recommend this profession to a fresher, she said:

'Being a doctor has been my sole dream from the beginning and I'm glad I could make it! This profession has taught me the importance of time and precision. Everything can change in a blink of an eye.

'It has also taught me to be a good listener, to be quick on my feet, to be precise in my handwork, but mostly to be an assuring and compassionate person. Personally, my job has made me more disciplined, focused but generally, a happy and content person.

'My daily activities include two to three hours in the Outpatient Department, quick rounds in the wards I've been assigned that day to check on the patients, constant attendance and care to the critical cases if any, to scrub in or watch the surgeries if required.

'This is a noble profession which makes a lot of difference in people's lives (though it calls for unreasonable hours and a lot of hard work). If not anything the look of gratitude on a person's face, when you ease their pain, is worthy enough!'

P&H 2 GENERAL NURSE

Job Description

While the doctor decides the treatment, it is the General Nurse who actually delivers the treatment when you are admitted to a hospital. A doctor may spend 10 minutes a day with the patient, but the General Nurse spends her entire day with the patients. Hence in many ways the General Nurses are the face of a hospital. Nurses also provide extensive psychological support to patients in times of need. They work in hospitals and even visit homes to help patients.

Typical Responsibilities

- Drafting patient-care plans as per the doctor's advice and implementing them.
- Monitoring blood pressure, temperature, blood sugar, and so on and dressing wounds periodically.
- Preparing the patients for operations.
- Giving injections and drips—as and when required.
- Scheduling and assisting patients during diagnostic tests.
- Briefing doctors on patient health.
- Responding in times of emergencies and providing necessary treatment before the doctor arrives.
- Providing support to the patient as well as his/her relatives.
- Supervising Junior Nurses and guiding them in learning nursing.
- Stocking of critical care consumables.

General Nurse: A Profile

Likely salary with 1–3 years of experience	Rs 120,000–Rs 250,000 per annum plus special allowances and overtime pay-outs. Government hospitals pay a higher salary than private hospitals.
Targets	Zero mistakes in implementing the patient-care plan. To ensure that ward discipline is maintained—ensuring relatives stick to visiting hours, and so on. Patient-care—responding to patients' needs on time and caring for them.
Challenges	Dealing simultaneously with multiple patients who have a variety of complex issues. Mistakes are very costly and so staying attentive during every minute of work is very challenging. The job is physically demanding and most General Nurses are overworked.
Skills	Nursing skills with the relevant degree (BSc Nursing). Excellent interpersonal skills. Attention to detail. Organizing skills.
Stress	Moderate to high.
Travel on the job	You will be stationed in the hospital where you work.

Impact on stakeholders	The hospital you work for and the patients are impacted by your work.
Career prospects	You can become a Head Nurse with five or more years of experience.
Future salary with 5–7 years of experience	Rs 250,000–Rs 350,000 per annum.

A Practitioner's View
Nurse, Ms Teresa, Hyderabad

Ms Teresa is working in a reputed hospital as a Nurse. When we asked her about her experiences, she said:

'I like doing my job as it is challenging and it gives me contentment as it is all about love and care. Professionally, I have learnt to be more organized, responsible, and how to manage matters during a crisis.

'Personally, I have learnt to be more compassionate, patient, sensitive, and humble. I enjoy doing this role as day by day it brings out the best in me. I recommend this job as it helps one to grow professionally and personally. It's a good career choice. My work has made me confident, strong, and taught me to give hope to everyone by my words and actions.'

P&H 3 EMERGENCY MEDICAL TECHNICIAN (EMT)

Job Description

As the name goes, an Emergency Medical Technician (EMT) provides emergency medical care to anyone who is critically ill or injured. EMTs are also responsible for transferring the patient to the medical facility as early as possible. They respond to the emergencies arising out of casualities from criminal violence, natural disasters, fires, air and land accidents, and so on. Most of them render their services in an ambulance vehicle.

Typical Responsibilities

- Reaching the accident spot or patient location at the shortest possible time.

- Assessing the patient's condition and communicating with professional medical personnel to obtain instructions for the right course of action.
- Provide medical first aid like controlling bleeding, bandaging wounds, preventing shocks.
- The medical duties performed by the EMT include providing cardiopulmonary resuscitation (CPR), opening a patient's airway to breathe, and providing ventilation assistance.
- Safely shifting the patient to the ambulance.
- Providing life support to the victim or patient while in the ambulance.
- Providing moral support to the family members in the ambulance.
- Communicating with professional medical personnel and nearest treatment facilities to arrange reception of patients.
- Maintaining order at scenes, including crowd disbursement and restraint of family and friends.
- Completing patient-care forms, insurance forms, evaluation forms, and all other forms in a competent and timely fashion.
- Clean and check the medical equipment and stock of supplies in the ambulance.
- Prepare a detailed report about the event.

Emergency Medical Technician (EMT): A Profile

Likely salary with 1–3 years of experience	Rs 150,000–Rs 250,000 per annum.
Targets	Number of patient calls attended. Quality and timeliness of patient-care provided.
Challenges	The biggest challenge is working under immense pressure without mistakes. Relatives of patients are often tense and managing their emotional pressure is a challenge.
Skills	Basic knowledge of biology is essential to absorb the technical training given to an EMT. Attention to detail. Good communication skills.
Stress	High.

Travel on the job	Every day you have to travel to the location of an emergency.
Impact on stakeholders	The victims/patients are impacted by the role.
Career prospects	This is a technical job. After a year of work experience as an EMT Trainee, you can become an EMT and after three to four years, you can become an expert paramedic. The next level is that of an Emergency Room Technician in a hospital.
Future salary with 5–7 years of experience	Rs 300,000–Rs 400,000 per annum.

A Practitioner's View
Emergency Medical Technician, Beena Joseph (name changed), Hyderabad

Ms Beena has been working in Hyderabad as an EMT over the last two years. When we spoke to her and asked her views regarding the job, she said:

'To be able to save a life is an amazing feeling. To do that day in day out is very satisfying. Situations can become complex at times, but through the support of fellow workers and thanks to the extensive training, things have gone smoothly for me. It is a good career option for people interested in becoming a paramedic.'

P&H 4 LABORATORY ASSISTANT/TECHNICIAN

Job Description

When you visit a hospital to get treated for an ailment, your doctor may prescribe some tests—like blood tests, urine tests, scans, X-rays in order to determine what exactly the problem is. So you are asked to visit a diagnostic centre where all these tests are conducted by Laboratory Assistants/Technicians. They ensure that all the lab tests are carried out under extremely hygienic conditions for the safety of patients as well as other visitors.

Typical Responsibilities

- Conducting tests strictly as prescribed.
- Explaining the diagnostic procedures to patients and guiding them.
- Maintaining the equipment.
- Train other juniors regarding equipment operations and patient-care.
- Constantly check and stock the inventory of materials required in the lab.
- Observing safety measures while conducting tests and dealing with infectious fluids.
- Conducting tests by keeping in mind the emotional condition of patients.

Laboratory Assistant/Technician: A Profile

Likely salary with 1–3 years of experience	Rs 80,000–Rs 150,000 per annum.
Targets	Quantity: Number of tests conducted. Quality: Accuracy of the test results.
Challenges	Handling infectious fluids: While handling these fluids (they can be blood, urine, or saliva), you need to take special care that you do not infect yourself. Repetitive job: You need to do the same tests again and again every day. So you need to know how to make your job interesting and learn new things while performing the role.
Skills	Basic technical skills. Attention to detail.
Stress	Low to moderate.
Travel on the job	There is no travel involved.
Impact on stakeholders	The patients, the doctors who trust your results, the reputation of the organization you work for, are all impacted by your work.
Career prospects	You join as a Junior Laboratory Assistant/Technician. After three years of experience you can grow up to the level of a Senior Lab Technician and thereafter, become a Supervisor handling the lab.

| Future salary with 5-7 years of experience | Rs 200,000–Rs 350,000 per annum. |

A Practitioner's View
Laboratory Technician, Sharad, Pune

Mr Sharad has been working as a Laboratory Technician for the last three years. When we asked him about his experiences and why he would recommend this profession to a fresher, he said:

'This profession has taught me a lot of things. While working in the role, I have learnt various lab techniques that have helped me do my job better. I get to deal with a number of patients on a daily basis. Some are very scared to get the tests done. So convincing them that the procedure will not hurt and why the test is important for his/her health is a challenge.

'I would recommend this role to any fresher whose motto is to pursue a career in this field as there are many things to learn and the opportunities are also high.'

P&H 5 QUALITY CONTROL CHEMIST (FACTORY)

Job Description

When a new drug is manufactured, it must meet stringent quality standards, every time. Who tests the quality of products/finished goods? It is the Quality Control Chemist (QC Chemist).

They mostly work in QC labs in pharma manufacturing companies. They carry out experiments using standard operating procedures under hygienic conditions and in accordance with industry protocols.

Typical Responsibilities

- Testing samples to check if they meet all the standard quality requirements.
- Checking the quality of incoming raw materials.
- Validating existing testing methods and developing new methods.

- Conducting a detailed review on the effectiveness of testing procedures.
- Using safety measures while working with hazardous substances to ensure workplace safety.
- Preparing documents on the tests conducted and submit reports to superiors regarding activities conducted during the day.

Quality Control Chemist (Factory): A Profile

Likely salary with 1–3 years of experience	Rs 120,000–Rs 200,000 per annum.
Targets	Quality: Accuracy of the results/reports. Timely submission of results.
Challenges	Repetitive job. Working under pressure: The Production Department will challenge quality failure reports. Regulatory liability: Pharmaceuticals' manufacture is highly regulated and many agencies are regularly testing the QC-approved products by taking samples from the market. The QC team will be under scrutiny by inspectors.
Skills	Technical skills in testing. Concentration and high attention to detail. Analytical skills. Good knowledge about regulatory requirements.
Stress	Moderate to high.
Travel on the job	This job does not involve travel. You will be stationed at a laboratory.
Impact on stakeholders	The public (consumers) at large and the company you work for, are impacted by your work.
Career prospects	You can start as a Junior Chemist and then grow up the ladder to become a Senior Chemist after three years; and become a QC Officer after five years of experience.
Future salary with 5–7 years of experience	Rs 300,000–Rs 500,000 per annum.

A Practitioner's View
Quality Control Manager, Vimal, Hyderabad

Mr Vimal is working in a pharma company. When we asked him about his experiences and why he would recommend the role to a fresher, he said:

'Most of us are quality conscious and prefer paying a price premium for the best quality consumer products. How do we know the quality? We trust the company that makes those products. Same is the case with medicines. My job is ensuring that the quality is maintained while manufacturing the product. It is a very vital and important role and I would recommend this to a fresher because it is a respectable position and the growth prospects are also bright.'

P&H 6 HOSPITAL BILLING EXECUTIVE

Job Description

If a patient is admitted to a hospital, the hospital would like to be sure that the payments for the treatments are guaranteed either by the patient or by the medical insurance company. The patient also wants to ensure that the billing is not excessive and that he can arrange the money required. The person who ensures both the above is the Billing Executive

Typical Responsibilities

- Discuss and agree about the payment plan with the patient/patient's relatives.
- Handling patient queries on the rates/charges for the services.
- Collecting payments made by patients and issuing receipts.
- Completing all the documentation and procedures for health insurance claims.
- Maintaining records of all invoices and payment receipts issued to patients.
- Sending 'payment due' alerts to patients and their relatives and collecting the amounts.
- Escalating to the management in case of payment defaults.

Hospital Billing Executive: A Profile

Likely salary with 1-3 years of experience	Rs 120,000-Rs 250,000 per annum.
Targets	Timely and accurate billing: Providing fair and transparent bills to patients. Accurate insurance claims: Minimize disallowance by the insurance company.
Challenges	Billing challenges: Sometimes it becomes very difficult to explain the billing to family members especially if they are unable to pay or if the treatment costs have overshot the budget. Dealing with nasty customers. Billing for insurance claims and government reimbursement schemes is a challenge because the norms and guidelines keep changing.
Skills	Exceptional data entry and computer skills. Good attention to detail. General mathematical skills to perform calculations.
Stress	Low.
Travel on the job	You will not need to travel since you will be working from the hospital itself.
Impact on stakeholders	The hospital you work for and the patients are impacted by your work.
Career prospects	You join as a Junior Billing Executive. After three years of experience you can grow up to the level of a Billing Co-ordinator. After that you can opt for a supervisory role in the administrative department of the hospital.
Future salary with 5-7 years of experience	Rs 300,000-Rs 400,000 per annum.

A Practitioner's View
Billing Executive, Chaya Kumar, Kolkata

Mr Kumar has been working as a Billing Executive for the past two and half years. When we asked him about his experiences and why he would recommend this profession to a fresher, he said:

'The role of a Billing Executive is not as easy as it sounds. My job involves capturing the right information regarding patients, explaining the various services that the hospital provides and charges pertaining to them. For example, our hospital specializes in heart care. So a lot of patients suffering from heart ailments visit us. We provide a wide range of treatments. So explaining the costs and billing them as per treatments is my main job.

'Some patients have special facilities like health insurance or health cards under government schemes. Therefore, I need to bill them in accordance with the cost that they need to pay, considering all discounts. So I need to maintain records and invoices of patients admitted across all wards. I like the job because I get to meet different people. I like addressing their concerns and guiding them in the right way.

'I would recommend this role to a fresher as a good starting point if he/she wants to pursue a career in the administrative field. There is lot of learning and the scope is also bright.'

P&H 7 MEDICAL TRANSCRIPTIONIST

Job Description

In the US, doctors while treating a patient or when conducting a surgery, dictate details of the patient's medical condition, surgical procedure, treatment protocols into a dictaphone. This is required by their legal system. As a Medical Transcriptionist, you will be responsible for listening to and interpreting audio files made by doctors/physicians and other healthcare professionals and transcribe them into accurate electronic medical records and other materials.

You will make use of a headset and a foot pedal in order to listen to the recordings. You need to be very careful while keying in data as they are important medico-legal documents.

ENTRY-LEVEL JOB ROLES IN INDUSTRIES / 341

Typical Responsibilities

- Listening to audiotapes containing data on patients.
- Documenting and recording medical information carefully by transcribing various types of information, in software, on a daily basis.
- Editing and correcting reports to make them complete.

Medical Transcriptionist: A Profile

Likely salary with 1–3 years of experience	Rs 90,000–Rs 180,000 per annum.
Targets	Quantity: Achieve daily transcription targets. Quality: Type and transcribe data with minimal errors.
Challenges	The main challenge you will face is interpreting medical data correctly and constantly staying updated regarding medical terminologies being used. This is a repetitive job with high levels of concentration required.
Skills	Strong listening skills. High levels of concentration. Fast typing skills.
Stress	Low.
Travel on the job	This job does not involve travel.
Impact on stakeholders	The doctors and the patients whose reports you type are impacted by your work.
Career prospects	You can start as a Junior Transcriptionist and in three years become a Senior Transcriptionist. In five years, you can become a Team Leader managing a group/team of Transcriptionists, or become a Quality Manager.
Future salary with 5–7 years of experience	Rs 300,000–Rs 400,000 per annum.

A Practitioner's View

Medical Transcriptionist, Syamala, Hyderabad

Ms Syamala was working as a Medical Transcriptionist for a few years. When we asked her about her experiences and why she would recommend this role to a fresher, she said:

'Working in this role has helped me a lot in improving my professional/medical editing skills. It is a very good career option for someone who wants to start a career in healthcare. There is immense scope for growth and so it is very attractive among youngsters as a career option due to its high flexibility.

'As we get to work with doctors directly, the learning quotient is very high. Yes, sometimes it does become a little stressful, but it all depends upon how well one is able to manage work.'

P&H 8 PHARMACY ASSISTANT

Job Description

When a doctor prescribes a medicine, you have to go and buy the medicine from a pharmacy. While many hospitals have in-house pharmacies, the bulk of pharmacies are independent chemist shops. When we visit pharmacies, Pharmacy Assistants look at the prescription and provide the medicines, bill you, and collect the money.

A Pharmacy Assistant helps the main Pharmacist by stocking shelves with medications, maintaining cash registers, attending to phone calls, and taking orders via phones, keeping track of the inventory, and carrying out billing.

Typical Responsibilities

- Attending to prescriptions and giving out the medicines after verifying the expiry dates.
- Generate computerized bills and collect payment.
- Check stocks/inventory at regular time periods and assist the Pharmacist in re-ordering.
- Ordering items like stationery for computers, and so on.
- Selling OTC or over-the-counter items.

◘ Guiding/helping customers by explaining the medication schedules.
◘ Receiving, loading, unloading incoming goods from stockists.
◘ Delivering pharmaceuticals and other goods to wards/departments/clinical areas in a hospital.

Pharmacy Assistant: A Profile

Likely salary with 1-3 years of experience	Rs 100,000-Rs 180,000 per annum.
Targets	Number of prescriptions attended to. Sales of non-medical items to customers, like shampoos.
Challenges	Understanding complex medical terms and drug names and dosages. Understanding a doctor's unclear handwriting.
Skills	Excellent memory for drug names and the purpose for which they are prescribed. Communication skills. Attention to detail.
Stress	Low.
Travel on the job	There is minimum travel involved in this role.
Impact on stakeholders	Customers are impacted by the role.
Career prospects	You join as a Pharmacy Assistant. If you have pharmacy qualifications you can become a Pharmacist in a few years. Thereafter, if you work in a pharmacy chain, you can go up the ladder and look after a group of retail stores.
Future salary with 5-7 years of experience	Rs 250,000-Rs 400,000 per annum.

A Practitioner's View

Pharmacy Assistant, Shiva, Hyderabad

Mr Shiva has been working in Hyderabad as a Pharmacy Assistant in a pharmacy for the last five years. When we spoke to him and asked him his views regarding the job, he said:

'It is a good role for someone who is looking to begin a career in the healthcare sector. It is challenging but at the same time, the learning is high. I get to do both administrative as well as clerical jobs. Freshers who like to pursue a career in pharma and healthcare should take up this role.'

P&H 9 MEDICAL REPRESENTATIVE

Job Description

When we visit clinics or hospitals, we often find people holding huge bags with samples of medicines. They are called Medical Representatives and are hired by pharmaceutical companies to market their products.

According to Indian regulations, most medicines (called prescription drugs) cannot be bought by a patient without a doctor's prescriptions from a chemist shop. Medical Representatives thus act like a link between pharma companies and doctors so that the company's drugs can be prescribed. They visit healthcare professionals on a one-to-one basis and give presentations to them. They also give samples of some medicines.

Typical Responsibilities

- Going to the main office, collecting samples, giving presentations, and discussing your plan of action for the day with your Manager.
- Organizing meetings with Pharmacists.
- Visiting hospitals, doctors, and giving presentations to them regarding new medicines, products, and medical equipment.
- Providing them samples of medicines along with other goodies offered by the company.
- Writing reports and submitting the same to the Manager on a daily basis.
- Achieving sales targets by maximizing sales in your particular territory.
- Organizing conferences for doctors and other medical staff; attending company trainings, meetings to keep yourself updated.
- Establishing strong contacts with healthcare professionals, Pharmacists, hospital staff.
- Developing innovative selling strategies to tackle competition from other players in the market.

Medical Representative: A Profile

Likely salary with 1–3 years of experience	Rs 120,000–Rs 300,000 per annum.
Targets	Your target will be to ensure that you meet the assigned sales targets. Track and report on competition.
Challenges	Meeting sales targets and deadlines. For example: You will be assigned a financial target to be achieved through sales within the territory assigned to you. It is not easy. Being prepared to wait for long hours in clinics and hospitals, because doctors prefer seeing their patients first and then meet Medical Representatives. It can be frustrating at times. Making your presentations interesting so that doctors pay attention to what you are saying. They meet many Medical Representatives from different companies on a daily basis. Therefore, you have to make smart presentations.
Skills	A passion for travelling and meeting people to persuade them to recommend a drug/medicine/product.
Stress	High.
Travel on the job	This role involves lot of travelling.
Impact on stakeholders	The healthcare community and the company you work for are directly impacted by this role.
Career prospects	You can start as a Junior Representative and then go up the ladder to become a Senior Representative and become an Area Manager in five to seven years.
Future salary with 5–7 years of experience	Rs 250,000–Rs 400,000 per annum.

A Practitioner's View
Medical Representative, K. Sudha, Hyderabad

Ms Sudha is working for a pharmaceutical firm. When we asked her about her experiences, she said:

'I like challenges and so I like doing this job. It is a very good career option for anyone who wants to set up a career in the field of medical sales. You get to meet a lot of people who belong to the same profession, so when you interact with them you get newer ideas, methods of marketing a product that can be incorporated in your way of work.

'Freshers receive a lot of guidance and training before they individually venture out so this gives you time to boost your confidence levels to go out and perform well.'

25

OTHER POPULAR JOB ROLES FROM THE FINANCIAL SERVICES SECTOR

ENTRY-LEVEL JOB ROLES

CODE	ROLE
FS 1	Equity Research Analyst
FS 2	Certified Financial Planner
FS 3	Financial Business Analyst

FS 1 EQUITY RESEARCH ANALYST

Job Description

Equity Research Analysts conduct research on stocks, organizations, and equity funds (such as mutual funds) to advise companies and even individuals on which stocks to invest in and which stocks to sell. They track company performances, the financial stability of Indian stock markets and global markets to arrive at their recommendations. There are many investors who subscribe to and study these research reports before investing their funds. Many large investment banks and banks managing funds of high net-worth individuals (HNI) hire Equity Research Analysts and offer their advice only to their clients. There are also several broking firms which create and send these reports to their clients as a value-added service.

There are three aspects to the research—Company Fundamentals, Industry Dynamics, and Stock Market Technical Research. Company Fundamentals deal with analyses of the company's balance sheet and profit and loss accounts. Industry Dynamics deal with competition performance, industry growth, and strategic factors. Stock Market

Technical Research deals with the demand for, and supply of, the company stock and factors that impact the stock market as a whole, such as the exchange rate and global recession.

It is well known that a stock market is very difficult to predict. Despite this, the Equity Research Analyst's job is to study all these factors systematically and recommend—buy, sell, or hold—on the stock. Most of the Equity Research Analysts work out of specialist research firms or banks.

Typical Responsibilities

You will spend most of the time conducting research on equity markets and specific portfolios of individual stocks. You will publish periodic (weekly or monthly) reports on findings. You will have to:

- Evaluate financial data for a company, industry, country, or region (for instance, the Asia–Pacific region).
- Study economic trends and stock markets across the globe.
- Recommend reliable investment ideas to investors, traders, and companies.
- Prepare reports of findings, illustrate data graphically, and translate complex findings into actionable recommendations.
- Write research notes and make, buy, or sell recommendations.
- Forecast capital market trends.
- Attend relevant group meetings and share investment ideas.
- Communicate ideas and knowledge to Portfolio Managers who make the investment decision.

Equity Research Analyst: A Profile

Likely salary with 1–3 years of experience	Rs 600,000–Rs 1,800,000 per annum.
Targets	Your main target as an Equity Research Analyst is to ensure that you generate accurate and reliable reports/analysis very often, based on part or incomplete information.

Challenges	Provide accurate and reliable reports. Investors risk their money based on your analysis. Stay one step ahead of your peer group (or other Equity Research Analysts) who are as smart as you are. Develop end-to-end knowledge about capital markets: you constantly need to keep yourself updated regarding various global and local happenings which impact the equity market. Digging for information which the company (that you are analysing) is trying to hide.
Stress	Moderate to high.
Skills	Good analytical and report-writing skills. Must be highly motivated, think out of the box, and have an eye for details. Sound in financial analytics. Have critical thinking abilities to answer complicated questions like 'what if this happens?', or 'how will the company finances be impacted if the existing government policies change?', and so on.
Travel on the job	Very limited travel.
Impact on stakeholders	Organizations and clients who rely on your research are highly impacted by this role.
Career prospects	Very bright as there is a heavy demand for this role. You could become a Team Lead in three years and Manager of the Equity Research Team within three years thereafter.
Future salary with 5–7 years of experience	Rs 1,200,000–Rs 3,600,000 per annum.

A Practitioner's View

Equity Research Analyst, Mansi Gosalia, Mumbai

Ms Gosalia is a Chartered Accountant with four years of experience in finance, business planning, strategy and equity research. When we spoke to her and asked her about her views on an Equity Research Analyst's role, and why she would recommend this role to a fresher, she said:

'Equity research as a career option is very exciting. It requires you to be on top of things all the time. It requires good technical skills—number crunching, financial analysis, and a passion for the stock markets. All the ups and down of the markets are based on news/events in the national and world economy that can potentially affect the stocks. One needs to have the ability to understand the business well and be able to relate these events and quantify their impact on a particular stock. The excitement and dynamism in the field will always keep you excited and the meetings with top corporate honchos will be a great experience. However, logical thinking and a strong conviction about the fair valuation of your stocks is very important. Monetarily too, it is a great place to be. So if you are up for a fast-paced, dynamic job with high risk and high rewards, this is where you should be.'

FS 2 CERTIFIED FINANCIAL PLANNER (CFP)

Job Description

A friend of mine made good profits in a property deal and suddenly received a lot of surplus cash. He wanted to invest it in financial instruments such as stocks, debt securities, government bonds to maximize his returns but at the same time ensure that he did not erode the principle. So he made the right decision and approached a Certified Financial Planner (CFP).

A CFP, also called a PFA or Personal Financial Adviser, is someone who helps individuals or organizations plan their savings, income, and investments effectively. She/he works for the investor and is, therefore, not biased towards any investment opportunity because of the commissions offered. A CFP certification is an internationally accepted financial planning qualification recognized and respected by the global financial community.

The Financial Planning Standards Board (FPSB) of India gives CFP certification. FPSB India is an affiliate of FPSB Ltd, which is a non-profit association that manages, develops, and operates certification, educational, and related programmes for financial planning organizations around the world.[86]

The job involves understanding the client's risk-taking capacity, liquidity (how fast the instrument can be sold and converted to cash) needs, and offering advice accordingly. You will have to very clearly understand the risk-return ratio of various types of financial investments in this job. You should also understand the various tax benefits offered by the government for investors. Most CFPs are self-employed but there are a few who work with banks and financial services firms.

Typical Responsibilities

- Continuously promoting and marketing oneself to identify prospects.
- Meeting prospects and converting them to become clients.
- Reading and watching financial coverage, including the financial newspapers and financial TV channels, to stay updated on the latest developments.
- Meeting and interviewing clients to assess their financial situation.
- Analysing financial markets and providing appropriate suggestions to clients.
- Advising on minimizing the tax burden on investments.
- Convincing clients to evaluate new financial products.
- Tracking client investments.
- Providing clients with periodic updates on investment portfolios, recommending and implementing changes in their portfolios.

Certified Financial Planner: A Profile

Likely salary with 1-3 years of experience	Rs 150,000-Rs 700,000 per annum, including commissions. If you are self-employed, your fee earned will vary based on the volume of business and the profit share negotiated.
Targets	Number of customers and their portfolio value. Return on investments earned.
Challenges	Acquiring new customers and retaining them. Clients have unrealistic expectations of high returns with low risk. So the real challenge is in educating customers without losing them. Staying updated on the latest tax laws and financial regulations is important.

Skills	Excellent networking skills to acquire new customers. Good analytical skills. Excellent influencing skills. Good understanding of financial and capital markets and taxation on investments.
Stress	Moderate to high.
Travel on the job	There is limited travel involved in this role.
Impact on stakeholders	The clients are directly impacted by this role.
Career prospects	Many CFPs choose to be in this role and grow in size (more customers, bigger investment budgets/portfolios). Some move up the ladder and become Managers who oversee the work of other CFPs.
Future salary with 5–7 years of experience	Rs 800,000–Rs 2,000,000 per annum.

A Practitioner's View

Certified Financial Planner,
Aijaz Khan(name changed), Hyderabad

Mr Khan is working in a financial services firm and has more than ten years of experience. When we asked him to share his experiences and tell us why he would recommend this job to a fresher, he said:

'My job is definitely not as easy as it sounds. I get to deal with various clients on a daily basis coming up with queries and enquiries regarding which stock to invest in and which to sell. Apart from this, I manage portfolios of clients who give us certain sums of money to invest. They completely rely on us regarding their investments. It is a very tough decision to make since you will be dealing with other people's money and so you need to be extra careful and study stocks of companies in which you invest. It is extremely interesting and at the same time involves high stress. So you need to be prepared to work for long hours to conduct a detailed analysis and research. The pay you can expect is very decent and so it is a good career option for students who wish to take up a career in capital markets.'

FS 3 FINANCIAL BUSINESS ANALYST (FBA)

Job Description

Businesses rely on sound analyses of financial data, analyses of areas such as profitability, costing, and cash-flows. The role of a Financial Business Analyst is to generate reports summarizing financial data for use by executives, Managers, and other stakeholders when making business decisions. These professionals require a combination of business and financial knowledge.

Let's take an example. Your competitor suddenly drops his price by 20 per cent. Now you have to respond to this. What should you do? Should you also drop your price and by how much? Is it possible to cut costs also? What would be the impact on the company's profits? Will lower profitability lead to cash-flow problems? The FBA's job is to study data and answer these questions, so that the Business Managers can take the right decisions.

Typical Responsibilities

- Assisting business leaders in achieving targets, by providing timely financial advice.
- Advising management officials to take proper decisions on financial planning and coming up with novel ideas to improve organizational efficiency.
- Analysing business trends, preparing reports, and presenting the same to top management, clients, and stakeholders.
- Presenting data analysis and interpretation in clear, compelling ways.
- Developing effective reporting tools for a business.

Financial Business Analyst: A Profile

Likely salary with 1–3 years of experience	Rs 200,000–Rs 500,000 per annum.

Targets	Timely submission of insightful reports.
Challenges	Suggestions for improvements have to be practical and implementable. To do this you need sound business knowledge at the company- and industry-level, in addition to financial analyses. Business leaders develop strong beliefs about their businesses. Getting them to change these beliefs requires a lot of data analytics and presentation and conviction in the recommendations.
Skills	Good analytical skills. Excellent communication and report writing skills. Critical thinking skills.
Stress	Moderate to high.
Travel on the job	There might be occasional travel involved in this role.
Impact on stakeholders	The business leaders you work for will be impacted by this role.
Career prospects	This job enables interaction with business leaders and hence provides excellent growth opportunities. After three years, you could move into an operational role in marketing, operations, or finance, depending upon your qualifications and inclinations.
Future salary with 5–7 years of experience	Rs 500,000–Rs 1,000,000 per annum.

A Practitioner's View

Financial Business Analyst, Prasanna, Andhra Pradesh

Ms Prasanna has around five years of experience working as a Business Analyst. When we asked her about her experiences and why would she recommend this role to a fresher, she said:

'I would like to make it clear that initially, freshers will be recruited as I Trainees because most of the companies prefer promoting their existing employees for this role due to its complexity. It requires a lot of understanding about the company processes, markets, competitors and also exceptional performance in what you are doing. Initially, I had a tough time understanding the intricacies of business analysis but once I started doing the role, things fell in place. Here, performance and efficiency is the key. I would recommend this role to any fresher who wishes to go up the ladder quickly by doing complex and crucial work, efficiently.'

A QUICK INDEX

S.No.	Sector/Function	Job Code	Job Title	Page
1	Marketing	MKTG 1	Market Research Analyst	22
2	Marketing	MKTG 2	Brand Executive	25
3	Marketing	MKTG 3	Media Executive	27
4	Marketing	MKTG 4	Creative Copywriter	30
5	Marketing	MKTG 5	Design Artist Assistant	32
6	Marketing	MKTG 6	Digital Marketing Specialist	34
7	Sales	SAL 1	B2B Sales Executive	45
8	Sales	SAL 2	Direct Sales Executive	47
9	Sales	SAL 3	Channel Sales Executive	49
10	Sales	SAL 4	Pre-sales Executive	52
11	Operations	OPS 1	Production Supervisor	60
12	Operations	OPS 2	Project Engineer/Trainee	62
13	Operations	OPS 3	Quality Control Supervisor	64
14	Operations	OPS 4	Customer Service Engineer	66
15	Finance and Accounting	FIN 1	Finance Executive	74
16	Finance and Accounting	FIN 2	Chartered Accountant	76
17	Finance and Accounting	FIN 3	Investor Relations Associate	80
18	Finance and Accounting	FIN 4	Budget Analyst	82
19	Finance and Accounting	FIN 5	Treasury Officer/Executive	84
20	Finance and Accounting	FIN 6	Forex Officer	85
21	Finance and Accounting	ACC 1	Accountant/Accounting Executive	87
22	Finance and Accounting	ACC 2	MIS Executive	89

S.No.	Sector/Function	Job Code	Job Title	Page
23	IT	IT 1	Network Executive	93
24	IT	IT 2	Instructional Designer (for e-learning)	95
25	IT	IT 3	Junior Web Designer	98
26	HR	HR 2	E-recruiter	104
27	HR	HR 2	Headhunter	106
28	HR	HR 3	International Tele-recruiter	109
29	HR	HR 4	Recruitment Data Analyst	111
30	HR	HR 5	Content Specialist	113
31	HR	HR 6	Corporate Trainer	115
32	HR	HR 7	Training Coordinator	117
33	HR	HR 8	Compensation Management Executive	119
34	HR	HR 9	Operations Executive	121
35	HR	HR 10	Industrial Relations Executive (Trainee)	123
36	Legal	LEGAL 1	Corporate Legal Assistant/ Secretarial Assistant	127
37	Legal	LEGAL 2	Company Secretary (Trainee)	130
38	Supply Chain	SC 1	Supply Chain Officer (Outbound)	134
39	Supply Chain	SC 2	Purchase Officer	137
40	Auto Sector	AUTO 1	Showroom Sales Executive	145
41	Auto Sector	AUTO 2	Service Supervisor	146
42	Civil Aviation	AVA 1	Trainee Co-pilot (Trainee First Officer)	152
43	Civil Aviation	AVA 2	Cabin Crew	155
44	Civil Aviation	AVA 3	Ground Staff	157
45	Banking	BANK 1	CASA Executive	166
46	Banking	BANK 2	Recovery Officer	168
47	Banking	BANK 3	Probationary Officer	170
48	Banking	BANK 4	Branch Customer Relationship Executive	172
49	Banking	BANK 5	Branch Operations Clerk	174
50	Education	EDU 1	School Teacher	181
51	Education	EDU 2	School Student Counsellor	183
52	Education	EDU 3	Student Mobilizer	185
53	Education	EDU 4	Skill Trainer	187
54	Insurance	INS 1	Insurance Agent/Adviser	194
55	Insurance	INS 2	Development Officer/Unit Manager/Agency Manager	198
56	Insurance	INS 3	Underwriting Executive (Trainee)	200

A QUICK INDEX / 359

S.No.	Sector/Function	Job Code	Job Title	Page
57	Insurance	INS 4	Claims Officer	202
58	Construction, Building, and Infrastructure Sector	INF 1	Project Civil Engineer	210
59	Construction, Building, and Infrastructure Sector	INF 2	Site Supervisor	212
60	Construction, Building, and Infrastructure Sector	INF 3	Interior Designer	214
61	Information Technology (IT) Sector	IT IND 1	Systems Integration Trainee	226
62	IT Sector	IT IND 2	Database Administrator Trainee	229
63	IT Sector	IT IND 3	Software Developer Trainee	231
64	IT Sector	IT IND 4	Quality Assurance Testing Engineer	234
65	IT Sector	IT IND 5	Remote Infrastructure Engineer	236
66	IT Sector	IT IND 6	IT Security Engineer	237
67	Information Technology-enabled Services (ITeS)	ITES 1	Inbound Call Centre Executive	244
68	ITeS	ITES 2	Outbound Call Centre Executive	246
69	ITeS	ITES 3	Process Analyst	248
70	ITeS	ITES 4	IT Tech Support Executive	250
71	ITeS	ITES 5	Geographical Information Systems Trainee	253
72	Logistics	LOG 1	Courier Executive	261
73	Logistics	LOG 2	Transport Logistics Executive	263
74	Logistics	LOG 3	Warehousing Executive	266
75	Media and Entertainment	M&E 1	Print Content Editor	272
76	Media and Entertainment	M&E 2	Radio Jockey	275
77	Media and Entertainment	M&E 3	News Reporter (Print/TV)	277
78	Media and Entertainment	M&E 4	TV Anchor/Presenter	280
79	Media and Entertainment	M&E 5	Public Relations Officer (PRO)	282
80	Retail Sector	RTL 1	Billing Executive/Cashier	289

S.No.	Sector/Function	Job Code	Job Title	Page
81	Retail Sector	RTL 2	Customer Service Associate	291
82	Telecom Sector	TEL 1	Fault Management/Support Engineer	299
83	Telecom Sector	TEL 2	Optical Fibre Splicer	302
84	Telecom Sector	TEL 3	In-shop Promoter	304
85	Telecom Sector	TEL 4	Service and Repair Executive (Handset)	306
86	Travel, Tourism, and Hospitality	HOS 1	Front Office Executive	312
87	Travel, Tourism, and Hospitality	HOS 2	Housekeeping Executive	314
88	Travel, Tourism, and Hospitality	HOS 3	Banquet Executive	315
89	Travel, Tourism, and Hospitality	HOS 4	Chef	317
90	Pharma and Healthcare Sector	P&H 1	Junior Doctor	328
91	Pharma and Healthcare Sector	P&H 2	General Nurse	330
92	Pharma and Healthcare Sector	P&H 3	Emergency Medical Technician (EMT)	332
93	Pharma and Healthcare Sector	P&H 4	Laboratory Assistant/ Technician	334
94	Pharma and Healthcare Sector	P&H 5	Quality Control Chemist (Factory)	336
95	Pharma and Healthcare Sector	P&H 6	Hospital Billing Executive	338
96	Pharma and Healthcare Sector	P&H 7	Medical Transcriptionist	340
97	Pharma and Healthcare Sector	P&H 8	Pharmacy Assistant	342
98	Pharma and Healthcare Sector	P&H 9	Medical Representative	344
99	Financial Services	FS 1	Equity Research Analyst	347
100	Financial Services	FS 2	Certiied Financial Planner (CFP)	350
101	Financial Services	FS 3	Financial Business Analyst (FBA)	353

NOTES

Chapter 4 (Sales Department)
1 http://www.tatasteel.com.

Chapter 5 (Operations Department)
2 http://en.wikipedia.org/wiki/Economy_of_India.
3 http://www2.deloitte.com/us/en/pages/manufacturing/articles/2013-global-manufacturing-competitiveness-index.html#.
4 http://www.ibef.org/industry/manufacturing-sector-india.aspx.
5 *The Times of India*.

Chapter 6 (Finance and Accounts Departments)
6 http://www.icai.org/post.html?post_id=1817.

Chapter 9 (Legal Department)
7 https://india.gov.in.

Chapter 11 (Automotive Sector)
8 Cited in http://www.knowindia.net/auto.html, which acknowledges source as OICA (The International Organization of Motor Vehicle Manufacturers 2013 Statistics).
9 OICA 2013 Statistics; NSDC skill-gap studies 2015.
10 http://www.ibef.org/industry/india-automobiles.aspx#sthash.QXNGgPIv.dpuf.
11 NSDC Human Resource and Skill Requirements reports.
12 http://www.jobaps.com.

Chapter 12 (Civil Aviation)
13 https://www.goodreads.com/author/show/332459.Orville_Wright; https://www.cia.gov/library/publications/the-world-factbook/fields/2053.html.
14 http://www.iata.org/Pages/default.aspx.
15 http://www.thehindubusinessline.com.

16 Indigo's inflight magazine.

Chapter 13 (Banking)
17 NSDC Human Resource and Skill Requirements reports.
18 http://www.banknetindia.com/jobs/carbank.htm.
19 http://bankexamforum.blogspot.in/.
20 http://www.cvc.nic.in/rkprofile.pdf;
http://www.bloomberg.com/research/stocks/people/person.asp?personId=35347152&ticker=121597.
21 Kumar, Ranjana. *A New Beginning: The Turnaround Story of Indian Bank,* McGraw-Hill Education (India, 2009).

Chapter 14 (Education)
22 NSDC Human Resource and Skill Requirements reports.
23 https://www2.deloitte.com/.../Deloitte/.../in-imo-indian-higher_education...
24 NSDC Human Resource and Skill Requirements reports.
25 Ibid.

Chapter 15 (Insurance)
26 http://typesofinsurance.org/.
27 Insurance Regulatory and Development Authority.
28 NSDC Human Resource and Skill Requirements reports;
http://www.irda.gov.in;
http://www.ibef.org/industry/insurance-sector-india.aspx.
29 *The Times of India,* 19 July 2015.
30 http://www.ibef.org/industry/insurance-sector-india.aspx.
31 www.insuranceacademy.org.
32 NSDC Human Resource and Skill Requirements reports.
33 http://www.prospects.ac.uk. (Even though the source is a UK-based company, the roles and tasks remain the same.)
34 Ibid.

Chapter 16 (Construction, Building, and Infrastructure Sector)
35 www.smithsonianmag.com.
36 www.ndtv.com.
37 NSDC Human Resource and Skill Requirements reports.
38 Ibid.
39 Ibid.
40 Ibid.

41 http://www.larsentoubro.com/media/30142/lt-earthmover-news-april-2012.pdf; http://economictimes.indiatimes.com/industry/indlgoods/svs/engineering/larsen-toubro-managing-director-and-ceo-kvenkataramanan-retires/articleshow/49181859.cms

Chapter 17 (IT Sector)
42 NSDC Human Resource and Skill Requirements reports.
43 http://www.ibef.org/industry/information-technology-india.aspx.
44 Ibid.
45 NASSCOM, Aranca Research.
46 NSDC Human Resource and Skill Requirements reports.
47 Ibid.
48 Ibid.
49 http://www.infosys.com/about/management-profiles/Pages/narayana-murthy.aspx.

Chapter 18 (IT-enabled Services)
50 http://economictimes.indiatimes.com/.

Chapter 19 (Logistics)
51 NSDC Human Resource and Skill Requirements reports.
52 Ibid.

Chapter 20 (Media and Entertainment Sector)
53 Wikipedia.
54 http://en.wikipedia.org/wiki/Entertainment_industry_in_India#cite_note-13.
55 NSDC Human Resource and Skill Requirements reports.
56 Wikipedia.

Chapter 21 (Retail Sector)
57 NSDC Human Resource and Skill Requirements reports; FICCI's sector reports.
58 The Boston Consulting Group and Retailers Association of India's report published in February 2015.
59 NSDC Human Resource and Skill Requirements reports.
60 http://www.futureretail.co.in/about-us/leadership-team-retail.Html.

Chapter 22 (Telecom Sector)
61 http://www.ibef.org/industry/telecommunications.aspx.
62 NSDC Human Resource and Skill Requirements reports.

63 Ibid.
64 Ibid.
65 http://jobsearch.naukri.com/job-listings-Fault-Management-Engr.
66 http://study.com/articles/Fiber_Optic_Splicing_Jobs_Duties_and_Requirements.html.
67 Telecom Sector Skills Council Qualification Pack, http://www.nsdcindia.org/sites/default/files/files/Optical-Fibre-Spilcer.pdf.
68 http://job-descriptions.careerplanner.com/.

Chapter 23 (Travel, Tourism, and Hospitality)
69 Wikipedia.
70 NSDC Human Resource and Skill Requirements reports.
71 http://www.livemint.com/Companies/FvHiSWXbodU42x779wpYYM/Hospitality-sector-to-attract-over-200-bn-in-next-3-years.html.
72 http://www.tophotelprojects.com/.
73 NSDC Human Resource and Skill Requirements reports.
74 Ibid.
75 http://www.bls.gov/.
76 http://www.rediff.com/money/2005/oct/21bspec.htm.

Chapter 24 (Pharma and Healthcare Sector)
77 Wikipedia.
78 NSDC Human Resource and Skill Requirements reports; *Forbes*, 27 June 2015.
79 http://www.ibef.org/industry/pharmaceutical-india.aspx.
80 http://www.mbaskool.com/.
81 NSDC Human Resource and Skill Requirements reports.
82 Ibid.
83 Ibid.
84 Ibid.
85 https://en.wikipedia.org/wiki/Kallam_Anji_Reddy; http://www.biography.co.in/biography-dr-k-anji-reddy.html.

Chapter 25 (Other Popular Job Roles from the Financial Services Sector)
86 www.fpsbindia.org.

SOURCES

The challenge in writing this book was accessing the latest data on jobs, job descriptions, salaries, and so on. Hence we had to refer to many sources. Among these sources, two sources were very critical and important for the book. We had received permissions to publish the extracts in the book from these two sources:

1. Human Resource and Skill Requirements reports published by NSDC, the Ministry of Skill Development and Entrepreneurship, Government of India. These reports were published on many sectors of the Indian economy. Specific permission was requested and granted by NSDC for publishing extracts. These reports were created by KPMG. So we are very grateful to NSDC and KPMG. The reports are available at www.nsdcindia.org/nsdcreports.
2. IBEF-India Brand Equity Foundation also publishes periodically reports on various sectors of the Indian economy, which are very useful. IBEF is a Trust established by the Department of Commerce, the Ministry of Commerce and Industry, Government of India. We have sought and received permission from IBEF for publishing extracts of the reports.

In addition to the above two, there were many information sources which were referred to. Appropriate citations have been given. The list of such sources are given below:

1. www.wikipedia.com
2. www.naukri.com
3. www.timesjobs.com
4. www.payscale.com
5. www.livemint.com/Companies
6. www.tophotelprojects.com
7. www.rediff.com

8. https://en.wikipedia.org/wiki/
9. www.oberoihotels.com
10. http://study.com/articles/Fiber_Optic_Splicing_Jobs_Duties_and_Requirements.html
11. http://job-descriptions.careerplanner.com/
12. www.totaljobs.com
13. www.bharti.com
14. http://www.futureretail.co.in/about-us/leadership-team-retail.html
15. www.ndtv.com
16. www.bluedart.com
17. www.dtdc.in
18. www.firstflight.net
19. www.gati.net
20. www.dhl.co.in
21. www.fedex.com
22. www.dtdc.com
23. www.deloitte.com
24. www.kpmg.com
25. NSSO Rounds.
26. https://india.gov.in
27. www.ICAI.org
28. www.timesofindia.com/articles
29. http://en.wikipedia.org/wiki/Economy_of_India
30. http://www.tatasteel.com
31. www.fpsbindia.org
32. http://www.larsentoubro.com/
33. http://economictimes.indiatimes.com
34. indiantollways.com
35. www.Iamrindia.gov.in
36. www.smithsonianmag.com
37. http://www.prospects.ac.uk
38. www.insuranceacademy.org
39. http://www.irda.gov.in
40. http://typesofinsurance.org/
41. https://www2.deloitte.com/.../Deloitte/.../in-imo-indian-higher_education...

42. http://www.cvc.nic.in/rkprofile.pdf
43. http://www.bloomberg.com/research/stocks/people/person.asp?personId=35347152&ticker=121597
44. http://bankexamforum.blogspot.in
45. http://www.banknetindia.com/jobs/carbank.htm
46. http://www.thehindubusinessline.com
47. http://www.apaoindia.com
48. http://www.globalbankingandfinance.com/Resources/List-Of-Investment-Banks-In-India.html
49. http://en.wikipedia.org/wiki/List_of_banks_in_India
50. http://www.allbankingsolutions.com/Links/List-of-Bank-in-India.shtml
51. http://www.iba.org.in
52. http://www.careerage.com/career/cc/aviation
53. https://www.goodreads.com
54. http://www.jobaps.com
55. http://www.herobpo.com/our_hero.html

ACKNOWLEDGEMENTS

There are many people I need to thank. Firstly, Ms Asha Donkar, who helped in the research and writing of this book. Secondly, my Editor, Ms Sneha Gusain, and my Executive Assistant, Ms G. Nagamani. Lastly, the multitude of practitioners who have shared their insights on their job roles.